...There are
things out there
that are good...
virtue comes from our
relationship to & love-
seeing that they thrive
and we contribute to
their flourishing."

# A THEORY OF VIRTUE

# A Theory of Virtue

*Excellence in Being for the Good*

ROBERT MERRIHEW ADAMS

CLARENDON PRESS · OXFORD

# OXFORD

UNIVERSITY PRESS

Great Clarendon Street, Oxford OX2 6DP

Oxford University Press is a department of the University of Oxford.
It furthers the University's objective of excellence in research, scholarship,
and education by publishing worldwide in

Oxford New York

Auckland Cape Town Dar es Salaam Hong Kong Karachi
Kuala Lumpur Madrid Melbourne Mexico City Nairobi
New Delhi Shanghai Taipei Toronto

With offices in

Argentina Austria Brazil Chile Czech Republic France Greece
Guatemala Hungary Italy Japan Poland Portugal Singapore
South Korea Switzerland Thailand Turkey Ukraine Vietnam

Oxford is a registered trade mark of Oxford University Press
in the UK and in certain other countries

Published in the United States
by Oxford University Press Inc., New York

© Robert Adams 2006

The moral rights of the author have been asserted
Database right Oxford University Press (maker)

First published 2006

British Library Cataloguing in Publication Data

Data available

Library of Congress Cataloging in Publication Data

Data available

Typeset by Laserwords Private Limited, Chennai, India
Printed in Great Britain
on acid-free paper by
Biddles Ltd., King's Lynn, Norfolk

ISBN 0–19–920751–8   978–0–19–920751–0

1 3 5 7 9 10 8 6 4 2

In memory of my parents
Arthur Merrihew Adams (1908–1979)
Margaret Baker Adams (1910–2005)

# Preface and Acknowledgments

For over thirty years I have been thinking and writing about the area some-times known as agent ethics, to which the ethics of virtue or character belongs. Until about six years ago most of my work in the area had not dealt with the evaluation of character as such, but with the closely related topic of the evalu-ation of motives. The focused work on virtue that has led to this book began with preparation for a graduate seminar on the subject that I gave at Yale in the second semester of 1999–2000. My choice of virtue as the topic for that class was inspired by the thought that it was a gap that deserved to be filled in the "frame-work for ethics" that I had published in 1999 in my book *Finite and Infinite Goods*. That book had a lot to say about motives, but little about virtue or charac-ter. The present book is intended to cohere with its predecessor (not least in the common themes of excellence and being for the good), but to be intelligible on its own.

An invitation to spend a week, and give three lectures, at Princeton University as a Stewart Fellow provided an occasion for me to write out my ideas about the nature of virtue at some length and present them to a very stimulating audience in March of 2001. I am very grateful to Princeton's Council of the Humanit-ies for the invitation, and to faculty and students of the departments of philo-sophy and religion for their hospitality and their very helpful comments and questions about my lectures. Material from them makes up important parts of chapters 1–2, 4, and 9–12.

A paper anticipating parts of chapters 1–2 and 4 was also presented to philo-sophical audiences at Yale, Georgetown, Vanderbilt, and Ohio Universities and the Universities of Michigan and Notre Dame. An ancestor of chapter 5 was a Coffin Lecture on Christian Ethics at the University of London, May 30, 2002, and more recent versions were presented to groups at the Universities of York and Oxford and Notre Dame and the University of California, San Diego, and to the Scots Philosophical Club, and as an address to the Society of Christian Ethics meeting in Miami, January 8, 2005. Versions of chapters 8 and 9 were presented to ethics discussion groups in Oxford and the Research Triangle area of North Carolina, and paired with a version of chapter 10 at the University of Cali-fornia, Riverside. An ancestor of chapters 9 and 12 was presented to the Pacific conference of the Society of Christian Philosophers in April of 2001.

Two chapters have a longer history, and contain the only extensive parts of the book that have been previously published.

Chapter 6 includes much material from my paper, "Common Projects and Moral Vir-tue," *Midwest Studies in Philosophy*, 13 (1988): 297–307, although the point of view as well as the framework is significantly different in the present version. Copyright © 1988 by University of Notre Dame Press. Used by permission.

Chapter 7 is a lightly adapted republication of my paper, "Self-Love and the Vices of Self-Preference," *Faith and Philosophy*, 15 (1998): 500–13. The substance of it is reprinted here with the permission of the journal.

In addition, chapter 8 contains two paragraphs adapted from my review article:

"Scanlon's Contractualism: Critical Notice of T. M. Scanlon, *What We Owe to Each Other*," *The Philosophical Review*, 110 (2001): 563–86. This material is used here with the permission of the journal and its present publisher, The Duke University Press.

I am grateful to the publishers of these papers for permission to reprint the material here.

The paper that became chapter 7 originated as the Joseph Butler Memorial Lecture delivered in Oxford on the 300th anniversary of Butler's birth, May 18, 1992. I am grateful to Oriel College, Butler's college, for the invitation to give the lecture and for their generous hospitality on the occasion. Versions of the paper were also presented to the philosophy department of the University of Vermont and to a conference on virtue ethics at the University of Santa Clara, and as the Ruth Evelyn Parcelles Memorial Lecture at the University of Connecticut, April 21, 1994, and the Franklin W. Matchette Lecture at Brooklyn College, May 5, 1994.

As the book neared completion, I had two exceptional opportunities to discuss it with groups of philosophers who had read drafts of part or all of it. In September of 2004, I met with a graduate seminar in moral philosophy at the University of North Carolina, Chapel Hill, whose members had read and discussed among themselves a complete draft of Parts I and II. I found this extremely helpful, and am very grateful to Geoffrey Sayre-McCord and Susan Wolf, the leaders of the seminar, for focusing on my work and inviting me to participate in this way, and further to Wolf for extended discussion of parts of the work, which also was extremely helpful. Then in February of 2005 I had a similar, and similarly rewarding, opportunity to meet with a group of graduate students and faculty in philosophy at the University of California, San Diego, who had previously read a draft of the whole book and discussed it among themselves.

With regard to all the occasions for speaking and discussion that I have mentioned, I am grateful for the invitations and hospitality that made them possible and enjoyable, and I am indebted to all who were involved in the discussions. Without their encouragement, criticism, and questioning, the book would be much poorer, if it would exist at all. Much the same can be said of the students in my graduate seminars on virtue at Yale in the spring of 2000 and the fall of 2001, and at Oxford in the fall of 2004.

As the preceding narrative may suggest, the number of discussants who have aided my thinking on this subject exceeds my ability to itemize them here. But I must not fail to mention Richard Arneson, David Brink, John Broome, Thomas Carson, John Cooper, William Costanzo, Jesse Couenhoven, Nina Davis, Roger Crisp, Stephen Darwall, Philippa Foot, Allan Gibbard, Lisa Halko, Gilbert Harman, Thomas E. Hill Jr., Megan Hughes, Shelly Kagan, James Kreines, Marc Lange, Gabriel Richardson Lear, Alasdair MacIntyre, Julia Markovits, Mark Murphy, Dana Nelkin, Derek Parfit, Thomas Pink, Mathias Risse, Nancy Sherman, Kelly Sorensen, Daniel Star, Jeffrey Stout, Georgia Warnke, Gary Watson, Ralph Wedgwood, Paul Weithman, and Annabelle Zagura. I am grateful to Marilyn McCord Adams for urging me to use my Princeton lectures as the nucleus of a book, and for her advice and help throughout the project.

At Yale my thanks are due not only to my students and colleagues in the philosophy department, with whom I talked through so many thoughts about virtue, but also to the university for a research leave for the academic year 2002/3, during which I accomplished important parts of my work on the book, and particularly on the psychological issues that provide much of the framework of Part III. Since my retirement from Yale, the University of Oxford has provided a wonderful environment for philosophical work. I am grateful to its faculty of philosophy, to Mansfield College, where I am a senior research fellow, and to my wife's college, Christ Church, where we live, for so much that stimulates and facilitates my research.

I am grateful also to Peter Momtchiloff, my editor at the Clarendon Press, for his advice and encouragement, and to two anonymous readers for the Press, whose helpful comments led to improvements in my final revision of the book.

The dedication of this book acknowledges my debt to my parents, who prepared me to think about human goodness by modeling a faith in God's good purposes for human life, combined with an unvindictive realism about human frailty and sin, and a will to reason about everything.

It is a pleasure to remember these debts of gratitude.

R. M. A.

*February 16, 2006*
*Mansfield College,*
*Oxford*

# Contents

# PART I
# WHAT IS VIRTUE?

# 1

# Introduction

## 1. THE SUBJECT MATTER

This is a book about the moral life. It is not a book about moral decision-making. The moral life involves much more than right and wrong decisions and actions. For example, it involves good and bad motives. Suppose you managed yesterday to do many morally right actions, and nothing at all that was wrong. Even on that assumption, your day will have gone better morally if your morally correct actions were motivated by concern for other people's well-being than if they sprang from fear of other people's disapproval.

Some motivational states don't last very long. Perhaps you are in a better mood today than yesterday, and your operative motives will be better today. Some motivational states are quite enduring, however. Perhaps you have had for many years a deep and strong commitment to do what you believe you morally ought to do. That would count as a *trait of character*, and a good one, a *virtue*. It would be a form of conscientiousness. Some traits of character are much worse than conscientiousness. One might have had for years a deep, strong, and controlling desire to accumulate as much wealth as possible. That would count as a trait of character too. If the desire is sufficiently overriding, it would be a bad trait, a vice, called avarice. Such good and bad traits are a major factor in how well your life (and not just your day) is going morally. Indeed, they constitute what is called *moral character*, and are commonly seen as determining the extent to which one is *a morally good person*.

A couple of points of terminology should be noted at the outset. (1) Despite the somewhat old-fashioned flavor that the word *virtue* has for many people, I use it to signify good moral character, or a good trait of character. It is so used in virtually all philosophical discussion of the ethics of character because such discussion is strongly connected with classic texts where that use of the word has a central role. (2) When I speak of "moral character" or a "morally good person," the words *moral* and *morally* signify only that evaluation is made with respect to faculties, states, and acts of will and motivation. Some moral evaluation in this broad sense may also be aesthetic or religious evaluation. It is no part of my project to draw sharp lines between moral, aesthetic, and religious value.

This is a book about the moral life, but not about moral decision-making, because it is about the ethics of character. The ethics of character is an important *department* of ethical theory. It is not the only department of ethical theory. Another important department is the ethics of right actions, which assesses principles of choice for voluntary action, seeking to determine, in a general way, what it is right and wrong to do. There is also the ethics of motives, and more broadly of attitudes. It is only partially separable from the ethics of virtue or character, inasmuch as some but not all motives and attitudes endure long enough to constitute traits of character.

Throughout the twentieth century the ethics of action held the lion's share of the attention in substantive ethical theory. Indeed, for most of the earlier part of the century it was generally treated, at least in anglophone moral philosophy, as virtually the whole of substantive ethics. 'What ought we to do?' was seen as *the* ethical question. For over forty years now there has been a vigorous movement calling attention to virtue, or moral character, as an important subject of moral reflection; but it can hardly be said that the ethics of character has attained parity with the ethics of action as a preoccupation of moral philosophers. These departments of ethics are not unrelated. Doing the right thing is an important part of having a good character, and considerations of character are sometimes relevant to our choice of actions. On the face of it, however, the ethics of virtue and the ethics of action are about different questions, and both sorts of question are important.

This obvious reason for studying the ethics of virtue is the one to which my present investigation seeks to respond. I am not responding to another motivation that is powerfully at work in the recent literature of virtue ethics. Some of the main contributions to that literature have been inspired by the idea that problems about meaning, justification, and truth in ethics which seem intractable in relation to the ethics of action can be better resolved by a return to the study of the virtues. Such problems about the nature of language and thought *about* ethical norms and values constitute the domain of what is called *metaethics*. It is distinguished from *substantive* ethics,[1] which actually engages in evaluation of ethically significant actions, attitudes, and traits of character. The two types of inquiry are not and should not be completely separate, but it can be useful to distinguish them. The present book is an essay in substantive ethics.

Metaethical motivation is obvious in G. E. M. Anscombe's famous paper on "Modern Moral Philosophy," which is widely credited with initiating the

---

[1] I prefer 'substantive ethics' to the more usual expression 'normative ethics' as a designation of the parts of ethical theory that are centrally engaged, in a general way, in actual ethical evaluation. That is because 'normative' too easily suggests that the whole subject matter is what we *ought to do*, whereas substantive ethics also includes evaluation of states of mind and traits of character as ethically better and worse. Substantive ethics is not necessarily less *general* than metaethics. Indeed, it normally focuses on fairly general principles, and on *types* of action, state, and character, rather than particular individuals.

renewed interest in virtue ethics. Anscombe's argument begins with the thesis that the concepts of moral obligation and moral duty should be abandoned by modern moral philosophy because they belong to "a law conception of ethics" that does not make sense without a belief in divine commands that will not be accepted by most moral philosophers. But it is possible to "do ethics" without such a law conception, "as is shown by the example of Aristotle."[2] And what Aristotle's example suggests is an ethics structured principally by the concept of virtue. Anscombe's paper does not go very far toward showing how metaethics might find a better sense for concepts of virtue than for concepts of moral obligation, but she seems to hold out at least the hope that it might be done with the aid of a better philosophy of psychology than any that existed in 1958.

It is a curious feature of Anscombe's paper that at the substantive, as distinct from the metaethical level, she seems much more concerned with the ethics of actions than with the ethics of traits of character. Concepts of virtue are to provide the terminology of moral assessment, but it is *actions* that she seems absorbingly interested in identifying as "untruthful," "unchaste," or "unjust." The most passionate concern of her essay is to defend a sort of moral absolutism about actions. She wants to find a way of excluding any possibility that it could be right, for instance, "to get a man judicially punished for something which it can be clearly seen he has not done." Because of the descriptive content or, as we might now say, the "thickness" of 'just' and 'unjust', she thinks "it cannot be argued that the procedure would in any circumstances be just." It is here above all that she wants us to "see the superiority of the [virtue] term 'unjust' over the [thinner, more colorless] terms 'morally right' and 'morally wrong'," which sometimes in fact have been used to admit as possible the conclusion she regards as evil.[3] In this way much of her argument supports a preference, not for evaluation of character as opposed to direct evaluation of action, but rather for ethical terminology in which evaluation is fused with rich descriptive content.

Similar observations apply to Alasdair MacIntyre's *After Virtue*. His argument begins with the claim that our culture suffers from a collapse of ethical thinking, a collapse that is clearly a *meta*ethical problem. It appears to be first of all an epistemological problem—namely, that "there seems to be no rational way of securing moral agreement in our culture." This epistemological problem, MacIntyre argues in his second chapter, has led to an emotivist view of the nature of ethical judgment. An argument too complicated to rehearse here, which turns on the concept of tradition at least as much as on the concept of a virtue, leads him to the conclusion that our best hope of escaping the collapse lies in a return to "the tradition of the virtues." Certainly he is interested in substantive ethical

[2] Anscombe, "Modern Moral Philosophy," pp. 33–4. Though the belief is not expressed in that paper, a large proportion of its first readers probably knew that Anscombe herself did believe in divine commands.
[3] Anscombe, "Modern Moral Philosophy," pp. 34, 40–4.

questions about traits of character as well as about actions, but it is noteworthy that his introductory examples of intractable ethical disagreement in our culture are all concerned with issues in the ethics of *action*. Indeed, they are largely about issues in the ethics of *political* action, such as legislation about abortion.[4]

It will be obvious that my theory of the nature of virtue is not proposed as a solution to metaethical problems. I identify virtue with persisting excellence in being for the good. In so doing I help myself to the concept of the good, and to the more specialized concept of excellence, which is regarded with particular suspicion by some metaethicists. Believing that these concepts ought to have a central role in ethical theory, I have given an extended metaethical account of them elsewhere (in my book *Finite and Infinite Goods*), and will not repeat that account here. But I do not suppose that a shift of attention from obligation to virtue will get us very far in metaethics; for all ethical and evaluative beliefs face fundamentally similar metaethical issues about their justification, meaning, and grounding in reality. I think those issues are difficult but not hopeless, and are well worth discussing; but my present concern is with issues of another sort about virtue.

## 2. VIRTUE AND RIGHT ACTION

Likewise I am not looking to the ethics of virtue for solutions to problems about the ethics of action. I am not trying to analyze or define the concepts of right and wrong in terms of virtue, nor to eliminate them in favor of concepts drawn from the theory of virtue. I call what I am offering here a contribution to the "ethics of virtue," but not a form of "virtue ethics." The latter expression has commonly been appropriated to designate the view that a theory of virtue provides the right foundation for all of ethics, and that the ethics of duty should be reduced to, or replaced by, the ethics of virtue.[5] That more imperialistic view seems to me at best misleading.

There are fundamental differences between judgments of virtue and judgments of obligation. One is that the former are evaluations of character while the latter are evaluations of action. And the value of an act can certainly diverge from the value of the character that produced it. Virtuous character is not *sufficient* to insure right action. For instance, lack of attention may cause one to fail to recognize a moral duty, but such a lack of attention will not always manifest a deficiency in virtue. For any human being's resources of attention are limited and one may have had good reason to focus one's attention elsewhere. But even in such a case, action contrary to the unrecognized duty is still a wrong action.

Virtuous character is also not *necessary* for right action. Suppose certain merchants deal honestly with you only because they fear dishonesty would damage

---

[4] MacIntyre, *After Virtue*, pp. 6–7.
[5] Cf. the Introduction to Crisp and Slote, eds., *Virtue Ethics*, pp. 2–3.

their business. You have no reason to complain that their *actions* violate an oblig-ation to you, though you may have reason to complain of their *attitude*, if you know of it. It can happen that only shabby motives of self-protection would in fact lead one to do what one has an obligation to do, whereas there is something else one could do instead from a good motive of kindness. In such a case one will act *badly*, in one way or another (either wrongly or from bad motives), no matter which one does. But it remains true that the *right* thing to *do*, with or without good motives, is the thing one is under obligation to do.[6]

There is an even more fundamental difference, in my opinion, between judg-ments of virtue and judgments of obligation. The concept of obligation, and the associated concepts of wrongness and guilt, involve the idea of an agent *owing* it *to* someone else to act or not act in a certain way. That idea does not flow in any obvious way from a general concept of excellent personal character, and one could have a concept of excellence of character without it.

Of course if we start with an idea of obligation we should expect something to flow from it into our complete theory of virtue. It is uncontroversial that a vir-tuous person will have a tendency to act rightly. Some particular virtues, such as those of conscientiousness, justice, and respect for the rights of other people, are mainly matters of responding well to considerations of moral obligation. These facts may tempt us to suppose that a morally wrong act, for example, could be defined as one that it would be characteristic of thoroughly virtuous persons not to do, as virtue ethicists have commonly suggested.

It is important to distinguish two claims that might be made about such a definition.[7] One is a claim of *equivalence*: the claim that the class of acts that are morally wrong is exactly the same as the class of acts that it would be characterist-ic of virtuous persons not to do.[8] The other is an *explanatory* claim: the claim that the fact that virtuous persons would characteristically not do them explains what the wrongness of morally wrong acts consists in. The second claim seems to me implausible. On the face of it, the thought that one owes it to someone else not to do an act seems more suited to explain than to be explained by the thought that one's own character, if virtuous, would lead one not to do it. But that's not an objection to the claim of equivalence, which if true might be of some importance for the theory of virtue.

In fact, however, the claim that every act that it would be characteristic of vir-tuous persons not to do is morally wrong is implausible too. Suppose excessive

---

⁶ I am responding here to an argument given by Michael Slote in *Morals from Motives*, p. 25. I do not mean that one is still doing the right thing if one is doing it mainly as a means to accomplishing something one has a greater obligation not to do.

⁷ Cf. Zagzebski, *Divine Motivation Theory*, pp. 141–5 and 159–60.

⁸ I leave undefined the strength of the supposed equivalence. The class of acts of which it is asserted must be understood as including acts that are realistically possible but not actually performed, as our discussion will rely on fictitious examples. But it should not be necessary to decide whether the equivalence extends to the farthest reaches of possibility, as I will try to avoid "far-fetched" examples.

timidity leads me to forgo an adventure that is important to some private personal project of my own. Yielding in that way to unreasonable fear is something I would not do without some deficiency in practical wisdom or courage, or probably in both. It is therefore an act that it would be characteristic of thoroughly virtuous persons not to do. But surely it does not follow that I would, in effect, be violating an obligation in doing it, or that it would be reasonable for me to feel *guilty* about it (though perhaps I might reasonably feel a bit *ashamed* of it).

We can escape this counterexample, and get a claim of equivalence that is at least more plausible, if we assume that unreasonable guilt feelings are not characteristic of a thoroughly virtuous person. On that basis we might say that a morally wrong act is one that is such that it is characteristic of a thoroughly virtuous person (1) not to do it, and (2) to feel guilty if (uncharacteristically) she has done it.[9] I need not object here to this more qualified claim of equivalence, though I am not sure it would survive all counterexamples. The main point I want to make about it is that it does not provide a *reduction* of obligation concepts to virtue, for it presupposes the concept of guilt, which is part of the obligation family of concepts. Moreover, we might think it more plausible to say that the virtuous person would feel guilty about the act because it is wrong, than that it is wrong because she would feel guilty about it.

The words 'right' and 'wrong' are used in a variety of ways. In some uses they do not express judgments of ethical obligation, as is obvious when we speak of "wrong answers" or "the right answer" on a test. The force of 'right' can differ widely, depending on the context, when advice is given in the form, 'I think that is the right thing for you to do in this situation.' This can sometimes mean that the recommended action is the one that agrees best with virtue, all things considered. But an action that is not "the right one" in that sense is not necessarily a violation of duty or obligation.[10] An act can be cowardly, as I have argued, and foolish as well, without incurring guilt. I believe the most important senses of 'right' and 'wrong' for ethical theory are those tied to the notion of obligation, for which an adequate account cannot be given in terms of virtue. My conception of moral obligation as obligation to someone else is doubtless controversial; but I will not turn aside to defend it here,[11] as this is not a book about the nature of obligation. My interest in the ethics of virtue, in any event, is in its own proper subject, the assessment of character, and not in its supposed potential for grounding or replacing the ethics of duty.

---

[9] This formulation is patterned on a definition proposed in Zagzebski, *Divine Motivation Theory*, p. 141. Zagzebski does not claim that it provides a reduction of obligation concepts to virtue, though she thinks that can be accomplished in another way.

[10] This point applies to all analyses of right action in terms of virtue with which I am acquainted—for instance, to those discussed in Christine Swanton's excellent article, "A Virtue Ethical Account of Right Action," including Swanton's own analysis.

[11] I have defended it in Adams, *Finite and Infinite Goods*, chapters 10 and 11.

Equally, on the other hand, I do not suppose that virtue can be defined as a tendency to act rightly, nor even as a tendency to *try* to act rightly. Such definitions have certainly been offered, and certainly we do expect the virtuous to try to act rightly. We also expect that they will usually succeed in doing so, except in the most difficult or confusing of situations. But a definition in terms of duty or right action offers us an impoverished conception of virtue, for two reasons.

The first is that the territory of virtue is larger than that of action and tendency to action. Virtue involves and depends on appropriate emotions as well as actions. This is still true where tendency to action is not an important aspect of the emotion, as in feeling sympathy for what deserves sympathy in the past, about which, in the most important respects, we cannot *do* anything. Even more importantly, virtue depends on motives and beliefs that shape actions. Claims about virtue and the virtues are not chiefly about the ethical classification and evaluation of actions performed, but rather about the ethical significance of *what lies behind our actions*. This is fortunate for the ethics of virtue; for, as we shall see in chapter 8, empirical evidence suggests that virtues understood as tendencies to right behavior are less consistently present in the lives of people that have them—and to that extent have less reality—than virtues understood in terms of morally good views and motives.

The second reason is that even in its manifestation in action, virtue is best understood as a kind of *goodness* rather than *rightness*. This may be a controversial classification. Even among philosophers who would not think of defining virtue in terms of duty, some still seem to conceive of virtue primarily as a matter of recognizing and enacting the right thing to do. John McDowell, for example, championing a virtue-centered approach to ethics as an alternative to a view that would define virtue as "a disposition . . . to behave rightly," nonetheless identifies virtue with a (motivating) sensitivity that detects "the *requirement* imposed by the situation" and is manifested in action that accords with the requirement.[12]

There is an irony here that should not go unnoticed. The current virtue ethics movement began with Anscombe's influential interpretation of Aristotle's ethics as one in which the notions of right and wrong and ought do not occur with the moral sense in which they signify being obliged or required "in the sense in which one can be obliged or bound by law."[13] I am prepared to grant that such a notion of moral *obligation* has at most a limited and arguably peripheral role in Aristotle's ethics. But plainly he did tend to think about virtue as a matter of getting it *right* in some sense—hitting the target,[14] choosing the correct action. It belongs to virtue, he says, to feel and act "at the time, and about the matters, and toward the people, and for the reason [or the end], that one should, and

---

[12] McDowell, "Virtue and Reason," pp. 141–3; italics mine.
[13] Anscombe, "Modern Moral Philosophy," p. 30.
[14] *Nicomachean Ethics*, II.v (1106b32).

as one should."[15] Aristotle says this in connection with his famous thesis that virtue lies in "the mean"—where the mean, of course, is not the mathematical midpoint or median or average, but the *right* point or the *right* degree. These features of Aristotle's conception of virtue are echoed by many virtue theorists today. Neera Badhwar is surely right in saying that "Aristotle's conception of virtue of character as a habitual emotional and rational disposition to feel, choose, and act in the right way for the right ends is accepted by many contemporary philosophers."[16]

This is one of a number of points at which my project in writing about virtue is not an Aristotelian project. One reason for that is that I am skeptical about the concept of rightness that is required for non-trivial Aristotelian views of the relation of virtue and rightness. "The right way" and "the right ends" that figure in Badhwar's characterization of Aristotelian virtue must surely be understood as invoking a broader conception of rightness than that of obligation of persons *to* other persons or social groups. But the characterization will be trivial or even viciously circular if "the right way" and "the right ends" mean merely those that accord with virtue.

The most influential neo-Aristotelian approach to these matters identifies the right ends, and the right ways of feeling, choosing, and acting in relation to them as those that are approved by *practical reason*. That is the point on which I am, as I said, skeptical. The conception of practical reason or practical rationality of which I think I can make the best sense simply identifies it with excellent thinking about practical matters. And a conception of virtue as responding in ways, and for ends, that would be approved by excellent thinking is uncontroversial to the point of triviality. In view of my skepticism, I do not intend to presuppose a more foundational conception of practical reason in this book, though I will not turn aside to argue that no such conception can be articulated and defended.

I also believe that Aristotle's emphasis on getting it right obscures one of the most interesting ways in which an ethics of virtue can differ from an ethics of duty. Assessments of virtue have a logical pattern more typical of judgments of goodness than of judgments of rightness. The concepts of the good and the right differ in the shape of the characteristic frameworks of evaluation they offer us, that of the good being much more tolerant of ambivalence and diversity.

If an action is right it is not wrong, but an action may well be good (in one way) and bad (in another). Saying that a certain action is "the right thing to do" normally implies that doing something quite different instead would not be right in the same sense. This is true even where saying it is "the right thing to do" does not express a judgment of duty or obligation. As Aristotle says, "there are

---

[15] Aristotle, *Nicomachean Ethics*, II.v (1106b21–23).

[16] Badhwar, "The Limited Unity of Virtue," p. 306. The thought is not peculiarly Aristotelian. I assume Julia Annas is right in saying that "all ancient theories understand a virtue to be, at least, a disposition to do the morally right thing" (Annas, *The Morality of Happiness*, p. 9).

many ways of going wrong [*hamartanein*]..., but only one way of getting it right [*katorthoun*]."[17] But saying that something would be "a good thing to do" by no means implies that there are not quite different alternatives that would be equally good. If we suppose that some action is the (one) right thing to do, we may naturally think that virtue will typically be shown in doing that thing. Nonetheless, notable forms of virtue may be manifested in actions that are in important ways good, even if they are not, all things considered, the right thing to do in the situation. A view of virtue as a kind of goodness rather than a kind of rightness makes it easier to see how there can be quite different alternative ways of being genuinely virtuous. This is a point of some importance in our world of cultural, religious, and ethical plurality.

## 3. OUTLINE

A brief outline of some of the main lines of thought in the book may help readers to orient themselves. As already stated, I identify virtue with persisting excellence in being for the good. This is a definition of virtue as goodness of character, as a holistic property of persons. Similarly I conceive of particular virtues, such as courage and benevolence, as excellent ways of being for (and against) things. However, I think that courage and some of the other virtues are not essentially ways of being for *the good*. Rather they are excellent strengths to have in governing one's life with a view to whatever one is for, and in that way are traits that *can* be part of excellent ways of being for the good. The articulation and defense of these conceptions of virtue and the virtues begins in chapter 2 and is the principal task of Part I, "What is Virtue?" Chapter 3 deals with the subject of vices and bad moral character. Chapter 4 defends my emphasis on excellence and being for the good against alternatives that would define virtue and virtues in terms of their benefits or their contribution to human flourishing.

For many moderns moral goodness is essentially altruistic, a matter of respect and care for the rights and the good of other persons. In contrast, my account of virtue as excellence in being for the good agrees with ancient philosophers in allowing that care for one's own good can be virtuous. Part II, "Self and Other," explores the place of altruism in such a conception of virtue. The first task, in chapter 5, is to argue that altruism is indeed excellent, and also to defend in this context the thesis that it must be intrinsically and not just instrumentally good if it is to be a virtue. Reflection on excellences of interpersonal cooperation leads in chapters 6 and 7 to the conclusion that some forms of self-love are virtuous, and cohere well with being *for* other people.

In view of my emphasis on excellence of character a reader might imagine that I have an extremely optimistic view of our moral capacities and inclinations. That

---

[17] Aristotle, *Nicomachean Ethics*, II.v (1106b28–31).

is not the case. I believe that such virtue as we may attain is never complete, always surpassable. Always fragmentary, it is often visible only from a certain angle, so to speak. At best we can be virtuous sinners. Actual human virtue is frail, and dependent on conditions beyond the voluntary control of the individual whose character is in question. Some may find that assessment of the human moral condition plausible but wonder how it can be consistent with belief in the reality of virtue as persisting excellence in being for the good, and in virtues as persisting excellences of character. How these views may be put together to obtain a realistic conception of virtue is the overarching theme of Part III, "Are There Really Any Virtues?"

Appealing to empirical findings of social psychologists, some contemporary philosophers have argued that there really are no virtues and vices, and indeed no traits of character. The empirical findings in question will be discussed in chapters 8 and 9. They support and inform my view of the limitations of human virtue, but I argue that they do not show that there are no actual moral virtues. Two general types of limitation of virtue will engage our attention.

In the first place, human virtue is in various ways *fragmentary*. It seems that a person can be more conscientious than generous, or more generous than conscientious. Experiments in social psychology seem to show that people rarely are broadly consistent in manifesting even behavior regarded as characteristic of a single virtue, broadly conceived. It seems they rarely are consistently honest, or consistently helpful to others, in different types of situation. This evidence is addressed in chapter 8. It is significant for moral psychology, but I believe it does not show that there are not actually any virtues. I try to identify types of quality with respect to which people do seem commonly to be consistent over time, and which seem otherwise to be promising candidates for recognition as virtues.

In the second place, psychological evidence indicates that supposed virtues typically are *frail* in some ways, and liable to be overwhelmed or subverted by the influence of social situations. The question then arises whether such traits lack a robustness they would have to have in order to be authentic virtues. Similarly, one might wonder whether in their origin and endurance they are too *dependent* on social support or social context to be attributed to an individual as a virtue. Are they really properties of the individual at all, or only of a group? Is too much "moral luck" involved in them for them to count as virtues, in that they are not acquired or maintained solely through an individual's own efforts but depend on factors outside the individual's voluntary control? In chapter 9 I argue that these issues should not keep us from regarding actual traits as virtues. I propose a perspective from which virtues are viewed more as gifts (and gifts which can sometimes be shared) than as a basis for earning or deserving anything.

In chapter 8 I do not argue that any human being is consistently virtuous in *all* respects, or has all virtues. In fact I believe that human virtue, though real, is typically *fragmentary*. Here I find myself in confrontation with the ancient doctrine of *the unity of the virtues*. Its most widely discussed implication is that one cannot have any of the virtues without having all of them. My reasons for rejecting the latter thesis will be explained in chapter 10. Other issues connected with the idea of the unity of the virtues will engage our attention in chapter 11. They include questions about the plurality of virtuous ways of life and the integration of moral character, which will also be central to the discussion of education for virtue in chapter 12, which concludes the book.

# 2

# Excellence in Being *for* the Good

I define moral virtue as persisting excellence in being for the good. Such a definition is worth little without explanation of its terms. That explanation is the business of this chapter.

The two central ideas in my account of virtue are those of excellence and being for the good. Whatever else may be said for a trait of character —however useful, agreeable, or desirable in other ways it may be—if we do not think it is excellent, honorable, or worthy of admiration, we will hardly call it a virtue. One recent writer on virtue goes so far as to say that "the central idea that virtue is an excellence has never been seriously questioned."[1] Few, at any rate, would flatly reject the claim that virtue is excellent, though it will be more controversial if it is taken to imply (as I do mean to imply) that virtue has an important value that is not merely instrumental.

Obviously not every sort of excellence constitutes moral virtue. Moral virtue is excellence of moral character. Here the idea of being for the good comes into play. How do we assess a person's moral character? By her actions, presumably. Behavior, including speech and facial expression, provides our only cognitive access to another person's character. But if it is character we are assessing, rather than the actions as such, we are concerned not just with what is done, physically speaking, but above all with what the behavior reveals of the person. What is the human significance of the actions? What motives, what feelings, thoughts, and intentions, lie behind them? What does the person try to do? What does she value, what does she want, what does she care about, what does she love? In the most general terms, what is the person *for* and *against*? A virtuous person, a morally good person, will of course be for good things and against bad things—and not in just any way, but excellently.

The claims that virtue is a matter of being for what is good and against what is bad, and that virtue is itself an excellence, surely have great plausibility. Even if these intuitively plausible theses are correct, however, it does not follow that I am right in thinking the nature of virtue is best understood in terms of them. There are other plausible general theses about virtue that some propose to use to explain its nature. Roughly speaking, most accounts of the nature or criterion of virtue define it either in terms of its *instrumental* value for promoting human

---

[1] Zagzebski, *Virtues of the Mind*, p. 85.

well-being or in terms of its *intrinsic* excellence. My theory is obviously of the second sort. These approaches need not lead to widely different lists of virtues, for excellent ways of being for the good typically are beneficial too; but the two types of theory represent importantly different ways of thinking about virtue and its place in human life.

Most obviously, excellence-based theories are committed to the view that moral goodness is worth having for its own sake. Typically they rank it high among the goods for the sake of which human life can be worth living. This view of the worth of moral goodness is one of the central commitments of my theory of virtue. Benefit-based theories of virtue, on the other hand, can be consistent with the view that moral goodness is not worth having for its own sake, but only for the sake of its extrinsic benefits.

In conceiving of virtue as a type of intrinsic excellence rather than of instrumental goodness I need not suppose that it has nothing to do with human well-being. On the contrary, I believe that virtue and other sorts of excellence are major constituents of human well-being. Few of us would wish for ourselves, or for others whom we love, a life of desire-satisfaction or enjoyment without regard to our judgments of the quality or intrinsic value of what is enjoyed. I would argue, indeed, that well-being is best understood as consisting chiefly in enjoyment of excellence.[2] In an excellence-based theory of virtue, however, virtue will not be measured by the level of well-being achieved. Rather, well-being may be measured in part by the excellence of virtue enjoyed.

Benefit-based theories in which virtue is defined in terms of its instrumental value deserve our serious attention. The relation of virtue to its benefits will be examined at some length in chapter 4. I will argue there that considerations of excellence and of being for the good are better suited than considerations of benefit to define virtue. First, however, in the present chapter, the content of my account of the nature of virtue must be developed more fully. There are three main concepts to be elucidated: those of being for, the good, and excellence; they will be the subjects of sections 1, 2, and 3, respectively. A fourth section will discuss the relation between virtue, in the singular, understood holistically as overall excellence of a person's moral character, and particular virtues such as courage and benevolence. A correlated account of vice will be presented in chapter 3.


## 1. BEING *FOR*

When I speak of "being for the good," *being for* is meant to cover a lot of territory. There are many ways of being for something. They include: loving it, liking it, respecting it, wanting it, wishing for it, appreciating it, thinking highly of it, speaking in favor of it and otherwise intentionally standing for it symbolically,

---

[2] This is argued in Adams, *Finite and Infinite Goods*, chapter 3.

acting to promote or protect it, and being disposed to do such things. I believe the breadth of this concept importantly reflects the difference between the ethics of character and the ethics of action.

When we start to think about virtue we may think first of obvious heroes, known for their noble deeds. But there are also less active dimensions of virtue, and they are important resources for living well the inevitably large parts of our lives in which we are relatively passive or even helpless. Let us focus therefore on virtue as it may be manifested in someone whose hands cannot reach the levers of the world. Think of someone very aged and infirm, perhaps unable to move her own wheelchair, and perhaps suffering such memory loss that someone else has to be responsible for many of the decisions in her life. Such a person, I believe, can still be virtuous, and even an inspiration to others. She can still be considerate of those who see her and care for her, and thus need not be altogether without a decision-making dimension of virtue. But if we see notable virtue in her, much of it surely will be in her attitudes, and they may be attitudes to things that she cannot do much about. Suppose she appreciates whatever good things she is still able to enjoy, is grateful to those who care for her, is delighted when she hears someone else's good news, and never enjoys hearing of another person's misfortune. I believe all of that is virtue—not because it shows a disposition to perform noble deeds, which may be mostly beyond her reach—but simply because those are ways of *being for* things that are importantly good.

I don't think that doing or being something that merely happens to be *causally conducive* to X is a way of being for X. Being for X is an *intentional* state, and must involve an action or attitude that *means* X or has X as an intentional object, or a tendency to such an action or attitude. Thus being for something is, or involves, a psychological or mental property. That is why viruses, for instance, are not, in the relevant sense, *for* disease. Their causing disease is not *sufficient* for being for it. Nor is being a cause of the object *necessary*, in all cases, for being for it. One can be for and against goods and evils that one cannot affect causally, such as those belonging to past history. The centrality of intentionality in the phenomena that concern us is underlined by the importance that standing for something symbolically can have as a way of being for it.

The point that there are broadly *intellectual* forms of being for something requires both emphasis and qualification. Believing that something is good or right or honorable is normally a way of being for it, and believing it is bad or wrong is a way of being against it. Conversely, if you say that you are *for* socialism, or "in favor of" it, we are normally entitled to infer that you believe in it, in the sense that you think it is the best way to organize an economy, or at least a good one. And one way of failing to be for people as one should is to *view* them, articulately or inarticulately, as inferior to others, or less important than others. We will have a lopsided view of people's character if we do not take account of such intellectual aspects of their being for and against things.

The main qualification this point requires is that *being for x* must involve dispositions to favor *x* in action, desire, emotion, or feeling. In that broad sense it must engage *the will*. Thinking Smith is the best candidate is normally a way of being for her—but not if you really care not at all about Smith and not at all about the election, and are not disposed to do anything about it. Largely cognitive states, such as believings, assents, and views, can be ways of being for something, but only if they engage the will in the indicated way. If they do so engage the will, however, they can constitute ways of being for something, and traits of moral character. Moral virtue is an excellence of the will, in the indicated broad sense.

I will not turn aside to enter the debate about the correctness or incorrectness of allowing, as I do, that there can be intellectual evaluations that are not ways of being for something because they do not involve the requisite motivating dispositions.[3] Such motivationally inert evaluations do not have a major role, anyway, in my account of virtue. As will appear in chapter 10, section 3, I do believe that there is such a thing as weakness of will, in the sense of acting contrary to evaluative beliefs that may be important to one's character. But such weakness does not show that those evaluative beliefs are motivationally inert or do not engage the will. It shows only that the motivational dispositions associated with the beliefs are not invincible in the clash of competing motives from which our actions commonly spring.

Debates about free will and determinism have tended to focus modern philosophical discussions of the will fairly narrowly on actions and decisions, understood as events. What I mean, however, by *the will*, of which moral virtue is an excellence, is not exclusively a faculty of such actions. Among its other functions, it is a faculty also of dispositions, of somewhat enduring causal states that influence action, and play a part, more broadly, in psychological processes of decision-making. In this I follow typical medieval conceptions of the will as an intellectual appetitive faculty [*appetitus intellectivus*]. It is broadly appetitive in having motivational states as well as decisions among its functions. It involves intelligence, and not merely sensation, inasmuch as those states and decisions involve some *understanding* of their objects. When I speak of being for or against something, I mean likewise to imply some level of understanding of the object. Emotions can be ways of being for or against something, but only insofar as the emotion has an intentionality that involves some understanding of its object. To "feel on top of the world," or to be gripped by nameless anxiety or grief, without

---

[3] The question is discussed in Adams, *Finite and Infinite Goods*, pp. 13–28. "Internalists," who hold that evaluative beliefs necessarily have internal to them a motivation to act as the belief indicates would be good to act, have no reason to disagree with my conditional claim that intellectual evaluative states must engage the will *if* they are to be ways of being for something. For the internalists hold unconditionally that intellectual evaluative states must involve dispositions of the will; and the conditional claim follows from the unconditional one.

any understanding of something one is glad or worried or sad about, is not yet to be for or against anything.

It would be difficult, if not impossible, to ascribe virtue to people without assuming that they are capable of being for and against goods and evils in disposition as well as in action. For virtue is not a merely momentary action or state of a person. One may be excellently, even heroically, for the good in a deed that takes but an instant, but that is not what we mean by virtue. That is why the full formulation of my definition of virtue is that virtue is *persisting* excellence in being for the good. It probably would not be fruitful to try to determine just how long virtue must persist in order genuinely to be virtue. A day is surely not long enough, but people who die five years after a conversion from vice may by then have been virtuous indeed. And it is hardly credible that one's being for the good would have the required persistence if one were not for the good in disposition as well as in action. The relevant dispositions will of course include states that have some tendency to *influence* action. This is not to say that they *completely determine* action. As I suggested above, they compete with each other, and may not be invincible.

There is no need to suppose even that all one's motivational dispositions taken together perfectly determine what one will do in any given situation. In the present state of our knowledge (including our reasons to accept quantum mechanics) I take it there is little reason to suppose that the world is completely deterministic. But the relevance of this point should not be exaggerated. It is obvious that human behavior, of sorts generally counted as voluntary, can often be predicted with high reliability, for better as well worse. David Hume makes the point very convincingly in Section 8 of his *Enquiry Concerning Human Understanding*:

> Were a man, whom I know to be honest and opulent, and with whom I live in intimate friendship, to come into my house, where I am surrounded with my servants, I rest assured that he is not to stab me before he leaves it in order to rob me of my silver standish; and I no more suspect this event than the falling of the house itself, which is new, and solidly built and founded.[4]

When we speak of virtues we surely mean to speak of enduring psychological states that can in some contexts play an influential part in more or less reliable predictability. This may give rise to uneasiness in moral philosophers who worry about deterministic views because they think that we cannot rightly be ethically evaluated except for what is within our control. Some misgivings about the relation of virtue to voluntary control will be addressed in chapter 9. Here I will simply note that there is little hope for any ethical outlook that cannot accommodate the fact that human behavior of apparent moral significance is often quite predictable.

---

[4] Hume, *Enquiries*, p. 91.

## 2. THE GOODS THAT VIRTUE IS FOR

What is the good that virtue is for? Or perhaps I should ask about "the goods" that virtue is for, in the plural. I believe there is something to be said for thinking of the good as one, or at any rate for trying to think of it as integrated in some way.[5] But we will be concerned, in most of our concrete thinking about virtue, with a great variety of particular goods.

What is most important about these goods, for the structure of my theory of virtue, is indeed their diversity. I hold a very broad view of the goods that virtue is for, including any goods that human beings can exemplify excellence in caring about. And when I speak of virtue as *moral* goodness, the territory of morality must likewise be understood very broadly. The word 'moral' is sometimes understood much more narrowly, in a sense in which *moral* virtue is exclusively goodness *to other people*, in caring about their well-being and being committed to respecting their rights. It is probably not profitable to debate whether a broader or narrower sense of 'moral' is right as a matter of linguistic analysis, as various uses of the word are quite common. My preference for a broader conception of moral virtue and the goods it is for is rooted rather in the perspective in which I believe it is most fruitful to think about character. That is a perspective in which we consider what kinds of person we should *admire*, and not only what personal qualities we should be *grateful*, on our own account, to other people for having. It is a perspective in which we think comprehensively about what kind of person we should want to be, in our valuing and caring and choosing, and what kind of person we should want people we love to be—and not only what kind of person we should wish, for our own sake, to find in a neighbor we must trust and rely on.

I believe we can treat more accurately the complex and subtle relations among our interests in diverse goods if we do not allow our theories of virtue to depend heavily on where a line is drawn between moral and other types of value. I am skeptical of sharp lines of that sort—between moral and religious value as well as between moral and aesthetic value. Those lines are not easy to draw in a clear and uncontroversial way. Caring excellently for the good of other people, for example, is a major virtue that we would expect to find on the "moral" side of any such line. But it seems that the excellence of such caring can be affected by the extent to which one recognizes, appreciates, and cares excellently for *any* of the goods that can enrich the life of another person. Won't that tend to pull the latter sorts of excellence over onto the "moral" side of the line too?

A broad conception of moral virtue has an attraction in promising to facilitate integration of character. It offers a comprehensive ideal of excellence in valuing,

[5] I have argued in Adams, *Finite and Infinite Goods* (especially chapters 1, 2, and 7) for an identification of the good itself with God, seen as a unifying object (though in many cases only an implicit object) of all virtuous motivation.

caring, and choosing which will include, as a proper part, an ideal of excellence in being for other people and being good to them. It must face, however, the question whether we can really do justice to the virtues of caring for the good of other people, and their rights, if we subsume those virtues as a proper part within such a comprehensive ideal.[6] I must argue that the comprehensive ideal provides ample room for an ideal of other-regarding virtue. Indeed, I will argue that the latter ideal finds its most adequate context within the more comprehensive ideal. That is a main task of Part II of this book, on "Self and Other."

Two aspects of the breadth I ascribe to virtue's concerns should be noted at this point. One is that the goods one is for in being virtuous will typically include *one's own good* as well as the good of other persons. Some views of morality suggest that only altruistic concerns are virtuous. But caring appropriately for one's own good, and more broadly for the values in one's own life, has also had a place in classical conceptions of virtue, and rightly so in my opinion. It is part of virtue to desire, for its own sake, that goods one cares about should be realized in one's own life. Of course it is not virtuous to care only about one's own good, or to have a swollen preference for one's own good in comparison with that of other people. That is not excellent. I will not offer a complete answer to the question whether, and to what extent, it is virtuous to prefer others' good systematically to one's own. At the extreme, however, an absolute and universal preference of others' good to one's own hardly seems virtuous. To risk one's life by plunging into a raging torrent to rescue a child's teddy bear would be an act of *folly*, in virtually any realistic situation, even if the teddy bear is quite important to the child. And folly is a vice, a lapse from excellence in being for the good.

A second aspect of the breadth of virtue's concerns is that they are not limited to the rights and well-being of persons—one's own or anyone else's. A deep concern for quality in intellectual and aesthetic pursuits for their own sake seems intuitively to be virtuous. The seriousness, sincerity, and disinterestedness of someone's love of philosophy may be among our grounds for admiring her character. And respect for the value of non-human creatures and of the natural relations among them seems to many a mark of virtue. One of the attractions of a broad conception of moral virtue is that it tends to make more of what matters to us accessible to ethical evaluation. However, the inclusion of impersonal goods among virtue's concerns certainly faces possible objections.

My view seems to imply, for instance, that *good taste* in aesthetic matters is morally virtuous. For it is certainly a way of being for some humanly important goods, and an excellent way of being for them. But is it really a moral virtue, a virtue in the same sense in which kindness and honesty are virtues? The conventional answer to that question is, 'No; it's not a virtue in the same sense as kindness and honesty. At most it's an aesthetic virtue, which is something quite different and much less important.' But I'm inclined to answer, 'Yes; good taste is

---

[6] For a classic argument for a negative answer to this question, see Wolf, "Moral Saints."

a moral virtue—a relatively *minor* one, but a virtue in the same sense as kindness and honesty.'

I could not tolerably give this answer if I held the ancient thesis of the unity of virtue and the virtues, according to which one cannot have any single virtue if one is not virtuous on the whole, and cannot be virtuous on the whole if one lacks any single virtue. For it is surely possible to have great moral virtue on the whole without good aesthetic taste, and with little or no interest in aesthetic values. And history sadly affords examples of people with exquisite aesthetic taste but bad moral character on the whole. This is not a problem of consistency for me, however, since I reject the thesis of the unity of virtue and the virtues for many reasons, as discussed in chapters 10 and 11.

While excellence with regard to aesthetic values can be separated from more general moral excellence in the ways just indicated, I believe it is a mistake to suppose it is so separate that it cannot enter at all into the excellence of our concern and care for other people. Consider two possible faults. (1) In the first case one cares about other people, and wants to be kind in one's dealings with them. One is considerate with regard to their feelings, so far as one is aware of them. But one is not perceptive in relation to their feelings, perhaps because one is very repressed and unaware of one's own feelings, because one is afraid of them. One is usually as kind as one is able to be, and that kindness is a virtue, but a virtue that is impaired by one's emotional imperceptiveness.

(2) In the second case one wants one's children to have good lives. Wanting their lives to be enriched by cultural values, one tries to introduce them to good art; but in fact one is introducing them to sentimental kitsch. One's parental benevolence and one's enthusiasm for cultural values are virtues; but the latter, at least, is impaired by one's bad taste. One fails to perceive accurately what sort of life, in aesthetic respects, would be best for one's children. And one's children have at least a little something less to be grateful for in one's parenting than if one had had the taste to introduce them to good art.

Both the faults I have just described are deficiencies in sensitivity or judgment regarding factors about which one has moral reason to be concerned. As such, both are deficiencies in practical wisdom, broadly understood. Both are forms of imperceptiveness regarding factors that enrich or impoverish human lives. Both result in one's being less helpful to other people than one meant to be. Most of us will be tempted to say that insensitivity to other people's feelings is a graver fault than aesthetic bad taste. Whether that is correct must depend, I think, on whether feelings are generally, if not universally, more important than aesthetic values as determinants of the quality of human lives and human relationships. For sensitivity to what is more important to the value of human life is more important for human excellence in being for the good.

We certainly can say that aesthetic values cannot *substitute* for duty and the good of persons as objects of virtue's concern. One who cares nothing for moral obligations or the good of other people is not a virtuous or morally good person even if he has the most refined and ardent love of beauty. But caring for people and commitment to duty can be enough for great virtue, even without any aesthetic interests at all. Why is that so? Given the framework of my account of virtue, I must say that the latter pattern of caring about goods is excellent enough to constitute virtue but the former is not. The concept of *vice* can be used too in comparing these cases. Not caring about the good of other people or one's duties to them is a vice, and a grave one. But though lacking aesthetic interests is lacking a virtue, it seems too harsh to call it a vice. Grounds for these judgments are explored in chapter 3, where an account of vice is developed.

My broad view of the types of good that virtue is for reflects my belief that what are commonly regarded as cases of moral and non-moral goodness can be treated illuminatingly as instances of *excellence* in the same sense, though not necessarily in the same degree. This has the advantage that the concept of excellence offers a conceptual framework in which narrowly moral goodness can be *commended* without circularity. In this context the question 'Why be moral?' becomes 'Why aspire to other-regarding virtues?' and receives the answer 'Because they are part of a more excellent way to be.' This answer is introduced at the end of chapter 4 and developed in chapter 5.

Four further points about the goods virtue is for should be noted. (1) The most fundamental of them is that when I speak of being for the good, I mean being for something that really is good. In the normal case of a virtuous attitude, what the virtuous person is for really is good, and the virtuous person thinks of it as good. Where these two conditions pull apart, we will get, at best, much less clear cases of the virtuous. If you are for something that really is good, though you believe it to be bad, that limits the excellence your attitude toward that good can have. Indeed, your thinking it bad may well constitute a way in which you are against it as well as for it. Whether there is anything virtuous about being for something because you believe it to be good, although it really is bad, is a more difficult question; a possible answer to it is suggested very briefly in section 4.

(2) The goods virtue is for will not always, nor I think even usually, be *states of affairs*. Among them will be persons and beautiful objects, for example. Being *for* the good, in many cases, as in loving or respecting a person, may not be reducible to attitudes toward states of affairs. This is one way in which my view is not one that relates ethical evaluation primarily to values of consequences; for consequences, in the relevant sense, are states of affairs.

(3) There seem to be goods there is no virtue in loving. The love of money, for example, is not a form of virtue. Money, of course, is a merely instrumental good, and we may be tempted to say that it is only in being for *intrinsic* and not merely instrumental goods that one is virtuous. Maybe some version of that claim is correct, but it cannot be right to exclude instrumental goods altogether from the concerns of virtue. Great virtue can be shown, for instance, in a passionate focus on securing for people goods that are plainly instrumental, such as an adequate income.

Perhaps the best way of getting at the fundamental issue about the love of money is to say that being for something good is not a constituent or manifestation of virtue if it is good only for certain reasons and one is for it only for other, unrelated reasons—and likewise in the case of being against something bad. For instance, if one is against Nazism only because Hitler is a vegetarian and one hates vegetarians, that is not a manifestation of virtue, but of intolerance, even though Nazism is certainly something one should be against. In the same way, if something is good only instrumentally, being for it may be a manifestation of virtue, but only if one is for it for the sake of good ends that it serves—and thus only if one is for the latter, more fundamental goods. The love of money that is no virtue is an interest in money that has become too independent of the more basic goods that money can serve.

(4) In characterizing the excellence of virtue as excellence in being for the good I do *not* mean to imply that the good the virtuous person is for must have a value that is greater or *more* fundamental or *more* primitive than the value of being for it. I think it would be a mistake, in particular, to seek such a superior or more fundamental value in pleasures (perhaps especially the pleasures of others) that one might be for. For most of the pleasures we value most are functions not merely of a sensory faculty, but at least in part of an intellectual faculty. They have an intentionality, and typically are constituted by a liking that is a way of being for an intended object. Enjoying an intended object is a way of being for it, and I believe the value of such pleasures depends largely on the value of the intended object. Their value, accordingly, is not of a more fundamental sort than the value of being for them, but is largely of the same sort. That these pleasures are states in which something good is *enjoyed*, rather than only longed for, may plausibly be regarded as enhancing their value. But that seems to me to be simply an *additional* dimension of value, rather than a *superior* sort of value. And it can be a dimension of the value of being for someone else's pleasure, since it is perfectly possible to enjoy another person's pleasure. Arguably there are also physical pleasures that do not essentially involve intentionality or valuing. Of them, however, it seems an implausible sensualism to insist that their value is almost always superior to higher-order valuings of them.[7]

## 3. EXCELLENCE AS CRITERION OF VIRTUE

Not every way of being for something good is virtuous or a virtue. One can seek goods selfishly, only for oneself; or unjustly, only for one's friends, without regard for the rights of strangers; or intemperately, losing track of one's own most central aims and values; or in ways that cheapen human life, preferring goods that

---

[7] In this paragraph I take myself to be in disagreement with the very interesting "recursive" account of the value of virtue in Hurka, *Virtue, Vice, and Value*, pp. 11 ff.

are easy or obvious and neglecting others that are more deeply meaningful. What distinguishes virtuous ways of being for something good from other ways? The criterion I propose is that virtuous ways of being for the good must be excellent.

To say that virtue must be excellent is not just to say that it must be good. Excellence is a particular type of goodness. It is not *usefulness*, or merely instrumental goodness. To say that virtue must be excellent is to insist that it must be worth prizing for its own sake. In its own right it is one of the things that make life worth living. Although it is thus a determinant of well-being, being excellent is never just being good *for* persons. Excellence is the objective and non-instrumental goodness of that which is worthy to be honored, loved, admired, or (in the extreme case) worshiped, for its own sake. What I have just said is not meant, however, as a reductive definition of excellence. I hope it will serve as an identifying description, but it would be circular for me to offer it as a definition, since I take the suitableness of responsive attitudes, mentioned in it, to be a case of excellence.

It is important to its role in my theory of virtue that excellence is a type of *intrinsic* goodness. I do not mean that excellence, nor perhaps any type of goodness, is intrinsic in the strongest possible sense, in which an intrinsic property of any thing must be completely independent of any relations to other things. Moral excellence is certainly not completely independent of relations in which the morally excellent person stands. I do not even mean that excellence is completely independent of the value of its consequences. I believe that helping other people, for example, is often a truly excellent, intrinsically valuable feature of a person's life—more valuable intrinsically than trying just as hard to help but failing through bad luck. Even assuming that those who needed help got it in both cases, we would rightly wish to be someone who actually helped rather than someone who only tried to help. Actually helping is worth prizing for its own sake and not only for the sake of the benefits received by the other people, though of course it is also worth prizing for the sake of those benefits extrinsic to it.[8]

I do not have a perfectly complete and adequate definition of the moderate sense in which I claim that the goodness of virtue is *intrinsic*, but I hope I can give sufficient clarification for the purposes of this book.[9] When I say that excellence of a quality Q of moral character is an intrinsic goodness, I mean at least that the excellence is not defined in terms of the value of consequences of having Q, and is not simply a function of their value. Consequences of having Q, in this context, are required first of all to be objects or states of affairs to whose occurrence a person's having Q contributes, or has some likelihood of contributing. In order to assure that consequences of having Q are extrinsic to having Q, I require, in the

---

[8] In what I say I do *not* mean in this paragraph, I am mindful of the arguments of Korsgaard, "Two Distinctions in Goodness," and especially Kagan, "Rethinking Intrinsic Value."

[9] Some other writers on virtue have sought recently to use 'intrinsic' in a similarly moderate sense. See Hurka, *Virtue, Vice, and Value*, p. 6; Zagzebski, *Divine Motivation Theory*, pp. 19–22.

second place, that it be possible in principle (in accordance with correct logical and evaluative principles) for them to occur, and have the same value, without any person of the relevant sort having Q.

When I say that excellence of a quality Q of moral character is an intrinsic goodness, I also mean that it is good and reasonable to prize Q *for its own sake*, and not merely for the sake of any consequences. One might try to express this by saying that what is excellent is good as an end in itself and not merely as a means to some ulterior end. But this would express my view only if it is *not* understood in accordance with Linda Zagzebski's statement that "the difference between goods as ends and goods as means is a difference in the way we value things."[10] For I assume that if Q is intrinsically good, even in the moderate sense of 'intrinsic' that I am trying to characterize, then it is good objectively and independently of our actually valuing or prizing it. (As this book is not about metaethics, I will not enter seriously into the question whether Q is good, indeed excellent, independently of *God's* prizing it.)

I will continue to describe the excellence I ascribe to virtue as a kind of "intrinsic" goodness. Sometimes also, I will characterize it as a "non-instrumental" goodness, particularly if instrumentality is prominently involved in an alternative I am rejecting. I hope I have said enough to make clear my use of 'intrinsic' is not meant to imply that the goodness of virtue is independent of all relations in which the virtuous stand, and that my use of 'non-instrumental' is not meant to imply that the goodness of virtue depends on our actually valuing or prizing it.

It will sometimes be helpful to speak of virtue as not only "excellent" but also "admirable." However, both of these words may suggest something exceptional, something *unusually* good, and my use of 'excellent' is not intended to have that implication. I have not found a better word than 'excellence' to express what I mean, but I wish to renounce any elitist connotations the word may have.[11] Certainly there are real excellences that are rare. Some forms of moral virtue are rare. But not all are. It is widely thought that in a successful democratic polity *most* citizens will have certain civic virtues, but we should not deny that those virtues are excellent. Human excellence is not in general found only in an elite group.

It is of great importance, morally, not to be so dazzled by excellences that are rare that we fail to appreciate the excellence of much that is ordinary. Healthy life, human or animal vitality, is a marvel and an excellence. So are simple pleasures. So is sincere love and friendship, however unambitious. It is a major part of moral wisdom to regard the excellence or worth that all persons have as beings capable of personal relationships, and of moral and other humanly significant choices and enjoyments, as having a claim on our respect and care that normally swamps reasons arising from more variable and contingent excellences persons

[10] Zagzebski, *Divine Motivation Theory*, p. 19.
[11] Aspects of the subject matter of this paragraph and the next are discussed more fully in Adams, *Finite and Infinite Goods*, chapter 4, section 5, on "The Value of Persons as Persons."

may have. In this regard it might be better to speak of the excellent often as "honorable" rather than "admirable," as there need not be anything very exclusive about the distribution of honor. But 'admirable' is more idiomatic in many contexts, and it would be pedantic to avoid it systematically.

It is especially important in the present context to resist the blandishments of *moral* elitism. Even with regard to the more variable and contingent excellences of persons, not all of them are moral, or excellences in being for the good. Physical vitality and beauty, grace of bodily movement, mathematical intelligence, are all non-moral excellences that are rightly prized. And though excellence in philosophy and music do involve excellence in being for the goods of those arts, they involve more than that. Much of what they involve is not moral excellence in even the broadest sense, but is still excellent to prize. Failure to recognize and value non-moral dimensions of excellence of persons is a prime example of *moralism* in a bad sense, allowing moral value to tyrannize over other sorts of value rather than enhancing them. It is a sort of idolatry of the moral.

For this reason I think we should avoid the common identification of (moral) virtue with "being a good person."[12] To be morally virtuous is to be a *morally* good person, but even a person who is not virtuous claims our regard for the excellence of personhood, and commonly for more variable excellences as well. Moral virtue is a truly worthy object of aspiration; it is right to want it very much. But it is deeply wrong to suppose that any degree of moral virtue could make one "worth more," or morally more important, than other people.

Saying that virtue must be excellent offers a framework for assessing virtue. It does not provide an algorithm for virtue, as we have no algorithm for excellence. The grounds for judgments of excellence of ways of being for the good are too varied, and often too subtle, I believe, for any algorithmic treatment. Reasons can normally be given for judgments of excellence, but the judgments must rely to a considerable extent on moral perceptiveness, and are not likely to form a deductive system. In terminology often used in metaethics, they are to some extent intuitionistic. The function of the concept of excellence here is not to give us a tightly defined criterion of virtue, but to point us in the direction of the appropriate sort of evaluation.

In the remainder of this section I will compare this approach with one that promises something more like an algorithm for determining which ways of being for the good are virtuous. Thomas Hurka's theory of virtue and vice is in some ways close to mine. For Hurka as for me, virtue is a kind of being for goods and against evils (loving goods and hating evils, as Hurka puts it), though he seems to assume (as I do not) that the goods and evils to be relevantly loved and hated will all be states of affairs. Hurka also holds something like my view of the intrinsic value of being for the good. He says, "If *x* is intrinsically good, [then] loving *x* (desiring, pursuing, or taking pleasure in *x*) for itself is also intrinsically

---

12  It is unfortunately not avoided in chapter 7 of Adams, *Finite and Infinite Goods*.

good."[13] But his conception of intrinsic goodness seems, at least initially, to play no essential role in his method of determining the presence and degree of virtue in different cases. It appears there are just two things that Hurka needs to know in order to determine whether and to what extent the attitude of a person *p* toward a good *g* is virtuous. How much does *p* love *g*? And how good is *g*? For Hurka finds virtue in loving goods and hating evils with an intensity *proportioned* to the degree of their goodness or badness.[14] This is surely not entirely wrong; we will often think that a person's attitude fails in excellence and virtue precisely because she prefers a trivial good to an important one.

The proportionality criterion, however, seems, at least initially, to have highly counterintuitive consequences, particularly regarding close relationships. For instance, Hurka's view seems to imply that it is contrary to virtue to care about particular persons and particular projects much more intensely than we care about other persons and projects with which we are less personally involved, when we know the latter are objectively as important and as valuable as the former. But there are well-recognized virtues, for instance of love and loyalty and friendship, that are bound up with such partiality.

Hurka proposes a way of accommodating such virtues of partiality within his scheme by recognizing "agent-relative values, ones that are good or evil only or to a greater degree from some people's points of view than from others'."[15] I appreciate the ingenuity and architectonic appeal of this line of thought, but it has a feature that seems morally unattractive at first sight. Hurka makes clear that the values he is talking about in this context are to be understood as "intrinsic" values. By one thing's being better than another from some person's point of view he does not mean just that the person subjectively values the former more than the latter. But while it seems quite appropriate, and normally virtuous, to care more intensely about a life partner's health than about most other people's, it would be repulsively self-centered to think that one's partner's health is intrinsically more important than other people's.

Hurka's ingenuity extends to his way of dealing with this problem. He suggests that agent-relative value makes sense if and only if we "analyze intrinsic goodness as what it is appropriate to love for its own sake or as what people have reason to desire and pursue. And," as he adds, "there is no reason why what is appropriate or rational for different people cannot be different."[16] I would resist this relativization of the value of things we may care about. However, it may leave Hurka's criterion of *virtue* not very different from mine, if appropriateness and rationality

---

[13] Hurka, *Virtue, Vice, and Value*, pp. 11–13.

[14] Ibid., chapter 3. I am simplifying here, focusing (legitimately, I think) on a feature of Hurka's view with which I wish to take issue.

[15] Ibid., p. 199. Hurka seems to avoid commitment on the question whether partialist virtues *should* be accommodated, arguing simply that he *can* accommodate them in the way he indicates (ibid. pp. 198–212).

[16] Ibid., p. 199f.

are understood in this context, as I think they should be, in terms of excellence of response to values and reasons. The proportionment demanded by virtue on this view will be the most excellent proportionment of one's concern to its objects, given one's relation to those objects.

That being so, I think we will be better able to deal with the full range of relevant considerations if we take excellence rather than proportionality as our comprehensive, framework-setting criterion for the virtuousness of ways of being for the good. We will have no reason to apply Hurka's proportionality principle in an agent-relative way until we have reason to think that some attitudes involving partiality are appropriate or rational (and thus, in my terms, excellent). The following, I believe, is an example of the best sort of reason that can be given for believing that.

What would we think must be lacking in the life of a human being who would relate to goods and evils only in the most impartial way? Such a person's energies and interests would be spread very thin. Being only human, she would not be able to engage in any depth *all* the valuable persons and projects within range of her potential interest. Being perfectly impartial, her caring would engage more or less *equally* all that are of roughly equal value, and would thus be quite limited in the depth to which she could be engaged in caring and commitment with any person or project. But depth of engagement in caring and commitment and in other dimensions of personal involvement with a particular good seems essential to the most excellent ways of being for a good. A vitally important sort of excellence would be missing from one's way of being for the good if one were not engaged so deeply with any person or project. But the excellence of such an engagement requires that one care about the good of the person or project with an intensity with which one would not be capable of caring about *all* similar goods. Thus it can be excellent to be in a position in which it is appropriate and rational, and thus excellent, to care more about the good of one person or project than about the good of other similar persons or projects.

In order to get to a position in which considerations of agent-relative proportionality are even relevant, this argument depends on considerations of excellence which are not considerations of proportionality. The considerations on which it relies involve other aspects of one's response which compete with proportionality as ways in which one's being for a good can be excellent.[17] Richness of understanding and appreciation of a particular good and durability of commitment to it, for example, are among the aspects of response that may outweigh impartial proportionment as grounds of excellence in being for goods.

I have been discussing a type of case in which Hurka's proportionality principle threatens to require too much impartiality. There are also cases in which it may seem to demand too much partiality. Suppose you have two children, Terry and Sandy, and Terry is much more talented than Sandy in almost every way,

---

[17] Swanton, *Virtue Ethics*, chapter 2, is helpful on this point.

so that the best life Terry can live is significantly more excellent in important respects than the best life Sandy can live. Would virtue therefore require you to desire the best possible life for Terry more strongly than you desire the best possible life for Sandy? Surely not. Indeed, it seems most virtuous for the strength of your desires for the best possible life for each of them to be equal—and (of course) very great (so far as such strength is quantifiable).

Can Hurka accommodate this intuitively plausible conclusion in his view? Should he reply that in fact the best life available for Terry is not better than the best life available for Sandy? Should he say that they are equally fine, or at any rate that any differences in possible value arising from their differences in talent are swamped by the huge value that each of their lives can have simply as a human life? There is considerable plausibility to this reply, but acceptance of such a view seems likely to make it difficult to apply a metric of values of desired outcomes in such a way as get from it the metric of virtuousness of desires that Hurka wants.

More fundamentally, the implication that we need to find an equality of value in the possible outcomes in order to justify equality of concern seems to me deeply disturbing. Is it really excellent for our love for a person to be measured or limited in proportion to the degree of value that we see as actual or possible in her life? Is it not better to love in a more open-ended and unconditional way? Is there no excellence of unstinting and overflowing grace?

In fact, I believe, the deepest appreciation of anything that is excellent is non-comparative. This is yet another factor that competes with proportionality as a ground of excellence in one's being for goods. It is not always a mistake to engage in rank-ordering of excellence, and it can be instructive; but there is something unappreciative about the exercise. Excellence is most truly appreciated for what *it* is, not for what something else isn't. What Martin Buber says about the Thou of an "I–Thou" relationship is true of anything whose excellence is truly and deeply appreciated: it "steps forth to confront us in its uniqueness. It fills the firmament—not as if there were nothing else, but everything else lives in *its* light."[18] This is the deepest reason for avoiding the competitiveness of elitism in our understanding of excellence, and perhaps also the most fundamental objection to Hurka's proportionality criterion of virtue.

It remains true that there is apt to be a notable lack of excellence in grossly disproportionate concern for trivial goods, or even in caring about a pet dog as one should about one's human children. But it is worth noting that disproportionment is not the only reason why it is not excellent for humans to care about dogs as much as we care about humans. What we understand as humans about human life is much richer than what we understand about canine life. We therefore cannot engage dogs, and their good, with anything like the depth and richness with which we can engage other humans and their good. This is another dimension

---

[18] Buber, *I and Thou*, p. 126 (*Werke*, vol. 1, p. 130). This point is discussed more fully in Adams, *Finite and Infinite Goods*, pp. 169–70.

in which our caring for other humans can be more excellent than our caring about dogs can be. Indeed, it is the very dimension that I have emphasized as providing a competing consideration that provides grounds for thinking that a motivational pattern including special concern for persons who are close to us can be more excellent than a more impartial motivational pattern that might be recommended by the proportionality criterion. The relevance of this dimension may be confirmed by the fact that there seems to be no deficiency of excellence in a dog's caring as much about another dog as about a human being. This may be explained by the consideration that the dog cannot engage the human being and the human being's good in a decisively deeper and richer way than it can engage with another dog.

Hurka may have a counterargument against relying, as I do, on an open-ended range of differently grounded judgments of excellence in being for goods. He accuses Michael Slote of "abandoning explanation" by relying on a similar diversity of judgments of admirableness, by "deny[ing] that there is any unifying feature that makes the virtues virtues; they are just the plural items on a list of admirable traits."[19] I take it that Hurka regards proportionality as a unifying feature of virtuous response to goods and evils, and as providing thereby an explanation of the desired sort.

Hurka's account, however, seems to me no less ad hoc and particularistic than Slote's or mine with regard to its most foundational judgments. For Hurka's account of virtue and its goodness "starts with a base-clause stating that certain states of affairs other than virtue are intrinsically good." Specifically, he states that "Pleasure, knowledge, and achievement are intrinsically good."[20] And I cannot see that he has any unifying feature to explain what makes those items intrinsically good.

His list of foundationally good items, which I have quoted, is shorter than the lists of types of foundationally admirable or excellent items that Slote and I will probably have to endorse. That might make Hurka's list less offensive to our explanatory aspirations. But it is not a very secure advantage of Hurka's view, for he says explicitly that his theory is not strongly dependent on his having identified the right base-clause goods. So far as I see, he has no basis for excluding the possibility that they are much more numerous. And even if we suppose that only pleasure, knowledge, and achievement are foundationally good, it is hard to see how we could plausibly have anything like an algorithm for determining the comparative value of particular cases and combinations of them. I have argued, in addition, that Hurka's strategy for accommodating strong intuitions of the virtuousness of partiality in some cases relies on judgments of appropriateness and rationality that are isomorphic with judgments of excellence on which I would

[19] Hurka, *Virtue, Vice and Value*, p. 244. The quoted claims about Slote specifically concern his book, *From Morality to Virtue*.
[20] Ibid., pp. 11–12.

rely. I doubt that a theory of virtue can be as parsimonious in foundational judgments as Hurka desires, without considerable sacrifice of plausibility.

## 4. VIRTUE AND THE VIRTUES

I do not think that relying on many diverse judgments of excellence or admirableness that cannot be reduced to a single principle amounts to abandoning explanation as such. No doubt it is incompatible with some forms of explanation to which one might aspire, but it can also be a result of a large and adventurous appetite for explanations. One's search for explanation might start with a question of the form, '$X$ seems excellent, but why?' The initial answer might have the form, 'Because $X$ has characteristics $A$, $B$, and $C$, which are excellent.' This naturally suggests the question 'Why are $A$, $B$, and $C$ excellent?' or 'What's excellent about them?' And reflection on those questions might turn up quite different grounds of excellence for $A$, $B$, and $C$; and further, possibly quite different, explanations might be sought and found for those grounds, and so on. Such a quest might not find a natural stopping point, and each step in it might well take one farther from being able to reduce all one's explanations of excellence to a single principle. But at the same time the process might well strengthen rather than weaken one's belief that one can give good reasons for one's judgments of excellence.

The process just described agrees well with the structure of traditional thinking about virtue. Whatever judgments may have been left without explanation in the tradition, the judgment that a particular person's moral character is good has not been one of them. For any such judgment explanations in terms of particular excellent traits in the person's character have been sought, and have normally been given. That practice of explanation is backed in turn by extensive discussion of the particular traits, in which further reasons for their excellence are sought—and so on.

If we hope for help from traditional thought about virtue in our thinking about which cases and ways of being for goods are so excellent as to be virtuous, and why, an obvious place to look for such help is in traditional accounts of the particular virtues. If we think that courage, generosity, and justice are virtues, we should suppose, other things equal, that it is more excellent to be for something good in a courageous way than in a rash or cowardly way, in a generous way than in a stingy or profligate way; more excellent to be kind in just than in unjust ways, and so forth. I would not propose an uncritical adoption of traditional ideas on this subject, but we should at least take them seriously if we do not want to lose touch with the concerns that lead people to think in terms of virtue in the first place. The project of this book in fact involves much reflection about traits traditionally regarded as virtues, and about some other candidates for the status. My final task in this chapter is to articulate a conceptual framework for such reflection.

Two different concepts are involved here, both legitimately expressed by the word 'virtue'. When I say that virtue is persisting excellence in being for the good, I am defining or explicating virtue in a sense in which it normally has no plural and does not take an indefinite article; we might call it "capital *V* Virtue."[21] It is the holistic property of having a good moral character. To have it one must not only have a number of excellent traits. One must also have them excellently composed into a whole. When we speak, on the other hand, of particular traits, such as benevolence and wisdom, as virtues, we use 'virtue' in a "small *v*" sense in which it has a plural and does take the indefinite as well as the definite article. In the present section I will try to frame an account of what it is to be a virtue in the small *v* sense.

The account does not follow trivially from my explication of capital *V* Virtue. Although I think that the particular virtues all indicate ways in which one's being for the good can be excellent, I do not think the status of a particular trait as one of the virtues always depends on the goodness of what one is for in having or exercising the trait. Courage is an obvious example. One way in which one's being for something good can be excellent is as being courageous. It seems natural, however, and I think it is correct, to say that a soldier may manifest courage in fighting for an unjust cause, and that the courage will still be an excellent trait and a virtue. This is a controversial view. I will defend it in chapter 10. Here I simply state it because my explication of the small *v* sense of 'virtue' must take it into account.

The two senses of 'virtue' are different enough to make it a good idea to start from the beginning in explaining what sort of trait can be a small *v* virtue. The most elementary point is that anything that is to count as a virtue for purposes of ethical theory must be a psychological property, and not a merely physical one, even though physical traits may play a part in the pursuit of good ends. A great singer's passionate devotion to the intrinsic goods of music is apt to involve an ethical virtue, or more than one; but the excellence of her vocal talent, the beauty of her instrument, cannot plausibly be counted as an ethical virtue. Muscular strength, likewise, is not a virtue in ethics, though strong arms may play a central role in virtuous deeds of courage.

Even among psychological properties, not all that are excellent could be virtues in ethics. For instance, a good memory for facts is not a moral virtue. Why not? Not just because it is an intellectual or cognitive property. Properties largely

---

[21] At one time I thought I would capitalize 'Virtue', when it occurs in this sense, from here on in this book; and this usage is followed in this section. I have found the device too artificial, however, and a source of awkwardness in discussing the work of writers who do not use it. Except in limited parts of the book, therefore, I try to avoid it, and instead to adhere to the following rule: 'virtue' in the "small *v*" sense is always used, and 'virtue' in the "capital *V*" sense never used, in the plural, or with a definite or indefinite article. Throughout the book 'virtuous' normally relates to virtue in the "capital *V*" sense.

intellectual or cognitive have not been excluded from the ranks of the virtues. Practical wisdom is one of the traditional cardinal virtues. Why treat factual memory differently from practical wisdom in this respect? The answer, I believe, is that a retentive memory does not engage the will in the sense explained in section 1. Remembering a fact does not involve any disposition to be for it or against it. Wisdom, on the other hand, is not practical unless it involves dispositions to action and concern for things that are worth being for. Practical wisdom engages the will sufficiently to count as a way of being for things, or of being disposed to be for them.

The relation between memory and practical wisdom is complex. One may be wiser in practical matters because of a good memory for relevant facts. In that case a good memory is, as it were, part of the machinery of practical wisdom. But the excellent memory does not in its own right involve practical wisdom's dispositions to action and concern, and is not itself a moral virtue. This is not a unique case. Sheer physical vigor can probably contribute to courage in something like the way that a good factual memory can contribute to practical wisdom. In that case the physical vigor may be thought of as part of the mechanism of courage, but is still not a virtue because it is not a psychological property, and a fortiori is not, as courage is, a disposition to govern in one way rather than another one's response to things one cares about in situations of fear or danger.

I say that capital *V* Virtue is persisting excellence in being for the good. One implication of this is that in ascribing Virtue, holistically, to a person I must in a general way commend her being for what she is for and against what she is against. But not all the particular virtues are essentially ways of being for and against things one should be commended for being for and against.

Some of them are. Some virtues are defined by motives which in turn are defined by goods that one is for in having them, as benevolence, for example, is defined by the motive of desiring or willing the good of others. We may call these *motivational* virtues. They would not be virtues if the ends they are definitively for were not goods, and goods that it is in general excellent to be for.

Other virtues—courage, for example, and also self-control and patience—are not defined in that way, by particular motives or by one's main aims, but are rather structural features of the way one organizes and manages whatever motives one has. We may call these *structural* virtues.[22] The excellence of structural

[22] The former sort of virtues are called "substantive or motivational," and the latter "virtues of will power," in a helpful discussion in Roberts, "Will Power and the Virtues," pp. 227–33; I have borrowed the term 'motivational virtues' from him. Wallace, *Virtues and Vices*, pp. 60–3, is interesting in relation to this distinction too. The term 'motivational' is applied to virtues in a somewhat broader sense in Brandt, "The Structure of Virtue," pp. 68–76. Brandt suggests that it may be that all virtues are motivational, but appears to mean no more than that all may be given an analysis in terms of roles that various motives do *and do not* have in a person's life.

virtues is a matter of personal psychic strength—of ability and willingness to govern one's behavior in accordance with values, commitments, and ends one is for. However excellent they may be as strengths, structural virtues by themselves cannot make one a morally good person. That depends above all on "having one's heart in the right place," on what goods one is for, and thus on motivational virtues. But without some of the strengths of structural virtues one can hardly be excellently for the good.

The classification of virtues as motivational and structural is not meant to be exhaustive. For instance, *practical wisdom* does not fit neatly into it. Practical wisdom is not defined by any particular kind of motive, but unlike courage and patience it is manifested largely, though not solely, in one's choice of one's main aims. In some cases we may be able to distinguish, though we commonly don't, a structural and a not merely structural virtue that go under the same name. Thus *conscientiousness* may be taken to be the virtue of excellent responsiveness to obligations one really has to other persons.[23] But there is also a more formal conscientiousness which consists in being strongly disposed to act as one *believes*, on whatever grounds, that one ought to act. The latter may be a structural virtue of psychic strength inasmuch as it enables one to use principles, commitments, and normative judgments to order one's life. Perhaps a similar structural virtue of excellence in ordering one's life by evaluative judgments may be manifested in being for something bad because one mistakenly believes it to be *good*. It is only in some such formal sense that one can speak, with a mixture of approval and disapproval, of someone as "conscientious but misguided." It may be, of course, that we will be unable to recognize even a structural excellence of conscientiousness in agents whose conception of how they ought to act is too entirely remote from anything we can approve.

Even the structural virtues are ways of being for and against things. Courage, for example, is a matter of how one orders one's values, and specifically, whether one overvalues considerations of safety and danger, and whether in the face of danger one is able to govern one's actual choices by one's main values. This is not to say that being courageous is a matter of the value of what one is most deeply for and against. At most it is required that there be enough good, and especially enough seriousness, in a courageous person's main aims, for it to be credible that they are indeed deeply held life-organizing aims of a normally competent human adult. Courage will not make one virtuous, or a morally good person, unless one's main aims, for the sake of which one manages one's fears, are good aims—and well-chosen good ones at that. However, if one is not only courageous, but in general excellently for the good, the excellence of one's courage is quite directly part of the excellence of the complex of properties that is one's being for the good. In that case being courageous is one of the excellent ways in which one is for the good.

---

[23] Cf. the extremely interesting fourth chapter of Wallace, *Virtues and Vices*.

These considerations suggest, as a working definition, that *a virtue* is an excellent way of being for and against things, a way whose excellence can be part of the excellence of capital *V* Virtue. I use the phrase 'can be part of' here, rather than 'is part of' because I believe that it is possible to have some particular virtues without having the holistic excellence of Virtue.

# 3

## Wickedness and Vices

### 1. VIRTUE AND THE VICES

Unfortunately, the nature of moral goodness can hardly be understood without some attention to the nature of moral badness. For instance (as noted in chapter 2, section 2), one can be a morally good or virtuous person without caring much about aesthetic values, but not without caring much about the rights and well-being of other persons. I have not said by any means enough thus far to explain this sort of difference. And pretty clearly part of what is to be explained in the cited case is why we think that not caring much about other people's rights and well-being is a *bad* trait in a way that not caring much about aesthetic values is not.

Bad traits of moral character have traditionally been called vices. My working definition of a vice is related to the sort of explanation sought in the previous paragraph. *A vice*, I take it, is a trait of character that is bad in such a way that if you have it, that counts (not necessarily decisively) against your having a good moral character or Virtue in the "capital *V*" sense, as I called it in the last section of chapter 2. In other words, a vice is a trait that counts against the overall excellence of the way you are for and against goods and evils.

Vice gets less attention in this book than virtue, because I believe that goodness is more fundamental than badness. Good and bad do not form a polarity in which each pole is as fundamental as the other. Rather, badness is parasitic on goodness and must be understood in terms of goodness, as lack of goodness or opposition to goods. In my underlying metaethics I think of the excellence of things in terms of their relation (of more or less fragmentary resemblance) to a transcendent standard (in fact, God) that is wholly good. This applies also to the excellence that constitutes human virtue. But I do not think there is a wholly evil being (or even the possibility of one) or a transcendent or counter-transcendent standard of wickedness.[1]

If badness of character, like badness in other domains of evaluation, must be understood in terms of its relation to goodness, what relations to the good can constitute vice? An obvious candidate is the relation of *deficiency*, in which badness is less of what goodness is more of. This seems to put badness and goodness

---

[1] Cf. Adams, *Finite and Infinite Goods*, chapter 4, especially pp. 102–4.

on a single scale in a way that satisfies some common expectations. And some vices can indeed be understood on this model. Incontinence is a lack of the excellence of self-control, callousness a lack of the excellence of sympathy.

But deficiency in an excellence that can constitute a virtue does not always constitute a vice. I believe that caring excellently about good art is a virtue, or a form of a virtue; but lacking such an interest need not be a vice, as already noted. I would say the same about loving excellence in athletics or in philosophy. The difference between a lack of excellence that constitutes a vice and one that does not is a main part of what I am trying in this chapter to understand.

We would find it hard anyway to believe that all vice consists only in *absence* of good. In some of the most appalling cases vice, or wickedness as we may call it, seems to be a presence of something terrifying or horrible, rather than merely an absence. In such cases the relation to what is good that constitutes vice may be seen as one of opposition, hostility, or violation, rather than just of deficiency. Vices of opposition to goods have the potential to make one an *enemy* of those who care about those goods, and that certainly affects our feelings about such vices. In view of the structure of my theory of virtue, however, I cannot rest too much on such potential enmity, but must insist that vices as such constitute deficiencies in *excellence* of character. Moreover, we shall see that vices of opposition to goods are not in all cases worse than vices of indifference, nor even particularly shocking.

## 2. VICES OF WEAKNESS AND OF EXCESS

In most of this chapter, particularly in sections 3–5, we will be concerned with vices that consist in not being for what is good—being simply indifferent to it, or actually being against it or for what is bad. But not all vices can be understood in that way. In this section we shall look, more briefly, at vices of weakness and vices of excess.

*Vices of weakness:* In the last section of chapter 2 I distinguished between "motivational" and "structural" virtues. Motivational virtues are defined in terms of goods one is for, or evils one is against, in having them, as benevolence, for example, is excellence in being for the good of other persons. Vices corresponding to motivational virtues will generally be vices of opposition or indifference to actual or potential goods. Structural virtues, such as courage and self-control, are not defined by particular goods or evils one is for or against, but rather by types of strength in rational self-government. A structural virtue is not a matter of having one's heart in the right place, but of being excellently able and willing to govern one's life in accordance with one's own central aims and values, whatever they are. Corresponding to structural virtues are what we may call *structural vices*. They consist not in opposition or indifference to specific goods, but in deficiency in strengths of self-government. Thus cowardice and incontinence, respectively, are deficiencies of strength in governing oneself in the face of danger or of temptation in general. In this way they are *vices of weakness*.

As such they do not normally make someone an *enemy*, but at worst an unreliable ally, of people whose hearts are in the right place. Likewise I think we should not classify them as forms of *wickedness*. A wicked person is someone whose heart is in a bad place, being for things it is very bad to be for and against things it is very bad to be against, or perhaps just not for things it is very bad not to be for.

Something similar can be said about some forms of *folly*. Folly or deficiency in practical wisdom can take the form of being for evils and against goods in a very fundamental way, which may be wicked. But it can also take the form of ineffectual planning for the achievement of good ends about which one cares appropriately. That sort of folly seems to be a vice of weakness and not a form of wickedness.

There are also *vices of excess*, in which (roughly speaking) one is too strongly for some good. Examples are workaholism, chauvinism, and various forms of idolatry. So are sensuality, avarice, and lust for social power and status. Vices of self-preference (to be discussed in chapter 7) generally consist in excessive concern for some good connected with oneself.

In all these vices concern for some good or type of good is badly swollen in some way. Typically, however, it would be imprecise to identify the vice with anything so simple as too strong a desire for the good at which it aims. I'm not sure there is any limit, for example, to how much one can like and crave the taste of chocolate without falling into the vice of *sensuality*. Sensuality is not a matter merely of strong likes and dislikes and vigorous appetites. It has more to do with the structure of one's aims and hopes in life. The sensual person invests too much of the meaning and value of life (for himself and perhaps for others too) in sensory pleasures and physical comfort. One can say that in general it is a vice rather than a virtue to be for a particular good in such a way that even the most compelling reasons would not lead one to give priority to another good.[2] But I think what is required for avoiding that type of vice is nothing so one-dimensional as constantly proportioning one's concern for different goods to their degrees of value, but is rather a more flexible responsiveness to considerations or reasons of various kinds.

I suppose that vices of excess, unlike those of weakness, can suffice for wickedness. But the most dramatic conceptions of wickedness, to which we now turn, focus on vices of another sort.

## 3. SATANIC WICKEDNESS

The concept of a wicked or evil person is both problematic and fascinating. It is clearly a dangerous idea, but one that is not easy to renounce altogether. I do not believe there can be a person so wicked as to be *entirely* evil, but it may be instructive to reflect a bit on the idea of a supremely, or perhaps even absolutely,

---

[2] There is more on this point in chapter 10, section 4.1.

evil being. In Western religious and cultural traditions such an idea has typically been an image or conception of Satan, as a person (of great power) who is against good and for evil. Milton famously represents Satan as saying, "Evil be thou my Good."[3] What might such a resolution mean? Could it actually be fulfilled in the life of a being endowed with intellect and will? Three interpretations will be considered here.

(1) On one rather extreme reading, Satan is resolving to count as good all and only those things that really are evil. It is difficult, however, to see how this resolution can be coherent, except as a relatively trivial decision to switch the names of good and evil. This conclusion holds even if it is just those things that have generally been *regarded* as evil that Satan resolves to count as good. For the meanings of 'good' and 'evil' are determined in no small part by the kinds of objects to which they have typically been applied. Of course *many* things that have been thought good may in fact be evil, and vice versa; but one can hardly say that *everything* that has been thought good is evil, and vice versa, without changing the subject.[4]

(2) On a more plausible interpretation, Milton's Satan is resolving to *treat* what he admits to *be* evil as one would normally treat what one takes to be good. Up to a point, this is certainly something he can do. It becomes impossible, however, if he means *universally* to treat *only* evils as goods—that is, to value and pursue only evils. Perhaps Milton's Satan does mean that. "To do ought good never will be our task," he declares, "But ever to do ill our sole delight" (I. 159–60). But good and being, I believe, are so connected that it is not possible for a voluntary agent to live and pursue coherent plans without valuing and seeking some goods. And in fact Milton's Satan is certainly portrayed as valuing a number of goods: for instance, strength, intelligence, and self-respect. This is part of the charm that his character has held for many readers. He derides weakness (I. 157), says it would be "low indeed" to beg for God's forgiveness (I. 114), and fears the shame of doing so (I. 115; IV, 81–6). What Satan says is "low" may not in truth be low. Milton would surely not say it is. But behind Satan's false values pretty clearly lies some valuing of true goods of strength and self-respect.

We also read in Milton's own voice that the other fallen angels praised Satan "That for the general safety he despis'd/His own: for neither do the Spirits damn'd/Loose all thir vertue" (II. 481–3), and that "Devil with Devil damn'd/Firm concord holds" (II. 496–7). These devilish virtues have an obvious importance for Milton's plot line, and also for any conception of a truly formidable embodiment of evil in (otherwise) rational agents. For strength, courage, patience, self-control, coordination, and firmness of purpose are needed for the execution even of evil purposes on any large scale. Voluntary agents will hardly be able to possess and utilize these assets without valuing important goods that are involved in them.

[3] Milton, *Paradise Lost*, IV. 110.
[4] This point is argued more fully in Adams, *Finite and Infinite Goods*, especially pp. 20, 246, 360.

(3) Perhaps the most plausible interpretation of Satan's resolution is that he proposes to treat *certain* evils as one would normally treat acknowledged goods. Specifically, he means to make it the organizing project of his life to attack the supremely good being, God; and this involves embracing the evils involved in opposing important goods favored by God. It is his "sole delight" to do evil "As being the contrary to his high will/Whom we resist" (I. 161–2). If, as I have argued, Satan is and practically must be for some goods, they will be goods that fit in plans opposed to God's plans, and many of them will be goods that God has decided against in favor of a better plan.[5]

In opposing God, of course, Milton's Satan does not just go for the wrong goods. In some cases, some important central cases, he pursues evil for the sake of evil. He attacks important goods and seeks to undermine and destroy them, not in order to achieve other goods that he prefers, but simply to spite God. And this is not just a *de facto tendency*. In saying, "Evil be thou my good," he self-consciously and voluntarily adopts it as a guiding *principle* to choose great evils *because* they are evil. Satan is *wicked*; and if wickedness is a form of vice, it is more than ordinary vice.

Does Milton's portrait of the prince of darkness show us anything about the worst degree of *human* wickedness and vice? Immanuel Kant might be taken as suggesting a negative answer to this question when he says that "the depravity [*Bösartigkeit*] of human nature is . . . not to be named *malice* [*Bosheit*], if we take this word in the strict sense, namely as a disposition (a subjective *principle* of maxims) to take up evil *as evil* as incentive into one's maxim (for that is devilish)."[6] That is, such malice may be ascribed to devils, but not to human beings. Kant is saying something quite incredible here if he means that human beings never have tendencies to want or do things that are bad for the sake of their badness.[7] People sometimes hate other people, or themselves, and want bad things to happen to those they hate, not so that good things may come of the bad, but just because they hate. There is sometimes found in human beings a vice of cruelty or abusiveness that is a settled tendency to aim at, and delight in, the pain and humiliation of others for its own sake. Kant himself discusses envy, vindictiveness, and *Schadenfreude* [delight in somebody else's misfortune] as vices of hatred of human beings [*Menschenhaß*];[8] they seem to involve being for evils for their own sake.

---

[5] One could consider a divine will theory of the nature of the good according to which whatever God has decided against in this way is not good because goodness consists in being willed by God. That is quite a different theistic theory of the good from the one defended in Adams, *Finite and Infinite Goods*. It would be too much of a digression to get into a discussion of such theories in the present context, in a book not focused on metaethical issues.

[6] Kant, *Religion within the Boundaries of Mere Reason*, Ak VI. 37.

[7] Cf. Stocker, "Desiring the Bad."

[8] Kant, *Metaphysics of Morals*, Ak VI. 458–61.

I believe Kant did not in fact mean to deny that human beings sometimes tend to desire, and do, evils for their own sake. His meaning is made clearer, perhaps, when he says that malice [*Bosheit*] cannot be a trait of character [*Charaktereigenschaft*] of a human being because "in that case it would be devilish; the human being, however, never *approves* of evil in itself, and so there is no malice from principles [*Grundsätze*], but only from departure from [principles]."[9] The malice that Kant thinks is "devilish" and *not* human is precisely that of making it consciously and voluntarily a *principle* to choose evils because they are evil, as Milton's devil does in saying, "Evil be thou my good."

I fear that we are capable of being worse even in this respect than Kant supposes. The fascination of Milton's Satan is due in no small part to the fact that it does seem humanly possible, in bitter resentment and despair, to make it a life-principle to try to do great evils because they are evil. We may hope that such immoralism is less frequently to be found in real life than in literature, but it remains at least a thinkable temptation, and part of the realm of possibilities in relation to which we define our moral identity. Such principled malice is certainly a terrible form of wickedness (if the evils at which it aims are grave ones, as we may expect them to be). But is it clear that no other form of wickedness can be as bad, as Kant seems to assume?

## 4. MALICE

By *malice* I shall mean being against goods, and for evils, for their own sake, and not merely for the sake of other ends to which the evils may be means. Though somewhat broader than the sense in which I think Kant uses the word, I think my use of the term 'malice' is not eccentric, and picks out a morally important class of phenomena. There are vices of this sort; I have already mentioned cruelty, vindictiveness, envy, and *Schadenfreude*. (There is also malice in some motives that are not persistent enough to constitute a trait of character nor, hence, a vice; but here we are concerned with malice that is sufficiently settled or habitual to be a vice.)

No vice seems more appalling to me than *cruelty*. It attacks great goods of personal life—its enjoyment and sometimes its persistence and even its very meaning—and takes satisfaction in doing so. Is cruelty even worse if it is principled? Suppose someone, from sheer malice, consciously makes it a *principle* to inflict pain and suffering on members of a hated minority group, whenever he can do so with impunity. Is he more wicked than someone who regularly perpetrates the same cruelties, but out of a more emotional malice, a hatred and sadistic inclination, rather than on principle? Maybe so; the principled cruelty seems more chilling and perhaps more horrifying. But we are dealing in either

---

[9] Kant, *Anthropology from a Pragmatic Standpoint*, Ak VII. 293–4.

case with cruelty of such magnitude that it may be neither easy nor profitable to assign comparative degrees of wickedness.

Can we say at least that malice is in all its forms, principled or unprincipled, the worst of vices? We may divide this into two questions. (1) Is malice always a vice? (2) Is it always worse than other types of vice?

(1) I take a severe view of malice. Goods compete with each other, not only for our attention, but also for space in the world, so to speak. Choosing one good often involves opposing another—not just being indifferent to the good not chosen. So we can hardly say that being against a good (because one is for another) is proof of vice, or even of lack of virtue. However, the competition of goods for our attention and for space in the world provides no similar justification or excuse for opposing a good (or favoring an evil) *for its own sake* and not merely for the sake of some other good. This is malice, and I believe that a settled or persisting malice is always a vice. The vices of envy, vindictiveness, and hatred (including self-hatred) are instances of it. (A merely occasional malice is bad too, but is not a trait of character, and therefore not a vice.)

Any misgivings about this severe verdict on malice are likeliest to focus on issues of *retribution*. Few will deny that there is a vice that goes under the name of *vindictiveness*, but many believe that retribution is an appropriate basis for punishment. Accepting a retributive basis for punishment seems to suggest that it is not necessarily a vice, and may even be a virtue, to be disposed to will that evils befall malefactors, not for the sake of any good that may come of it, but just because they did evil in the past.

This is not a place to discuss how far a retributive theory of punishment may be correct, but I believe that in any event such a theory need not imply that malice can be virtuous. For the retributivist may believe that just retribution is not only infliction of an evil but also intrinsically involves an important good, or else constitutes avoidance or removal of an important evil. One might believe this if one thinks that retribution vindicates the honor of the malefactor's victims, or that someone's having "gotten away with" a major act of injustice is a serious evil (either in itself, or as constituting a serious breach in a just system of social relations). Apart from some such belief, however, I think we ought to conclude that willing retribution for its own sake is indicative of the vice of vindictiveness, and cannot be virtuous. (Whether retribution can be willed virtuously by someone who *falsely* believes that it is intrinsically connected with an important good is a harder question which I will not try to answer here.)

Even where only evil is sought in willing retribution, it may be that the desire for retribution is largely inspired by love or loyalty or sympathy for people who have been injured. The latter may be a largely or wholly good motive, as a way of being *for* great goods. Vindictiveness in this case is still a vice, I think, but its gravity may be mitigated by the value of motives from which it springs. The motivation of a human attitude or action often cannot be completely understood in terms of ends at which it aims. The attitude or action may spring in part *from* other motives—motives that resist analysis in terms of ends of the attitude or action.[10] I doubt that the value of these motives can be decisive for the goodness or badness of the attitude or action itself; but all such motives deserve a role in assessment of the bearing of the phenomena on the goodness or badness of a person's character on the whole.

In saying that settled malice is always a *vice* I mean that it always counts against the *excellence* of a person's moral character. I ascribe to malice a negative value that is not merely instrumental or relative to other persons' interests. Malice obviously tends to harm other persons and to unfit the malicious person for alliance with those who love the good, but I do not think that fully explains our disapproval of it.

In this connection I think of my reaction to Neil La Bute's movie *The Company of Men*. I found it as painful to watch as any film I can remember seeing. This was a reaction enhanced, no doubt, by the exceptionally realistic and unglamorized staging and acting of the film,[11] but responding primarily to the malice of the central character, Chad. He gratuitously, and all too successfully, seeks to hurt people he works with, making sport of betraying and humiliating them, and causing serious economic and professional harm to one of them—but probably not doing anything that would render him liable to a long prison term.

I found him far more revolting than Michael Corleone, the central character in the *Godfather* series of films. Michael Corleone is not without malice; he becomes implacably vindictive, as well as remarkably ruthless. We have to suppose that he causes far more harm to other people than we see Chad causing, and he is no more an ally of well-intentioned persons than Chad is. But Chad seems *vile* to a degree that Michael Corleone does not. I think that is because one can see some excellence intertwined with Michael's malice, inasmuch as his vindictiveness springs, at least initially, from loyalty to members of his family who have been betrayed or wronged. Chad's malice, on the other hand, though far less deadly, seems utterly gratuitous, and thus more thoroughly and unambiguously a matter of being for evils and against goods for their own sake. Its gratuitousness contributes to grounding a vileness in his character, a negative relation to excellence, that is neither a function of its harmful consequences, nor relative to other people's interests.

(2) Though I think malice is always a vice, I do not think that every form of malice is worse than every vice of other types. *Schadenfreude* by itself, for example, does not seem one of the gravest vices, malicious though it is. *Ruthlessness* can be much more serious, though it is not a form of malice. The word 'ruthless', in its broadest sense, can signify any willingness to sacrifice other goods in the pursuit of one's main ends. It is sometimes applied to a commendable willingness to prune one's shrubbery or one's prose. In its most usual sense, however,

---

[10] Cf. Stocker, "Values and Purposes."
[11] With lots of awkward pauses in conversation, for instance.

it signifies an *excessive* willingness to sacrifice specifically *other people's* good, and is a vice. The ruthless person as such is willing to damage or destroy important goods, but is not necessarily opposed to them for their own sake. That is why ruthlessness is not a form of malice. The ruthless person may also be malicious, and even cruel, but malice is not of the essence of ruthlessness. The main aims of the ruthless person, pursued for their own sake, may be malicious; but they also may not be. In themselves they may be good aims, even aims that it would be virtuous to pursue if only they were pursued with due regard for the interests and rights of other people.

Even without malice, ruthlessness can be very wicked. If we do think worse of one who kills another person from hatred (and thus with malice) than of one who kills another just to get their money, that is not one of the deepest and clearest differences in moral evaluation. And if the parties knew each other well, we may even think that the ruthless killing shows a more inhuman character than the act of hate.

Why do we condemn *Schadenfreude* less severely than ruthlessness without malice? The obvious answer is that *Schadenfreude*, even where it is a settled vice, does not necessarily involve any willingness to contribute causally to the evils in which it finds delight. Being for or against goods in thought or attitude or feeling deserves less weight in the overall evaluation of character if it remains passive, involving no tendency or will to show itself in ethically important action or inaction. One who is not disposed to contribute causally to the realization of an end, if that were possible, is less strongly for it. This is a distinction in ways of being for and against goods that cuts across the distinctions that define malice.

## 5. VICES OF RUTHLESSNESS AND INDIFFERENCE

The cases of ruthlessness envisaged in the previous section were cases in which the ruthless person opposes or even attacks an important good, being willing perhaps even to kill another person as a means to some desired end. Such opposition is not essential to ruthlessness, however. Those who scatter landmines in an inhabited country may be charged with ruthlessness for pursuing their military end by means that may cause injury and death to innocent non-combatants long after the war is over. The charge of ruthlessness does not imply that they are *opposed* to the good of the potential civilian victims. They are not *trying* to kill them. Ruthlessness in such a case consists rather in *indifference* to harm that may be caused, or in *not caring enough* to avoid what may cause it.

It can surely be as ruthless and *as bad* to pursue one's end by means (such as landmines) that will cause foreseen though unintended harm as by intentionally producing similar harms. According to the much debated "principle of double effect," the former is not always *wrong* where the latter would be. But even if that is correct, it is not obvious that our judgments of ruthlessness are or should be very sensitive to such a difference in wrongness. For the primary evil in ruth-lessness seems to be contempt or disregard for the *good* of other people. Where the primary evil is contempt or disregard for moral *obligations*, it seems more apt to speak of unscrupulousness or injustice than of ruthlessness. We may even think that an act might be right but ruthless, perhaps indeed one that ought to be done but could hardly be done without a ruthlessness that must remain morally troubling.

Not caring enough for important goods is ruthlessness when it subordinates those goods to other ends. But there is also simple *indifference*, or just not caring enough, which is not exactly ruthlessness because it is not motivated by the needs of any serious project. Such indifference can be as appalling as ruthlessness, as when parents allow disorganization of their lives to result in disastrous neglect of their children's health and safety. This is clearly a case in which a *vice*, incompatible with good moral character, is constituted by an *absence* of concern for an important good, rather than by the presence of an opposition or hostility.

How that can be is one of the deepest mysteries about moral excellence and badness. Part of the mystery is that *not all* lack of concern for goods is vice. Not caring much about the goods of philosophy, for example, or of music or literature would not be a vice in most situations. How is it that not caring about some goods counts heavily against the excellence of one's way of being for the good, considered as a whole, and not caring about other goods does not? The obvious suggestion is that our relation to some goods is more important, for the meaning and excellence of our lives, than our relation to others; and I think that must be right. What in a trivial relationship might be just not relating well can be relating badly, and important, in an important relationship. The demandingness of ethical facts suggests further that this sort of importance must be independent, to a large extent, of our wanting those relations to be important, though it is surely not entirely independent of the situations in which we find ourselves. Resolutely treating a relationship as trivial doesn't make it so.

For such relational reasons virtue may not be seriously compromised by unconcern about even a very great human good that is very remote from us, such as the well-being of farmers in medieval Europe. But a similar indifference to the good of people among whom we now live would be a serious blot on our character. Such comparative judgments of significance are intuitively plausible in many cases, but we may well wish to have a rationale for them.

A persuasive rationale is available, I believe, for rating a concern about cultural goods, such as those of philosophy, music, or literature, as less important than a concern for the good of persons. This rationale begins with the thought that interests in some goods find their context in interests in other goods in such a way that one cannot relate well to the former without relating well to the latter. That is true of interests in goods of literature, music, and philosophy. Loving or caring about such impersonal goods mostly takes the form of wanting persons, including oneself, to participate in those impersonal goods, to appreciate them and enjoy them. Indeed, the goods of philosophy, literature, and music cannot even exist without a context in the life of persons. Written records of excellent works in those cultural categories could certainly survive the extinction of the human race. But their characteristic excellence would survive only as the possibility of other, non-human persons someday deciphering and appreciating them. To care about such goods is to care about them as they exist in the lives of persons.

Is that true also of such creations of the visual arts as paintings and sculptures? Some of their aesthetic values certainly depend on cultural meanings whose reality necessarily depends on actual or possible understanding by persons. But it might be thought that beauty of their physical form could survive and be excellent in itself apart from any possibility of being seen or appreciated by persons in the future. That's a controversial thought, but I won't dispute it here. It's enough for my present argument to point out that love for art and objects of art virtually never includes caring very much about the possibility of that kind of survival. It virtually always involves some sort of desire for the possibility of a person, or persons, appreciating the art.

It does not follow that such cultural goods cannot be valued and loved except as means to the well-being of persons. On the contrary, their contribution to human well-being depends heavily on their being valued and loved for their own sake. Typically, in our interest in specific cultural goods, we care about both the persons involved and those particular cultural goods for their own sakes. We know that people could find enjoyment and excellence in many other cultural goods. But still we particularly want them to enjoy *philosophy*, or perhaps *Mozart*, as the case may be. Those particular cultural goods are more to us than means to the more general end of happiness or well-being for persons.

These considerations set the stage for an argument that caring well for cultural goods such as those of philosophy, literature, and music cannot be an adequate substitute for caring well for persons as a ground of excellence in one's motivation. Caring about cultural goods, I have argued, virtually always involves caring about their role in the life of persons. It is caring about an aspect of the life of persons. But surely the way in which one cares about the life of persons is not excellent, on the whole, if one does not care for the persons, and their good, for their own sake. The good of persons is a central object of interest in human life. The interest in it is one with which most interests in any aspect of human life, including cultural goods, are subtly intertwined. Particular cultural goods are more peripheral objects of interest in human life. One can have an excellent interest in human life, on the whole, without any interest in music (for instance, if one is "tone deaf"). But one's interest, however refined, in cultural goods will be part of a bizarre and misshapen pattern of interests in human life if one is indifferent to the well-being of the persons with whom one has to do, or deaf to the cry of their needs. No doubt some sense of the greater importance of the good of persons is implicitly presupposed in this judgment of bizarreness. But I hope that this rationale may still help to make judgments of the more limited importance of the cultural goods intelligible.

I do not claim that *all* the judgments of comparative importance on which assessments of vice must depend can be explained by a rationale based on the way in which our interests in different goods structure each other's contexts.[12] Such a rationale will play a part in my argument for the excellence of altruism in chapter 5. But no single form of rationale will be sufficient to deal with the complexity of an adequate comprehensive treatment of excellence in caring about persons, which will be the subject of Part II of this book. I have no formula to propose as generally adequate for determining when our relationship to a good is so important or salient as to make it a vice not to be strongly for that good.

This is another point at which consequentialists might charge that my position commits me to excessive reliance on intuition. But I think they are no better off on this point. For the importance and unimportance of relationships is a major determinant of the values of outcomes in human life, and not merely causally so, on any but the most flat-footedly hedonistic view of those values. Consequentialists, depending heavily on evaluation of human outcomes, have, I think, no good way of avoiding judgments of non-instrumental importance and value about relationships. And consequentialism gives them no advantage in making or justifying judgments concerning *non-instrumental* importance and value. There is much more to be said, however, about consequentialist views of virtue. They will be a major topic of the next chapter.

---

[12] How plausibly can such a rationale account for the widely held view that caring for impersonal goods that are natural rather than cultural (for example, the goods of biodiversity) can be excellent but is decisively less important than caring for persons and their good? Some think it is excellent, perhaps even imperative, to care for such goods independently of their actual and possible place in the lives of persons. That is a controversial view, but I think there is something right about it. What I think is right about it is that it is excellent to *respect* such goods independently of their place in the life of persons, and a vice not to. But I think that *love* for such goods normally is and should be in part a matter of caring about their place in one's own life and the lives of other persons.

# 4

# Virtue and its Benefits

I have defined virtue, or goodness of moral character, as persisting excellence in being for the good, and particular virtues as traits whose excellence can be part of the excellence of virtue. In defining virtue, and virtues, in terms of excellence, I imply that they are valuable for their own sake, and not just instrumentally. A further implication of my definition is that virtue depends largely on the value of what one is for, intentionally, rather than on the value of what one actually causes, or is likely to cause. There are very influential theories of virtue, however, that define virtue in terms of a value that is largely instrumental. This chapter is devoted to a critique of that approach. Examining the relation of virtue to its benefits, we will ask whether considerations of benefit are better suited than considerations of excellence and of being for the good to define virtue and the virtues.

## 1. HUMAN FLOURISHING

The benefits of virtue have been the object of much philosophical discussion. Most controversial has been the question whether virtue is necessarily or reliably beneficial *to its possessor*. Socrates, Plato, and the Stoics held that it is, and indeed that the nature of virtue is such that it necessarily makes its possessor a happy or flourishing person. Aristotle held the more moderate view that only the virtuous can truly flourish, but that favorable circumstances, as well as virtue, are required for flourishing. Kant vigorously rejected Stoic views about the relation of virtue to happiness. He insisted that "there is not the slightest ground in the moral law for a necessary connection between the morality and the proportionate happiness of a being belonging to the world as part of it and hence dependent upon it."[1]

Setting aside for discussion in section 3 the thesis that virtue is beneficial specifically for its possessors, let us focus on the more widely accepted view that virtue is beneficial for humanity in general, or for communities to which virtuous people belong. The plausibility of this view is well exhibited in the concluding

---

[1] Kant, *Critique of Practical Reason*, Ak V, 111–13, 124. This is part of Kant's larger argument that morality has a need for belief in a God who will assure that happiness is proportioned to virtue. However, this connection between virtue and happiness is supernatural, not one that flows from the nature of virtue.

paragraph of one of the best systematic books about virtue that I know, James Wallace's *Virtues and Vices*.

All of these traits [of conscientiousness, benevolence, courage and restraint] perform functions that are, in one way or another, essential to human life. If such traits were lacking altogether in a group of people, they could not live together the sort of life characteristic of human beings. When these traits are developed in an individual to a noteworthy degree, they are virtues, human excellences. When such traits are so perfected that they are virtues, the traits tend to enhance human life, to make it flourish. This is not to say that a good human being invariably flourishes. Rather, the more good people there are in a community, the better life generally in the community is apt to be.[2]

I don't doubt that the virtues are generally beneficial to human communities in much the way Wallace says they are. That they are is an important fact that should be accounted for in a plausible theory of the nature of virtue. The question before us, however, is whether this fact should be used to explain the nature of virtue. An affirmative answer is given in some of the most important recent philosophical discussions of virtue. Another example is Philippa Foot's "admittedly fragmentary" account of "the concept of a moral virtue" in a well-known paper contemporaneous with Wallace's book. As the first step in it, she offers the thesis that "virtues are in general beneficial characteristics, and indeed ones that a human being needs to have, for his own sake and that of his fellows."[3]

For some writers, including Foot, this approach has metaethical motivations—naturalistic ones. These motivations may help to explain the popularity of the term *flourishing* in the contemporary literature of virtue ethics, where it is widely used as a rendering or counterpart of the *eudaimonia* of the ancient Greek philosophers. *Eudaimonia* is notoriously difficult to translate, and the traditional rendering, 'happiness', is far from perfect. 'Flourishing' is arguably a better fit semantically,[4] but etymologically there is a mismatch. The origins of 'flourishing' are botanical, connected with flowering or blooming, but the origins of *eudaimonia* are connected rather with religion, evoking the idea of a favorable *daimon* or supernatural being.

The botanical connections of 'flourishing' seem in fact to be part of the appeal of the term for some neo-Aristotelians. G. E. M. Anscombe's 1958 essay on "Modern Moral Philosophy" may well have started the fashion of using the term as the counterpart of *eudaimonia*.[5] The claim that one can tell in a quite factual

[2] Wallace, *Virtues and Vices*, p. 161.
[3] Foot, "Virtues and Vices," pp. 164–5. I think the same thought is implied in Foot's much more recent book, *Natural Goodness* (see especially its chapter 3), but she actually introduces the concept of virtue there in a way that, though not inconsistent with this thought, could be carried in other directions (pp. 12–14).
[4] For the argument, see Cooper, *Reason and Human Good in Aristotle*, p. 89n.
[5] Cf. Cooper, *Reason and Human Good in Aristotle*, p. 90n.

way what a *plant* needs in order to "flourish" is used there as a way of establishing the metaethical possibility of a "transition from 'is' to 'needs'."⁶ Naturalistic metaethical motivations are at work in much of the recent interest in the ethics of virtue. I believe the fashion of speaking of "flourishing" reflects a widespread hope that it may be possible to identify in naturalistic terms a human good or human *telos* (end or purpose) that is to be served by human beings who function well, and that can be used to define the virtues as traits that are conducive to that good.

Foot certainly cherishes such a hope. She claims it is "possible that the concept of a good human life plays the same part in determining goodness of human characteristics and operations that the concept of flourishing plays in the determination of goodness in plants and animals."⁷ Wallace shares the hope too, and he too uses biological examples. He claims that "a knowledge of what it is for certain kinds of creatures to live well, to flourish," is an indispensable part of biological science. This is clearly part of a metaethical strategy. Wallace is trying "to show that the value we place upon certain traits of character can be given a naturalistic basis."⁸ If what it is for a type of creature to flourish is in general a natural fact of the sort it is the business of biologists to know, then what it is for human beings to flourish will presumably also be a natural fact. Then if virtues are defined as traits, or capacities and dispositions of will, that humans need, in a general way, if they are to flourish as social creatures, a trait's being a virtue will also be a natural fact.

Wallace seems to claim fulfillment for this metaethical hope when he says, "By studying [human] life, ... we can come to understand what it is for a human being to live well and what characteristics of a human being contribute to living well." He also recognizes the possibility of a simultaneous approach "from the opposite direction," in which one asks, "On the assumption that certain virtues are human excellences, what must human life and human good be like?" Such an approach from the opposite direction might be inspired by the plentiful indications in Wallace's account that human flourishing is not only *causally* dependent on virtue in various ways, but also *consists* in large part in activities that are virtuous. Wallace says he will "proceed in both ways," but his naturalistic metaethical aspirations seem to depend on the approach that proceeds from an understanding of living well to the conception of the virtues.⁹

Aristotle, as I read him, tends to proceed in the opposite direction, from recognition of the virtues to an understanding of living well.¹⁰ Accounts of the nature of virtue in terms of conduciveness to human flourishing have

---

⁶ Anscombe, "Modern Moral Philosophy," p. 32. On the biological background of 'flourishing' and its possible relation to metaethics, cf. Darwall, "Valuing Activity," pp. 176–7, 180–1.

⁷ Foot, *Natural Goodness*, p. 44.

⁸ Wallace, *Virtues and Vices*, pp. 19, 159.

⁹ All quotations in this paragraph are from Wallace, *Virtues and Vices*, p. 38.

¹⁰ My reading is not eccentric; cf. Swanton, *Virtue Ethics*, p. 9.

tended to be self-consciously, though not slavishly, Aristotelian or, perhaps more accurately, neo-Aristotelian. Wallace focuses particularly on Aristotle's idea that human beings have by nature a characteristic *ergon* (work or function), and that "the virtue of a human being will . . . be the state [*hexis*] . . . by virtue of which he performs his function [*ergon*] well."[11] Wallace "propose[s] to characterize the human *ergon* as a social life informed by convention, rather than [in Aristotle's terms] as activity in accordance with *logos*."[12] It is social life informed by convention whose "flourishing" Wallace takes to be the characteristic result that can be used to define virtue.

Aristotle's more or less biological concept of natural function [*ergon*] in fact does not go very far toward providing a naturalistic foundation for his theory of virtue. He does identify virtue as the personal quality manifested in performing well the human *ergon* of activity in accordance with *logos*. But equally he defines "the human good" as "activity of the soul in accordance with *aretē* [excellence or virtue]."[13] Combining the two definitions, we get the conclusion that human good consists in rational activity of the soul, done well, and that virtue is the personal quality manifested in doing it well. If this is a foundational formulation, the key foundational concept in it is obviously that of performing *well* the rational activity of the soul. In practice, Aristotle tends to start with judgments about what sorts of activity are fine or noble [*kalos*], and hence virtuous, and draw from them conclusions about *eudaimonia* or human good, rather than arguing in the opposite direction.

Aristotle's actual procedure is, I think, more promising than one that starts with judgments about *eudaimonia* in order to use conduciveness to *eudaimonia* as the criterion of virtue. We may grant that human good will be found at least largely in rational activity and in social life informed by convention. But that leaves open a vast array of questions about what constitutes doing it *well*. And I think we cannot expect naturalistic (for instance biological) investigations of "human nature" to answer these questions convincingly. Even if Aristotle's biological teleology had given him more of an answer to them than I think it did, we cannot today expect help on this point from biology. If there is a teleology intrinsic to *our* biology, it is one in which the *telos* served in fact by evolving organisms is the propagation of their genes; and efficacy in serving *that telos* has, I think, no plausibility as a measure of ethical virtue.[14] I would not wish to exclude the concept of an ethically valid purpose (or *telos*) for human life,

---

[11] Aristotle, *Nicomachean Ethics*, p. 42 (II. 6/1106a22–24); I have slightly modified the translation.

[12] Wallace, *Virtues and Vices*, p. 37.

[13] *Nicomachean Ethics*, I. 7 (1098a16–17). The definition (generally taken as also a definition of *eudaimonia*) is amplified there, but this brief version will serve for our present purposes. Like Wallace, Aristotle seems to think that it follows from our biologically given nature that our life is to be lived in a social context; we are "political" beings by nature [ibid., I. 7 (1097b11); cf. IX. 9 (1169b18), VIII. 12 (1162a15ff.)]. But that still leaves us with the questions about doing it *well*.

[14] Cf. FitzPatrick, *Teleology and the Norms of Nature*.

but if we can discern such a purpose, I think we must do it, at least in part, *by* discerning potentialities for excellence. We cannot plausibly hope to discern excellence *by* discerning objective purposes in human life. Even theology, I think, cannot plausibly make judgments of natural purpose epistemologically prior to judgments of excellence.[15]

No doubt these judgments reflect my commitment to conceiving of value in terms of its imitative or participatory relation to a transcendent good. Value, I believe, is not to be defined by the demands of the merely biological (as if they really were demands in any normative sense), but by approximation to an object-ive ideal or transcendent standard. We have to seek and find and love the good in our lives within the possibilities and necessities that biological and other natural facts establish in our lives. But in deciding what, within those possibilities and necessities, is good and to be loved, we must look higher.

A more plausible account of what constitutes human good (or, if you will, human flourishing) will have to start, as Aristotle's does in practice, with some judgments about what is intrinsically good or excellent in human life. Many of these judgments are likely to involve the excellence of virtue. Suppose we ask why one would not want one's great-grandchildren, say, to grow up to live lives of duplicity. I think part of the most plausible answer will be that one believes more honest lives would be (intrinsically) more excellent. The point can be made as strongly about the good of a human community as about that of an individual. A flourishing human community will not simply be one that is materially pros-perous and free of the most devastating plagues and conflicts. It must be one in which people live *well*, enjoying great value that is not merely instrumental in their private and public projects. And an important part of that non-instrumental value, in a truly flourishing community, should be the excellence of virtue.

It is frequently remarked, in discussions of virtue, that a community needs cer-tain virtues in its people in order to sustain a good social and political life. Among the virtues important for the good of a free and democratic society, for example, are public spirit, honesty, reasonableness, tolerance, fairness, and respect for gen-erally good laws. It is less often noted that such virtues do not make some of their most important contributions to the community's life if they are valued only instrumentally rather than for their own sake. In any large and vibrant com-munity, especially a free and democratic one, there are always large and small conflicts going on—non-violently, we hope. In these conflicts there is naturally apt to be disagreement about which outcomes would be best. It is crucial to the social function of the civic virtues in such a context that our interest in them tran-scends our interest in the outcomes about which we disagree. They help us to maintain our social union, and just institutions, through the inevitable clashes of interest and opinion, precisely because we care more about the virtues than about

---

[15] Cf. Adams, *Finite and Infinite Goods*, pp. 78–9, 304–9, 365–6; "Platonism and Naturalism"; and "Human Nature, Christian Vocation, and the Sexes."

most of the outcomes that may or may not follow from them, and can respect and admire the virtues even in political opponents. This would be less likely, I think, if we saw only instrumental value in the virtues.

## 2. VARIATIONS ON TRAIT CONSEQUENTIALISM

The project of defining virtue in terms of its benefits is not restricted or limited to Aristotelian or naturalistic forms, or to the concept of human flourishing. In a very general and abstract perspective it is a typical expression of what we may call *trait consequentialism*. Consequentialisms are theories that assess the ethical value or rightness of some morally assessable factor in terms of the value of the consequences resulting, or apt to result, from that factor. The best-known type of consequentialism is act consequentialism, which applies the test of consequences to acts, typically defining a right action as one whose consequences, comprehensively considered, are at least as good as those of any relevant alternative action. But the test of consequences can be applied to other factors: to rules, to social policies, to forms of ethical culture, and to motives, for example. Quite different, even substantively divergent, ethical theories can be built around these different applications of the test of consequences. It is an important fact that these applications in general, and trait consequentialism in particular, need not imply act consequentialism.

Trait consequentialism assesses the ethical value of traits of character on the basis of the value of their consequences. It holds that one trait or personal quality is better than another to the extent that the consequences of the former are better than the consequences of the latter. In this context the having of a trait is counted among its own consequences, along with everything that follows logically or causally from it. So the value of a trait need not be *purely* instrumental. But instrumental value will typically have a large role, and can certainly have a decisive one, in consequentialist evaluation of traits.

Trait consequentialism will count a trait as a virtue if its consequences are good enough by the indicated criterion. That obviously leaves open questions about how good is good enough. Must a virtue have better consequences than any possible alternative? That seems an implausibly high standard (and invites questions as to how possible an alternative must be to be relevant). I will bypass this set of problems. I think Julia Driver shows good judgment in formulating her avowedly "consequentialist theory of virtue" as claiming simply that "virtues are character traits which produce good effects . . . [A]s long as the trait generally produces good, it is a virtue."[16] In other words, virtues are defined as traits that are generally beneficial. We will find enough issues to discuss about such a theory without

[16] Driver, "The Virtues and Human Nature," p. 124. This view is reaffirmed in Driver, *Uneasy Virtue*, pp. 60–1.

worrying about how beneficial the virtues must be, from a trait consequentialist point of view.

My disagreement with trait consequentialism is fairly subtle. I agree that virtue is generally beneficial, as are most if not all particular virtues. I do not agree that this fact aptly explains the nature of virtue. I think rather that the generally beneficial character of virtue is explained by its nature as excellence in being for the good. One explanation is obvious and straightforward. If virtue consists in excellence in being for the good, it follows that virtuous people will be for the good, and will care about it. We must expect them to have a strong desire that their lives should be beneficial. And the excellence of virtue typically includes traits such as courage, temperance, and practical wisdom, which are apt to insure that the virtuous will be disciplined and judicious in their efforts to do good. Merely human excellences cannot absolutely guarantee the success of such efforts. But these considerations do support the expectation that virtuous people will generally try to do good and will generally tend to be reasonably successful in doing good (relative to what their circumstances make possible).

This does not show, nor should we expect, that virtue will be *always* or *maximally* beneficial. The plausible thesis that virtue is *generally* beneficial is not as extreme as that. I also do not mean to suggest that a desire to *cause* good is the only effective motive that will arise from virtue. There are other, less consequentially oriented, excellent ways of being for the good—admiring it, respecting it, aspiring to express it or stand for it in one's life; and these may give the virtuous person strong motives that may compete with those that aim more straightforwardly at causing good results. Still it seems extremely plausible that virtue, as I conceive of it, will have strong beneficial tendencies.

Analogy with arguments against act consequentialism suggests that trait consequentialism might be most convincingly refuted by counterexamples showing that being generally beneficial is neither necessary nor sufficient for a trait's being virtuous. In fact I think the claim of sufficiency for the trait-consequentialist criterion can be refuted in this way. The situation regarding its claim of necessity is more obscure. I take up first the question of sufficiency.

Conclusions drawn from counterexamples will not be uncontroversial. One of the most striking cases is actually proposed by Driver in expounding her trait-consequentialist view. She firmly accepts the implication I find so counterintuitive. She imagines a society of people she calls Mutors, who have learned that "for them, beating one's child severely when it is exactly 5.57 years old actually increases the life expectancy of the child by 50 per cent." They could not bring themselves to do this were it not that "some Mutors have a special trait—they intensely desire to beat children who are exactly 5.57 years old," and in fact find "an intense pleasure" in doing so. "That it is good for the child is irrelevant to them." Other Mutors bring 5.57-year-old children to the beaters to receive the life-prolonging treatment they need. Is the special trait possessed by the beaters a virtue? Driver argues that it is, "because others would value it, it actually does produce good and a specific social benefit, and the trait is specific enough so as *not* to produce *any* bad consequences."[17]

I find it impossible to think of this "special trait" as a virtue, even in the circumstances described, though I admit that parents in such a case might have morally sufficient reason to take their children to be beaten. We think, to be sure, that it may be virtuous for a doctor to administer a painful but life-prolonging treatment to a child; but here there is a crucial difference from Driver's case. The virtuous doctor intends good for the child, but the beaters in her example intend nothing but bad for the child. In judging of virtue in these cases my intuitions seem to respond to the good or bad intended and not merely to the good or bad consequences, and I doubt that my intuitions are eccentric in this respect. They suggest that predictably good consequences of a trait or disposition of the will are not sufficient to make it a virtue. They also support my view that virtue is chiefly a matter of being for the good, and that a standing desire cannot constitute a virtue except insofar as it is motivated by something that's good about its object.

This example might be questioned for its reliance on special circumstances. It is admittedly not realistic. More importantly, Driver's description of it does not suggest that the beaters' trait is *generally* beneficial, as she agrees in other contexts that a virtue must be. It is described as occurring only in a part (presumably a minority) of the population, and manifesting itself only in very special circumstances. And that may be significant. Trait consequentialists, I think, would be well advised not to imply that traits are virtues, or not, in any situation, however unusual, according as they are beneficial or not in that situation. It is too well-established and plausible a truism that virtue and success can lead in very different directions in particular situations.

What is more plausible is that virtue is *generally* or *typically* beneficial. Indeed that is surely true to some approximation about comprehensive virtue or goodness of moral character. Let us suppose that the trait consequentialist therefore defines a virtue as a trait that *generally* or *typically* has good consequences. This may give rise to difficulties in determining when a situation is typical enough to pose a relevant test, but it is a move that is reasonable enough to be taken very seriously. So I wish to consider an example in which the question is what we should say about a certain trait on the assumption that it is beneficial in *typical* human circumstances. The question will be whether having generally good consequences is *sufficient* to mark the trait as a virtue. We are not yet dealing with the question whether it is *necessary* for a virtue to be typically beneficial.

Suppose that *competitiveness* is a generally and typically beneficial trait, as some forms of capitalist economic theory might suggest. Does it follow that

---

[17] Driver, "The Virtues and Human Nature," p. 120. The example is used again, and its thesis about the virtue of the beaters reaffirmed, in Driver, *Uneasy Virtue*, pp. 55–6.

competitiveness is a virtue? Or can "public benefits" flow reliably and predictably from "private vices" that remain vices, as Bernard de Mandeville's famous subtitle suggests?[18] Setting aside the question how beneficial competitiveness really is, it seems to me that even if it is typically beneficial to society, it is not a virtue, not the sort of trait that makes one a morally good person. That is because of considerations about being for or against the good. Competitiveness, as normally understood, involves a sort of hostility to the interests of other people (a hostility limited to certain contexts, to be sure). That can hardly be a virtue, even if it has good consequences. To wish to do *well* seems virtuous (a motivational virtue). But competitiveness is a matter of wanting to do *better than others*, which involves a wish that others do less well, which is hardly a mark of virtue, even if it has good consequences by spurring us to productive activity. And the need to use others' failure or falling short as a measure of one's own success is a form of weakness rather than of strength.[19]

This is not to deny that a virtuous person may sometimes compete, and even be quite competitive in some contexts. It is not to say that we could not have morally sufficient reason to encourage children to become competitive if it really is beneficial. It is no part of my theory that the interest in virtue trumps all other moral considerations, or that every virtue is to be encouraged at all costs. What I am saying here about competitiveness is just that it is not itself a virtue, and does not of itself contribute to making one a morally good person, because it is not directed toward the good in an excellent way. Virtue, if one is competitive, will be shown rather in managing one's competitiveness well and limiting appropriately its field of operation.

The examples considered thus far support, I believe, my contention that *being for the good* is central to the nature of virtue. The importance of the consideration that virtues must be intrinsically *excellent* can be illuminated, I think, by another example suggested by Driver. She proposes *chastity* as exemplifying "the fact . . . that when we . . . see that we have misjudged the consequences of a trait, we change our judgment of the trait's status as a virtue." Claiming that "chastity is not generally considered a virtue any more, though it used to be considered one," she asks, "Why the change?" She proposes an account "in terms of people's perceptions of the consequences of the trait," mentioning a popular sociobiological account of why "chastity in women" was regarded as a moral virtue. The suggested explanation is that it was thought that "if women were not chaste, men would have no confidence in paternity, and would not support children," which would have disastrous social consequences. The "opinion that chastity is a virtue" has changed, she argues, because with better technology in the reproductive sphere, paternity can be established without chastity, or because we have come

---

[18] *Private Vices, Public Benefits* is the subtitle of Mandeville's *Fable of the Bees*.
[19] For a much more admiring evaluation of competitiveness, expressed with eloquence but without offering clearly articulated premises for discussion, see Nietzsche, "Homer on Competition."

to think that the old "picture of the social consequences of chastity" never was correct.[20]

This is a very interesting example. There clearly has been a remarkable change of thought and feeling about chastity in our culture, in roughly the direction that Driver indicates. Yet I find her explanation unconvincing. The most glaring objection to it, perhaps,[21] is that the changed climate of thought and feeling about chastity has endured in the face of the AIDS epidemic. AIDS gives any knowledgeable person plenty of reason to think that chastity is likely to be generally beneficial for the foreseeable future. Chastity as a strategy looks pretty good in terms of its consequences, even if "safe sex" is an only moderately riskier alternative that can be considered. For many people, however, this has only confirmed (if confirmation were needed) that in many situations the virtues of practical wisdom and self-control will be expressed in sexual abstinence. It has not led to a revitalization of the belief that chastity as such is a virtue. That, I submit, is because what changed, fundamentally, in views of chastity, were people's assessments, not of its consequences, but of its intrinsic value. Chastity never was valued primarily as a beneficial trait, but as an *honorable* quality. It would never have carried the emotional load that it has carried if it had been regarded merely as useful. What has changed is that far fewer people now see personal excellence or honor as depending on the behavioral patterns traditionally classified as chaste.

Chastity remains a controversial topic. The word 'chastity' may not have a bright future as the name of a virtue, but the thought that there is such a virtue as it has been taken to name is far from dead. This is true especially if we take chastity as belonging properly to the ethics of virtue and not primarily to the ethics of action. In the ethics of virtue chastity is not just a pattern of overt behavior, but a personal quality of some motivational depth and complexity, belonging to men as well as women. It has certainly been understood in that way in spiritual traditions that have been main sponsors of the idea of chastity. People who are skeptical about traditional precepts of chastity may still think it a virtue to honor one's own sexuality and the sexuality of others, and may well believe that some forms of sexual indulgence and lust are contrary to such honoring. T. M. Scanlon, for example, without seeming to be more traditionalist than Driver on this subject, argues for taking seriously, as a broadly moral matter, the question "how sexual relations should be understood and properly valued."[22] Someone who understands and values sexuality appropriately, and fittingly expresses that valuation in emotion and action, may be credited, I think, with the virtue that chastity was supposed to be.

---

[20] Driver, "The Virtues and Human Nature," pp. 125–6 is the source of all the quotations in this paragraph. This discussion of chastity is echoed in Driver, *Uneasy Virtue*, pp. 84–5, 88.
[21] Another objection is that the kind of disloyalty and deception of a partner whose prevalence would give rise to doubts about paternity still is generally regarded as wrong and contrary to virtue.
[22] Scanlon, *What We Owe to Each Other*, pp. 174–6.

It will be hard to obtain agreement at present about the shape that such a virtue should have concretely—that is, about how the value of human sexuality should be honored in attitude and action. Some have very traditional views on the subject. Many others would place less emphasis than traditional views do on the institutional structure of marriage as a framework for sexual relationships. They might give primary emphasis to love and autonomy as factors in relationships that honor the sexuality of the parties. Most people have strong feelings about some types of interaction (most obviously rape) that they would regard as dishonoring their sexuality. The question I want to highlight here about this debate is not who is right in it, but what it is about. I think it is clear that the disagreements are not mainly about the good and bad consequences of different attitudes to sex, but about how human sexuality may be honored excellently, in ways that are intrinsically good. That is quite understandable, given the degree to which most of us care about the significance and value intrinsic to our intimate relationships. That is reflected historically in the emotional resonance of issues about chastity as a virtue.

I believe these examples support the view that extrinsic benefits of a motivational or behavioral trait are not *sufficient* to make it a virtue. Specifically I think they support the theses (1) that virtues must be excellent in a way that is more than merely instrumental, and (2) that the value of the objects intentionally favored by a motive or attitude can outweigh the value of its actual or probable consequences in determining whether it is a virtue. It remains a question, however, whether being beneficial is a *necessary* condition of a quality's being a virtue. In addition to being excellent and actually or possibly a way (or part of a way) of being for the good, *must* a virtue generally have good consequences? It is hard to find examples that give a clear test on this issue. This should be expected, I think, due to a complex of subtle relationships among the relevant benefits and excellences.

I have argued that virtue, on my view of it, should be expected to be generally beneficial. My argument turned on the benefits of the *actions* that may be expected to arise from virtue. Being for the good, the virtuous will want their lives to be beneficial. Being excellent in their being for the good, they will be disciplined and judicious in their efforts to do good. Their actions, therefore, will typically be beneficial. That a character is productive of actions that are foreseeably very harmful on the whole will therefore be a strong reason for thinking it gravely deficient in practical wisdom if not in other virtues.

A further reason should be noted here. It is a fact, very important to the difference between trait consequentialism and act consequentialism, that the consequences of *having* a trait or personal quality may be more extensive, and much more or much less beneficial, than the consequences of actions arising from it.[23] It is therefore significant that among the contributions that *having* excellent personal qualities makes to the determination of human well-being

---

[23] This is argued at length in Adams, "Motive Utilitarianism."

(over and above the contributions made by actions flowing from the qualities), the most reliable and the most confidently identifiable is always beneficial. Human good, I believe, consists chiefly in enjoyment of the excellent, and the virtues are among the most important of human excellences. Intrinsically excellent social relationships are also among the excellences that have the largest part in constituting human good. And excellence of the parties' character, attitude, or motive in being for the good is typically an integral part of the excellence of social relationships. The excellence of virtue therefore constitutes, in itself and quite apart from its causal consequences, a significant contribution to human good or well-being. This contribution is vastly more certain and easier to evaluate than many of the causal consequences of personal qualities. So it will typically be hard to be confident, about any intrinsically excellent personal quality, that it is not generally beneficial.

It may, nonetheless, be possible to find motivational or behavioral traits that it is plausible to count as virtuous but not generally beneficial. I think there may even be cases in which it is in *action* that the virtuous trait fails to be beneficial. For there are other excellent ways of being for the good that may compete with the desire to produce the best outcome. May they not still be virtuous if they fail, by a moderate margin, to be beneficial on the whole?

Here are two possible cases. The first is the virtue of *justice*. Philippa Foot remarks that:

Justice, in the wide sense in which it is understood in discussions of the cardinal virtues, . . . has to do with that to which someone has a right—. . . and rights may stand in the way of the pursuit of the common good. Or so at least it seems to those who reject utilitarian doctrines.[24]

As Foot's "at least" suggests, this is a point at which consequentialism about traits may be linked with consequentialism about actions. But those who oppose act consequentialism may indeed have reason to say that justice would be a virtue even if its consequences on the whole would be somewhat less good than those of a somewhat more ruthless zeal for the common good.

The second case concerns *integrity*. We may think it can be manifested in a tendency to prefer open expression of one's convictions, above success in one's efforts to produce good, if one is forced to choose. If not carried to fastidious or catastrophic extremes, this tendency seems to many of us to be admirable, though it is not clear that it is typically beneficial. Perhaps for that reason, we are not likely to demand it of everyone, but I think it is still plausible to count it as a form of virtue. We may admire the agent's integrity and consistency in speaking out, even if we disagree with the views expressed. And I think we are especially likely to regard the tendency as virtuous where we think the values involved in the

---

[24] Foot, "Virtues and Vices," p. 165.

convictions expressed are good ones. In assessing virtue in such cases we are typic-ally moved more by what the person is *for* than by the expected consequences of the trait.

It is significant that we are often more confident in judging that a trait is or is not virtuous than in our judgment as to whether its consequences will be bene-ficial. In practice we seem ready to suppose that virtue is surer than its benefits. This is naturally explained if what we regard as decisive for virtue is not the value of a trait's consequences but its intrinsic excellence and whether its aim is toward something good. The point is important for the usefulness of the concept of vir-tue in evaluating character. For the well-known difficulty facing consequential-isms, that it is often difficult or impossible to determine the actual or expectable consequences, applies to traits as much as to actions.

I grant, nonetheless, that considerations of benefit provide reasons for valuing virtues more or less highly in some ways than we otherwise would. A sense of fun, for example, may be no less excellent in itself than industriousness, and might be valued at least as highly in a society that had little economic need for hard work. I suppose that in assessing intrinsic excellence a just judgment might rate a good sense of fun as highly as industriousness. In most actual human circum-stances, however, consequential considerations give ample reason for regarding industriousness as more important, more desirable, and to be fostered with more urgency than a sense of fun.[25] We care about the virtues for more than one reas-on—for the sake of their excellence in responding to real values, yes, but also for the sake of their benefits. These reasons are distinct (though only partly so, as I have argued), and it is virtuous, on any plausible account, to care about them for both reasons.

## 3. DOES VIRTUE PAY?

I promised to return to the question whether virtue reliably benefits its possessor. This is an ancient question; Plato's *Republic*, for example, is organized around it. It is also one of the most urgent questions about morality. If we have easily assumed that we can live with an ideal of virtue that is not good for the virtuous, we might yet be disturbed by the terms in which Nietzsche argues that virtue is bad for its possessors. He claims that "the virtues (such as industriousness, obedience, chastity, piety, and justice) are usually *harmful* for those who possess them," being valued for their consequences for others and for "society." He says that "when you have a virtue, a real, whole virtue (and not merely a mini-instinct for some virtue), you are its *victim*."[26] This is ironic use of the term 'virtue'. In the context Nietzsche is clearly attacking the supposition that the mentioned traits

[25] As persuasively noted in Roberts, "Will Power and the Virtues," p. 233.
[26] Nietzsche, *Die fröhliche Wissenschaft* [*The Gay Science*], section 21, p. 53. There are also contexts in which Nietzsche uses the term 'virtue' for traits he does admire.

are admirable, deriding preachers of selflessness as motivated (in his estimation) by the hope of profiting from others' self-sacrifice. We do not seriously have a morality if we do not encourage people (including those we love) to be morally good. But how can we do that (and live with ourselves) if we do not believe the good will be happy?[27]

This is a difficult issue. It is not hard to make a case that people who are at least moderately virtuous are likely to lead more successful and more satisfying lives. For they are likely to have better personal relations; and such virtues as wisdom, self-control, and courage, will make them stronger and better organized to achieve whatever ends they have. But experience suggests that virtue can also be dangerous to the virtuous, leading sometimes to suffering, failure, and even death. Might it not be to one's own advantage to be like the virtuous person in most contexts but hold open an escape hatch of selfishness for occasions on which virtue would be too costly? Perhaps most of us have done that in some context or other. How are we to be dissuaded from doing that, and from hoping that other people whom we love will do that? More than a few thinkers have concluded that unqualified advocacy of virtue does require faith in the sure reward of virtue, and that this must involve belief in a life after death and in something like karma or divine providence. Can the advocates of virtue find adequate support in more this-worldly views? I will not try to answer that question here, but I will sketch a couple of lines of response to the challenge; they are not mutually exclusive.

(1) One might suppose that virtue is a not sufficient condition of well-being for its possessors, but that it is a necessary condition of the best sort of happiness or well-being. Aristotle is widely taken to have believed that, and Philippa Foot says that "there is indeed a kind of happiness that only goodness can achieve, but that by one of the evil chances of life it may be out of reach of even the best of men."[28] Can we think that the virtuous are quite likely to attain the best kind of happiness, and that failure of well-being for the virtuous is rare? Would that be basis enough for urging all to be virtuous?

(2) Here is another line of thought about the issue. I won't try to prove all its premises, but I think they are appealing. It is something that Plato did not quite say, but came tantalizingly close to saying, in the *Republic*; and I find it more convincing than what he did say on the subject.

His interpretation of justice as an obviously desirable harmony of the soul leaves him with a crucial difficulty. He claims that one who possesses this virtue, as an inner harmony, will also seek the public good and treat other people in ways ordinarily recognized as just. But it seems very doubtful that he has adequate grounds for this claim. Why wouldn't the desirable inner harmony be consistent

---

[27] This point is made forcefully in Hursthouse, *On Virtue Ethics*, pp. 174–87. I will return to it in chapter 5.

[28] Foot, *Natural Goodness*, p. 97.

with much more selfish decisions?[29] Note that in Plato's argument virtue is a state of the self that is seen as advantageous for its possessor, and then the problem is to connect that state with actions that might have seemed to be disadvantageous to the agent. The connection Plato claims is that the just person *will* do actions recognizable as just. The argument I propose for him has the same features, except that the connection is the weaker one that the person who has the intrinsically rewarding state of virtue has a *motive* to perform, even at great cost, actions recognizable as virtuous, and a basis for seeing *reason* to perform them.

The argument I think Plato should have given us will have obvious religious resonance for theistic Platonists who identify the Good with God, but I think it is not alien to the thought-world of Plato's own *Symposium* and *Republic*. It begins with his belief that the supreme benefit to which a person can aspire is knowledge of the Good. One for whom it is a supreme benefit must surely be one who loves or enjoys the Good for its own sake. This argument finds the crucial intrinsic reward of being virtuous, not in the structural virtue of inner harmony, but in the inclusive motivational virtue of being for the Good. What sort of behavior will this virtue inspire? Among particular goods, will it lead a person to care only for those that are part of his or her own life? Or for *all* goods? Won't we expect it to lead a person to cherish and protect good wherever it may be found, and thus to be altruistic and public-spirited? This is not an argument that altruism "pays" in the sense that the virtuous person is better off for acting altruistically. Rather it gives reason for thinking that virtue offers a supreme benefit that is inseparable from having a strong motive for altruistic action.

A variant on this argument is suggested by Plato's statement that one "whose thoughts are truly directed towards the things that are" will "imitate them and become as like them as possible" (*Republic* 500 B–C). One who enjoys the supreme benefit in loving the Good will have a motive to imitate the Good, and therefore to become as excellent as possible.[30] This will be a motive for aspiring to be altruistic, if altruism is a particularly excellent way of being for the good.

The excellence of altruism will be the topic of section 1 of the next chapter. It will provide both a concrete case in which the importance of excellence as a criterion of virtue can be further examined, and an occasion for a fuller response to Nietzsche's challenge.

---

[29] Cf. Sachs, "A Fallacy in Plato's *Republic.*"

[30] Cf. Lear, *Happy Lives and the Highest Good,* chapter 4, which argues that "when we love something, in the sense relevant to [Aristotle's] *Metaphysics,* . . . we strive to approximate [or imitate] it insofar as that is possible for us" (p. 72). My thinking about Plato as well as Aristotle in this matter owes much to conversation with Lear.

# PART II
# SELF AND OTHER

# 5

# Altruism

Altruism is both an important topic in its own right for a theory of virtue, and an interesting test case for my thesis that virtue is best defined in terms of its intrinsic excellence rather than in terms of its benefits. What I mean by 'altruism' in this context is other-regarding benevolence. It signifies any motive that takes as its end or goal the good or well-being of one or more or all persons other than oneself. Or perhaps in some cases the goal, less grandly, is simply something that is good for another person. I will also take note of ways in which one may be motivated to do something *for* other persons though not exactly for their well-being. They may not be central cases of altruism, but they are important for relating well to other persons.

A dichotomy between egoism and altruism, between one's own good and the good of others as motives, has had an organizing role in modern moral philosophy since Hobbes; and the majority have seen altruism as central to moral goodness. The ancient Greek philosophers, on the other hand, emphasized the contribution virtue makes to the well-being of the virtuous. They often seem to modern readers to assign too peripheral a place in their theories of virtue to altruism and regard for other persons. Some may have similar misgivings about my account of virtue as excellence in being for the good, and of the particular virtues as personal excellences. If altruism finds a place as a virtue in my theory, it will presumably be as what I have called a *motivational* virtue, an excellent way of being for something good. Does that afford a satisfying account of altruism?

That altruism, as I have defined it, is a way of being for something good is obvious. That altruism is *excellent* is a claim that requires more discussion. To say that something is excellent is to say that it has a kind of intrinsic and *non-instrumental* goodness that makes it a suitable object of honor, love, admiration, or perhaps (in the extreme case) of worship. It might be thought, however, that the main advantage of altruism is its *instrumental* value in enhancing the lives of other people. That presents me with two challenges.

One is a challenge internal to my theory. What's so excellent about altruism? How is it virtuous on my account? It is likely that we will approach this subject thinking it obvious that altruism is virtuous, and excellent; but we should not let this assumption pass without examination. Section 2 of this chapter will be devoted to discussion of reasons for thinking that altruism is indeed excellent, and a virtue. Sections 3 and 4 will address further questions about what sort of altruism is excellent.

First, however, I must address the more external challenge, which questions the need for a response to the internal challenge. Why should we care whether altruism is excellent in the indicated sense? In thinking about altruism (of all things) isn't there something perverse about a mode of evaluation that looks toward the admirableness of the agent rather than simply toward the benefits received by others? These questions will be the subject of the first and longest section of the chapter.

## 1. DOES IT MATTER WHETHER ALTRUISM IS EXCELLENT?

Why isn't it enough for the praise of altruism that it is generally beneficial? The benefits of altruism seem obvious. Wouldn't we all be much worse off if nobody cared about our well-being? Don't we depend on each other's good will? At a purely emotional level, is it not a great comfort to know that someone cares about our good—even if they cannot do very much about it? Would it not be chilling indeed to believe that it didn't matter to anybody else whether we fared well or ill?

To be sure, the benefits of altruism are not altogether uncontroversial. Some might argue that in a fair and well-ordered society self-interest would be given sufficient incentives to provide all important goods. And most of us in practice seem to think that many of the most urgent goods are best assured by giving some people self-interested motives to provide them, by paying them to do so. Still it is hard to deny that altruism is generally beneficial. How many of us would prefer to live in a society so cold-hearted that only self-interested motives would impel our neighbors to benefit us or avoid injuring us?

This motive for praising altruism would fit well with a conception that defines virtues as traits that are generally beneficial. I call that conception "trait consequentialist" because it evaluates traits of character by the value of their consequences.[1] I am not alone in opposing such a conception. A trait-consequentialist conception of virtue is taken by Nietzsche as a target in his attack on the morality of altruism, which figured in the last section of chapter 4. He agrees that people often identify human goodness with whatever qualities are useful to most people, and that these include altruistic qualities such as "compassion, the welcome helping hand, the warm heart," and "friendliness." But this "morality of usefulness" he identifies with "slave morality."[2] Its conception of human goodness, he thinks, is far inferior to that of an aristocratic morality that values noble life and noble action as good without concern for usefulness.[3]

---

[1] As explained in chapter 4, section 2.
[2] Nietzsche, *Jenseits von Gut und Böse*, p. 156 (IX. 260).
[3] Id., *Genealogy of Morality*, p. 12 (I. 2).

Nietzsche does not despise everything that might be considered altruistic. He praises a type of friendship (an aristocratic type) and a "gift-giving virtue."[4] But he does object to treating altruism or "the unegoistic" as a moral value;[5] and he does not admire a comprehensive, systematic, or consistent altruism. Nietzsche adores the ancients, and particularly thrills to the non-altruistic aspects of their conceptions of virtue. Altruistic qualities, he argues, are praised by the weak in order to seduce the strong into sacrificing their greatness by behaving in ways that are indeed useful to the less gifted majority, but that are not honorable. Disturbingly, he ascribes nobility to powerful warriors whom he sees, to be sure, as capable of friendship, but whom he also likens to predatory birds and beasts, giving free rein to impulses of cruelty.[6]

Diverse reactions to Nietzsche are possible. Mine are mixed. My strongest reaction to these aspects of his thought is revulsion at the passages in which he appears to celebrate cruelty. Yet his arguments leave me convinced that we will damn altruism with graceless praise if we extol it only as useful and not also as excellent and admirable. In the face of his powerful evocation of aesthetic issues about moral life it is very hard to remain content with a supposed virtue that is not beautiful, not admirable or honorable. No matter how useful we think altruism is to society, how wholeheartedly can we embrace it for ourselves, or urge it on those we love, if we do not honor or admire it?

An important question suggested by Nietzsche's arguments is whether one is regarded as a means or as an end when one is seen as virtuous. Nietzsche suggests that people are regarded mainly as means to the ends of others when they are praised for altruistic qualities. To be regarded mainly as a means and not as an end in oneself is degrading; and whatever else a virtue should be, the praise of it should not be degrading. So *is* one regarded mainly as a means when one is praised for altruistic qualities?

We may approach this question by considering how one regards *oneself* if one desires to have altruistic qualities, or indeed to be useful to other people. For example, Leibniz wanted to be *useful*. In so desiring was he regarding himself merely as a means and not an end? Was it only for the sake of other beings that he wanted to be useful, and not also and very much for his own sake? Should we imagine that he would have been gratified to discover that he had been useful to other people by serving as the butt of their jokes? Surely not; what he wanted, no doubt, was to *accomplish* something useful—and not something usefully contemptible, but something usefully excellent.

Why do we want to create, to achieve, to accomplish something good? Is it not that that is a way of participating in the good? That may be what we want most of all for ourselves. A classic representation of such a motive is the idea of

---

[4] Id., *Thus Spoke Zarathustra*, pp. 173–4, 186–8.
[5] Id., *Genealogy of Morality*, p. 64 (II. 18).
[6] Ibid., I. 11, 13, pp. 25, 28; cf. II. 6–7, pp. 45–9.

a deep desire literally or figuratively to "procreate in beauty" that is prominently featured in Plato's *Symposium*. It is clearly a desire to *participate* in the good, and specifically in beauty, and is a form of love for beauty. A very similar motive can apply in relation to other forms of good, and under other conceptions of the good.

The desire to be of service to other people is different from the desire that they be served, no matter by whom. The latter may be a desire purely for their good, for their sake. But you may also want to be one of those who serve other people; that may be something you want for its own sake. If you love another person, you are particularly likely to desire, for its own sake and from love, to be someone who does something for the person you love. These desires to be one who serves have an undeniable self-regarding aspect; there is something there that you want for yourself for its own sake.[7] We might debate whether it is good for you, or wanted as good for you; but even if it is not, I think it is clear enough that you may want it *for yourself* in a broader sense. It is a desire in which you regard yourself as an end and not merely as a means. It does not follow that it is not also an altruistic desire. Your serving others may be something you want for yourself for its own sake, and also something you want for the sake of the others, desiring their good for its own sake. Indeed I suppose that is the typical case of a desire to serve.

Why might you want such a thing for yourself? Because you might want to contribute to something good that you care about, to have some responsibility for it, and in that way to participate in it. I believe the way in which we commonly desire such participation makes clear that we regard it as enriching our lives with a value that is not merely instrumental, but is something over and above the benefit that is received by the other person.

If we can see how we may desire altruistic activity for ourselves, for our own sake, perhaps that will help us to see how we may desire altruistic motivation and action for others whom we love, for their sake. This is important for the role of altruism as a virtue. If we cannot sincerely encourage loved ones to be altruistic, either we do not really regard altruism as a moral virtue, or our attitude in the matter is disturbingly amoral. But if their being altruistic is not something we can want *for them*, and if in encouraging them to be altruistic we are treating them only as means to the good of other people, then so encouraging them hardly seems a loving thing to do to them. If we are to encourage people we love to be virtuous, then it is not enough to praise virtue as beneficial to others.[8]

It will be said, of course, that people generally are better off for being altruistic, because they will have happier social relations and get more cooperation from other people; and no doubt that is true, up to a point. But altruistic motivation

---

[7] Cf. Adams, *Finite and Infinite Goods*, pp. 88, 139–41.

[8] A similar argument is made forcefully in Hursthouse, *On Virtue Ethics*, pp. 174–87, though her conclusion, that virtue must be expected to be beneficial for the virtuous, is somewhat different from mine.

sometimes leads people to do things that cost them something of their own good, and that may plausibly be thought to leave them worse off. Should loving parents therefore encourage their children to be altruistic only when it is not particularly costly to them on balance? But such carefully limited altruism is not much of a virtue. Parents do not seriously desire altruistic virtue for their children unless they are really willing for the children to be disposed to give up something of their own good for the sake of other people. Is that something they can support for the sake of their children, and not just for the sake of the *other* people who may be benefited?

I believe it is. Note first of all that a person's good or well-being is not the only thing one can want or favor or support for that person's sake. In many cases, if you have asked me to do something, I can do it *for you* even if I don't think it will be good for you. That can be an expression of my *respect* or *friendship* for you. Similarly, I can want something *for you* because it will further a main project of yours, even if it won't benefit you because your project is self-sacrificing. Perhaps in such cases I will have some ambivalence because of the cost to you, but what I do or want can still be for you. Being *for your good* is only one of the ways in which I may be *for you*.[9] This is important for my theory of virtue, inasmuch as being for persons is one of the main ways in which we can be for what is good.

Another thing you can want *for* people you love is that they should be *worthy* of love and esteem. In short, you can want them to be excellent. Indeed, we might think love deficient if it didn't involve that desire. It is likely to be something you want for your own sake too, for the sake of your loving. But it needn't be only for your own sake. It can be an expression of your caring about *them*, in which you want them to be worthy whether or not you are there to know about it. I think this motive is probably at work in most cases in which one wants persons one loves to be altruistic, for their sake. If so, this is a way in which the excellence of altruism is important to altruism's role as a virtue.

Is caring about the excellence of people you love, for their sake, just a form of caring about their good? This is a question of some intricacy, though I think in the end it will not be crucial for our present investigation. Our response to it is bound to be shaped by our view of what constitutes a person's good, which is a controversial issue in moral philosophy. I believe, and have argued elsewhere, that the principal constituents of a person's good are enjoyment and the excellence of what one enjoys.[10] Suppose you agree with me about that, and think that enthusiastic altruism, uninhibited by self-concern, enjoys supreme excellence in itself. Then you may believe that you can desire such altruism for people you love, *for their own good*, regardless of other goods it may cost them. If you do believe all that, I needn't argue with you, for you already accept the main conclusions of this chapter: that altruism is excellent and its excellence is important.

---

[9] These points will be discussed more fully in chapter 6, section 3.
[10] Adams, *Finite and Infinite Goods*, chapter 3.

Most people, however, will probably believe that in thinking about a person's good, our own or anyone else's, we should balance considerations of excellence and of enjoyment, and different excellences that could be enjoyed. So believing, they may think that whatever excellence the altruist may enjoy in what would generally be regarded as an act of self-sacrifice might well be less than the enjoyment and excellence of other goods she thereby gives up. I believe that myself, but I still think that if the relevant sort of altruism is excellent enough, you could be glad that a loved one has it, for her sake, though not exactly for her own good.

You may have noticed that I put that in terms of being *glad*, for her sake, that a loved one has the excellence you see in altruism. I think it is also something you could *desire* for her sake, but that is attended with additional moral dangers. In some cases parents' zeal for their children to acquire certain excellences seems oppressive, compromising their love.[11] Not necessarily that what they desire is for their own good rather than for their children. But there seems to be too much of self in their concern, too much self-will, not a pure enough focus on the loved one, not enough appreciation or understanding of her difference. I believe that what is offensive in such cases is the insensitive imposition of parental preferences, rather than the preference for excellence as such. If parents' determination that their child should enjoy a safe and comfortable life stands in the way of the child's actual autonomous preference for a life of more generous or more arduous and adventurous excellence, that can be offensive, I believe, in much the same way. If a loved one clear-sightedly chooses a path of excellence that seems likely to be less enjoyable on balance, and perhaps less good for her, than a less arduous path would be, that is something you ought to be able to support for her sake.

Some may be tempted to object that this whole effort to find non-instrumental value in altruism is frivolous. Whatever non-instrumental excellence we may see in altruism, the objector suggests, it pales into triviality in comparison with the importance of the good that altruism may produce for its intended beneficiaries. But attention to the importance of valuable *relationships* among persons suggests that non-instrumental excellence of altruism and other moral qualities is anything but trivial. If we think of an interest in the non-instrumental value of altruism as derogating from an interest in its benefits, we are likely to be thinking of the benefits on the model of *commodities*. An interest in the distribution of commodities certainly has an important place in ethics, and especially in political philosophy. Much human good does depend on commodities; there is in fact much suffering due to the lack of them, and much injustice in their distribution. The distribution of commodities is a topic of moral urgency.

We have a very truncated conception of the goods of human life, however, if we conceive of them chiefly as commodities, or a function of commodities. We need some commodities if we are to live at all, and we need additional commodities for many of the good projects we might have. But if people ask how

---

[11] I am indebted to Julia Markovits for raising this issue with me.

they can live the best kind of life, few of us will think it good advice to reply, "Just get as much as you can of material goods." There are goods that contribute to the value of life out of proportion to the amount of material wealth they require—goods of meaningful activity, of friendship, community, religion, culture, of beauty seen or heard or created. If one is poor in these goods it may not matter much how rich one is in commodities. Many of these goods essentially involve relationships among persons, and most of them are not separable from the motives with which we enter into them. Friendship involves an interest specifically in the friend's well-being and in the friendship. Finding meaning and happiness in activities, cultures, and communities typically involves caring for their own sake about goods specific to them.[12]

The intrinsic and non-instrumental value of moral qualities is an integral part of the intrinsic value of many phenomena of personal relationship. I will discuss two examples of this connection in ancient writings, beginning with Aristotle's ideal of friendship. He devotes two of the ten "books" of his *Nicomachean Ethics* to a treatise on friendship. This is significant for the social dimension of Aristotle's virtue-centered ethical theory. Friendship provides him with a context in which the intrinsic excellence of virtue can be socially as well as individually valued. Raising the question whether a virtuous and happy human being will be so self-sufficient as not to need friends, Aristotle answers that he will need friends. At the center of his argument is an idea of the value of participating, even vicariously, in excellence. It is, specifically, the thought that good people are happy in being conscious that they stand in some connection with good actions. They find this happiness in contemplating not only their own actions but also, and perhaps more clearly, "the actions of virtuous people [*spoudaioi*] who are their friends"[13]

My second example is drawn from a very different, less aristocratic ancient literature. It is the role of personal moral excellence and its relation to self-giving in the New Testament. Some Christian writers have been highly suspicious of ethical emphasis on individual excellence. But in fact personal excellence, notably including moral excellence, frequently appears in the New Testament as a central part of the framework for ethical aspiration and exhortation. The excellence can be characterized in aesthetic or quasi-aesthetic terms, as when St Paul presents an exhortation so to act "that you may become blameless and pure, unblemished children of God amid a crooked and misshapen generation, in which you shine like stars in the universe" (Philippians 2:15). The language of purity is connected with ancient practices of worship, and specifically with sacrificial practices. A sacrificial offering must be pure, without blemish, something excellent. This can be seen in the biblical statement, "Christ. . . loved us and gave himself up for us as an offering and sacrifice to God, for a sweet fragrance" (Ephesians 5:1–2). Here

---

[12] These points will be argued further in chapter 6, section 2.
[13] Aristotle, *Nicomachean Ethics*, IX. 9 (1169b28–1170a4).

the sweet fragrance is a metaphor for an aesthetic or quasi-aesthetic excellence of Christ's self-offering that is important to its role in sacrifice.

Why is the excellence of what is sacrificed so important? Because it is a gift. The point of the sacrifice is not that something is destroyed but that something is given. Sacrifice in a literal sense is an ancient religious practice, a form of worship. The New Testament speaks of offering oneself as a sacrifice, perhaps a "living sacrifice" (Romans 12:1), as a way of describing a love in which the gift that is given, *and* the gift that is received, is the self of the giver. This gift is not a commodity, and it is not truly received if it is received only as a means to some ulterior end of the recipient. One who truly receives this gift must value it as an end, for its own sake. It is important that such a gift be excellent—and hence that the giver be excellent, since the giver *is* the gift.

Surely such gifts of self are rightly prized in profane as well as sacred contexts. Like an Aristotelian friendship, a relationship in which we are able to exchange such gifts with each other must be one in which the excellence of each person matters not only to herself but to all the parties. It is a relationship in which excellence of a person, including such excellence as altruism may have, has intrinsic importance as part of the excellence of the relationship, which may constitute part of the good of all the parties to the relationship. In such a relationship it is surely not frivolous to care about the excellence of moral qualities.

My argument in this section is part of my case for thinking of virtue, and the virtues, as excellences, of not merely instrumental value. The context of social relations in which we situate the moral point of view is of fundamental importance for our conception of moral values. The momentousness of such a context emerges strongly, I believe, in Julia Driver's defense of her trait-consequentialist account of virtue against the objection that it commends traits that "simply can't be virtues, since they don't seem to contribute at all to the agent's flourishing," and that "it's difficult to see how we could *recommend* that anyone adopt such traits—especially since one may not want one of these traits for oneself." Driver's reply distinguishes between moral virtue and other kinds of virtue. On her view "the connection between virtue and flourishing. . . is that moral virtue contributes to the flourishing of others—and perhaps [only perhaps!] of oneself. . . So personal flourishing is not the aim of the moral virtues, though other virtues (prudential ones) will be so directed." Driver also distinguishes between commending and recommending. "There are many traits in people that are commendable," she says, "indeed, that I think are of considerable worth, yet are ones that I would be reluctant to recommend to others or want for myself—for example, the courage to risk life and limb to save others in distress. I particularly doubt that I'd recommend such traits to my children."[14]

I don't expect to be alone in finding Driver's response on these points disturbing; but it gives unusually clear and forthright expression to an outlook that has

---

[14] Driver, *Uneasy Virtue*, pp. 38–9.

been very influential in modern moral thought. It is an outlook in which the moral point of view is situated (implicitly) in a system in which the *interests* of the agents are seen as in competition rather than community with those of other agents. To praise an agent from that point of view is to praise the agent for consequences external to the agent's own life. It is praise for benefits that others derive from the agent's qualities, states, and actions, without regard to whether the agent's life is happier or better in any intrinsic way for those qualities, states, or actions. Such praise is what Driver calls "commending," and she identifies it with *moral* praise. She recognizes, of course, another, less competitive, more loving relational point of view from which personal traits can be "recommended," but she does not regard that as *moral* praise. These are emphatically not comments about the character of Driver's or any other moral theorist's actual social relationships. I suppose that anyone who thinks about these things has some relationships that are loving and trusting and some that are less trusting and more competitive. The issue is which sort of social context we think ourselves into for purposes of thinking about virtue.

Situating the moral point of view in a primarily competitive social context, and identifying virtue with qualities of an agent that are useful to others, leaves us obviously exposed to Nietzsche's challenge to morality, and without a satisfying answer to the question why one should desire moral virtue for oneself or for anyone that one loves. I believe that a conception of moral virtue, or virtue in social relations, that is worth aspiring to must be answerable to a point of view that would be situated in quite a different system of relationships. From such a point of view it is natural to identify virtues with qualities of will and personal relationship that would be prized in a community of persons who love each other, want to have well-founded admiration for each other, and want their social relationships to be excellent. Such a point of view supports a conception of virtue as most fundamentally a form of excellence rather than of usefulness.

## 2. WHAT'S SO EXCELLENT ABOUT ALTRUISM?

*Is* altruism excellent? Does it in fact have the sort of intrinsic and non-instrumental value about which I have been speaking? That it does may seem obvious to some of us. I mentioned that I react with revulsion to passages in which Nietzsche seems to celebrate cruelty. My revulsion is in part an aesthetic reaction. I find the opposite of altruism ugly. Do I likewise see beauty, and more broadly excellence, in striking cases of altruism? I think so. Say that I have a partly aesthetic conviction that altruistic motivation is admirable. Call it an intuition, if you will, in current philosophical parlance.

Be they intuitions or convictions, I take such apprehensions of value seriously. I doubt that we can have a good appreciation of excellence that is not largely formed by them. But such a basis for believing that altruistic motivation is excellent does not answer the moral philosopher's question, what is excellent about it—as an intuitive aesthetic judgment that a work of art is beautiful does not answer the art critic's question, what is beautiful about it.

As a step toward answering the question about altruism, we may remind ourselves that altruistic motivation is normally a form of being for the good. The goal of an altruistic motive is something that one wants for the sake of a person or persons other than oneself, and we may reasonably count as altruistic only motives whose goal is good. In central cases of altruism the goal is the good or well-being *of* one or more or all other persons. For present purposes we may add the proviso that the goals of the altruistic motive really are good, and not merely regarded as such by the altruist. To what extent *misguided* altruism may be excellent and a virtue, is a subsidiary question which I will not try to answer here.

As a way of being for the good, altruism satisfies half of the condition I laid down at the outset, that if altruism is a virtue, it will be as an excellent way of being for something good. The other and more difficult half of the condition, excellence, is our current concern; but the consideration that the altruist, as such, is for something good may also get us a further step on our way to the conclusion that altruism is excellent. I believe there is a conceptual connection between value and valuing. Not that either can be defined simply as a function of the other; but if something is good there is a way in which it is good—indeed excellent—to value it.[15]

But surely it is not simply as a case of being for something good that we admire altruism. Selfish people may be *for* good things that they want only for themselves. We think the altruist is for the good in a much more excellent way than that. What is it that is *more* excellent about altruism? I believe we can discern at least four ways in which altruistic motivation is more excellent than wanting good things for oneself alone.

(1) If it is excellent to be for what is good, would it not be more excellent to be for more rather than less of what is good? Altruism has an advantage here. An altruistic interest in the good of other people can have wider scope than my interest in my own good can have, since there are many other people to care about and there is only one of me. And surely in typical cases altruism's interest in human well-being will *in fact* have wider scope in this way. Conceivably not in *all* cases. It is quite possible in self-hatred to wish oneself ill, or in depression or exhaustion to lose the will to pursue one's own good.[16] Since it is possible not to care for one's own good, we might think of a form of altruism in which one cared about the good of only one other person, and not at all about one's own good, or the good of any third party. This would be far from admirable, however, involving, among other things, a failure of appreciative response to some of the

---

[15]  Cf. Adams, *Finite and Infinite Goods*, pp. 20 ff., and Anderson, *Value in Ethics and Economics*.
[16]  For convincing argument on this point, see Stocker, "Desiring the Bad."

goods and possibilities of good with which one is, inescapably, most intimately acquainted. It is far from obvious that it would be more excellent than a totally egoistic motivational pattern. Both seem bizarre and unattractive, at least partly because the scope of concern in both is too narrow.

Even if altruism as such does not necessarily have the advantage of larger scope, it is clear that altruism *can* have wider scope than egoism can. And wider scope of being for what is good is more excellent, other things being equal. Because of our limited capacities for knowing, caring, and acting, of course, other things often are not equal. But if we ignore human limitations, what would we take as our ideal of benevolence? It is hard to see any reason for not idealizing good will that is universal in scope and profound in understanding and intensity, if we suppose it to be possible. Such benevolence would embrace the good of every person, including the benevolent person's own good, with the passion and sensitivity to detail that is characteristic of the most intimate love. That seems as excellent a way of being for the good of persons as I can imagine. Such profound and universal love is commonly (and I would say rightly) ascribed to God; but it is obviously impossible for mere humans.

It does seem possible, however, for us to participate less perfectly in both the universality and the depth of divine love. We can participate more superficially in the universality, having some regard for the rights and well-being of all persons. And we can participate more selectively in the profundity, caring in a more intense and focused way for the good of some persons, including ourselves but not only ourselves. I believe the most plausible ideal of human benevolence will include both these ways of responding to possibilities of good for human beings.[17] If humans can indeed have both some concern for the good of all and a richer, more particular concern for the good of some, why would it not be best to have both? We will be lacking one or another important dimension of motivational excellence unless we do have both. If we accept this ideal, we have reason to think that the altruistic motivation involved in it is excellent.

(2) But is it really possible to combine these two dimensions of excellence? How much narrowness of scope is required for truly profound concern for a particular person? An argument for egoism that takes off from this question will end up helping us to see the central place of altruism in excellent motivation.

I have acknowledged that there are excellences of profundity and intensity of good will that are possible for humans only in focusing on the good of a relatively limited number of persons. Perhaps an egoist will argue that the greatest excellence of profundity and intensity of good will is possible for us only in focusing exclusively on our own good, because it is the one instance of human good with which we are most intimately acquainted. The egoist's claim would be that an exclusive engagement with this best known of all goods promises an excellence so great as to win the prize of virtue in competition with altruism's wider focus.

---

[17] Cf. Slote's views about balanced caring, in his *Morals from Motives*, ch. 3.

Most of us will probably find this suggestion intuitively implausible. The most clearly decisive objection to it, perhaps, is that one's engagement with one's own good will be truncated and impoverished so long as one has no altruistic motivation. That is because so much of the good we can enjoy in life depends on the breadth of our interests, and particularly on our benevolent interest in other persons. Unless we are as unluckily isolated as Robinson Crusoe without his man Friday, there will be a great proportion of our own possible good that we will not have engaged in any depth if we do not care about the good of others. It is not a focus on one individual's *good* as such that gives a richer object for a deeper love. The rich object of love is the individual's *life*, which will be much richer if it is rich in aspects that you cannot care about without caring about the good of other people. Thus my caring, however intensively, about my own good alone could not have sufficient richness to compensate for its narrowness. Really excellent self-love must be integrated with unselfcentered concerns. In this way it resembles really excellent love of cultural goods, which (as I argued in chapter 3) must be integrated with concern for the good of persons.

(3) An important part of what is to be accounted for here is that we do not just think altruistic motivation excellent; we think not caring for the good of other people, for its own sake, is morally *bad*—in extreme cases even wicked. If it is a settled motivational pattern, it is a *vice* (in the sense explained in chapter 3), and not just the absence of a virtue. Most of us think a purely egoistic pattern of motivation is morally bad. One reason for thinking it so is that it seems *idolatrous*. It lacks a certain flexibility and readiness to subordinate one interest to another, when appropriate, that we rightly expect of excellent motivation. We may count it idolatry, in a moral sense, to be so bound to any particular good or type of good as object of concern that one is not sensitive to reasons for diverting attention to some other good, or even for preferring the other good. Such idolatry compromises, or even cancels, the excellence of caring for the good that one does care for. Because of the salience and magnitude of other goods that can compete with one's own personal well-being as objects of concern, a settled pattern of motivation that is purely egoistic can hardly fail to be an idolatry in this sense. And not only that, but even a qualified egoism will be idolatrous in the indicated sense if it allows altruistic motives but confines them within the straitjacket of the constraint, 'But me first, always.'

(4) Another way in which it is bad not to care at all, for their sake, about the good of other persons within the range of one's knowledge, is that it is a way of *relating badly* to them. Conversely, and positively, there is an *excellence of personal relationship* in altruistic motivation. Whether or not it is reciprocated, caring for another person's good constitutes an interpersonal relationship (in a broad sense) which is richer and more excellent than the more reflexive relationship to oneself involved in caring for one's own good.

This is not a minor point. If the *other*-regarding character of altruism is a ground of excellence, that is most plausibly attributed, I think, to its role in constituting goods of personal relationship. The consistent egoist is to a large extent a practical solipsist, living as if alone in the world. He is one for whom the reality of the other, the beyond-the-self, is at least subjectively devalued. Those who care for the good of others live in a larger and richer universe of relations. In giving oneself unreservedly to other persons or to larger goods one escapes from isolation. One moves with freedom, and probably with much richer perceptiveness,[18] in a space of values in which one's life can have significance in relation to those other persons and goods and not merely in relation to oneself. That is excellent.

The importance of goods of relationship as grounds of our judgments of virtue and vice regarding the presence and absence of altruistic interests is signaled by the responsiveness of such judgments to facts of proximity and remoteness. Consider two possible Robinson Crusoes, both of them deprived of all human company for some years past and for the foreseeable future. Crusoe 1 still thinks much about the family and friends from whom he is separated. We may suppose he prays for them every day, as also for other concerns in the human world that he carries with him. This is admirable. What about Crusoe 2? He no longer concerns himself much, even inwardly, about other people, not expecting to have anything to do with them again. He is almost totally absorbed in his new environment on the island—not just in finding food and safety there, but exploring, appreciating and enjoying the wonders of its non-human creatures, its geology and biology.

It would be narrow-minded, I think, to call this *vice* in Crusoe 2, or to consider it incompatible with being virtuous on the whole. In this respect we may compare Crusoe 2 with a reclusive human individual living amid other people but avoiding substantive interaction with them, and having little or no concern for them. The unconcern of the latter, reclusive individual may well be a *vice*, compromising any claim to good character he might have on the basis of his relating well to the non-human world. If it is a vice, the reason, I believe, is that it constitutes *relating badly* to other people with whom he stands in relations that are important for the meaning and value of the present phase of his life, however much he tries to starve those relations out of existence.

## 3. IMPURE BENEVOLENCE AND JUSTICE AS A VIRTUE

As announced at the beginning of this chapter, I am counting as altruistic any motive that aims at the good of one or more other persons for its (or their) own sake. Some may think I am using the terms 'altruism' and 'altruistic' in a rather broad sense. It is certainly a current, ordinary sense of the term, and I think it is the dominant sense in analytical moral philosophy. Discussion, however, has

---

[18] I am indebted to Valeria Chiappini for urging this point on me.

convinced me that the word is also used sometimes in another sense to signify a doctrine of pure and universal altruism.

Insisting on *universal* altruism, such a doctrine refuses to count as altruistic any motive that is bound up with a "special relationship" such as those of friendship and family. I do count motives of the latter sort as altruistic.[19] An important part of my argument for the excellence of altruism relies on considerations of excellence in interpersonal relationships. And I have argued that an important dimension of depth and richness will be absent from our altruistic motivation if we do not care about the good of some persons in special ways in which we do not have the capacity to care about the good of all.

In its advocacy of *pure* altruism, the doctrine I reject here is opposite to egoism but similar in structure. The purely altruistic motivation it advocates is motivation with which absolutely no fundamentally self-regarding motive is mixed. I do not believe there is any such thing as purely altruistic motivation. I don't think we have radically pure motives at all. Motives are always mixed, in the sense that they work together with other motives or motivational states. We may not be conscious of some of these—for instance, of our proneness to be influenced by certain situational factors (which will be a major topic of discussion in chapter 9).

At any rate, in speaking of altruistic motives, I don't mean to exclude motives that aim at other ends (such as one's own excellence or happiness) *in addition to* the good of other people. It's enough that one aims at another person's good for its own sake and not only as means to one's less altruistic ends. I think this also fits the views of classic defenders of the reality of altruistic motivation in British moral philosophy of the eighteenth century, particularly of Shaftesbury and Butler.[20]

The most extreme idealization of "pure" altruism would favor a total pattern of motivation completely uninfluenced by (intrinsically) self-regarding motives. This seems a very unrealistic moral fantasy, but it has been a haunting ideal for many. Even if it were possible, I do not think such a totally selfless motivational pattern would be truly excellent. For, as I have already indicated, it would not be possible without colossal insensitivity or unresponsiveness to significant goods in one's own life with which one can hardly fail to be acquainted.

The possible, and desirable, complexity of interest in goods is very inadequately represented by the popular dichotomy between egoism and altruism—which is to say, between motives that aim at one's own well-being and motives that aim at the well-being of others. For there are other goods to be aimed at besides the well-being of persons, and some of them are worth prizing for their own sake, and

---

[19] See Blum, *Friendship, Altruism, and Morality*, for fuller defense of a similar view.

[20] Shaftesbury, *Inquiry Concerning Virtue, or Merit*, Book 2; Butler, *Fifteen Sermons*, Sermon 11. Even Hutcheson, who insists that "if there be any benevolence at all, it must be disinterested," allows that "as all men have self-love, as well as benevolence, these two principles may jointly excite a man to the same action" (*Concerning Moral Good and Evil*, II. iii, p. 86). Cf. the commentary on Hutcheson in Darwall, *The British Moralists and the Internal 'Ought'*, pp. 207–43.

not merely as means to someone's well-being. Some of the goods one may aim at, not just for the sake of someone's well-being, do involve oneself, however. One's motive is *self-regarding*, in a broad sense, insofar as one aims, for its own sake, at an end that essentially involves oneself. We may say that motives are *self-interested* only when they aim specifically at one's own *well-being* for its own sake.[21]

Self-regarding motives play important structuring roles in any form of life that one could easily wish any person to have. Being a friend, and caring therefore how one is related to one's friend, typically (and I think ideally) involves a motive that is self-regarding but not strictly self-interested—namely, an interest in the relationship for its own sake and not just as a means to either party's well-being. The desire to be of service to others, discussed in section 1, is likewise a self-regarding but not necessarily self-interested motive.

Typical forms of both consequentialist and non-consequentialist ethical theories commend, or appeal to, self-regarding motives. This is true of those consequentialist theories, for instance, that think one's most fundamental and decisive goal should be to maximize either the total or the average of human well-being, counting each person's well-being equally, including one's own. They obviously imply that one should have at least some degree of self-interested motivation aiming at one's own well-being. And trait consequentialists must be expected to commend a more than minor desire for one's own well-being, in view of the huge part that taking care of oneself plays in sustaining and advancing human well-being.

Typical non-consequentialist theories are committed to what some philosophers call "agent-centered restrictions" on the pursuit of best consequences.[22] These are restrictions that prohibit one from causing certain harms oneself even in order to maximize the sum of human well-being by preventing greater harms from being produced in some other way. An example would be a moral constraint against torturing a child in order to extort morally needed cooperation from a grandparent.[23] Constraints of this sort are a well-established part of the common morality of our culture. The term 'agent-centered' rightly signals the deeply self-regarding character of a commitment to such restrictions. The commitment is not necessarily self-interested, as it need not involve concern for one's own well-being. But it is self-regarding, as the actions it is to govern are one's own and that is essential to the nature of the commitment. It is hard to see how one could be firm in such a commitment without caring in a special way about one's own behavior for its own sake.

What excellent and attractive motive could inspire commitment to such self-regarding constraints? Among the most plausible candidates for that role are

---

[21] In terms of a distinction to be introduced in chapter 7, which need not concern us yet, these are *narrowly* self-interested motives.

[22] The term was introduced (without unambiguous endorsement of such restrictions) in Scheffler, *The Rejection of Consequentialism* (1982).

[23] This example is from Nagel, *The View from Nowhere*, p. 176.

desires to *relate well* to other people. Consider, for example, T. M. Scanlon's non-consequentialist account of the morality of duty, or, in his apt phrase, of "what we owe to each other." There is something very appealing about his argument that the main and most appropriate motive for doing our duty to other people is "the positive value of living with others on terms that they could not reasonably reject,"[24] and thus of being able to *justify* one's conduct to them. It would be quite unfair to call this a *selfish* motive. As Scanlon emphasizes, it is a matter of valuing "a valuable relationship with others"[25]—a relationship that should be good for the other persons involved as well as for oneself. Nonetheless, this is not an unambiguously altruistic motive. It is other-regarding in part, but also, and decisively, self-regarding, though not exactly self-interested. The decisive consideration, for it, is that one's own action be justifiable—that one have reasons for it that cannot *reasonably* be rejected by others to whom one relates.[26] What is at stake in this decisive consideration is the excellence of one's way of relating to other persons, rather than one's good or well-being; but it is excellence of one's *own*. The desire to relate well to other people will similarly be a crucial motive for aspiring to the virtue of altruism, on my account of the matter.

For reasons of this sort I believe that the motives that root other-regarding morality in a virtuous character cannot be expected to be *purely* altruistic, but will include a self-regarding interest in relating well to other persons. This is important in accounting for the status of *justice* as a virtue, and of injustice as a vice. A just person is one who has a pretty accurate awareness of what her moral obligations are, cares about them and is committed to fulfilling them, and in fact generally fulfills them. That corresponds to one historic way of using the word 'just' to name a virtue—not the only one, but one that will serve us well in the present context. We can likewise say that someone who is not just is *unjust*. It must always seem at best very questionable to regard an unjust person as morally virtuous. In other words, injustice is a *vice*, and a very grave one. I face, therefore, the question what is so importantly excellent about justice that not only is it a virtue, but the lack of it is a vice.

This question cannot be answered purely in terms of the excellence of altruistic motivation. For, as rights generate agent-centered restrictions, respecting the rights of other persons is not necessarily good for them. The wait-staff of a restaurant, for instance, respect the rights of customers by bringing them the food they ordered, which may quite clearly not be the food that is best for them. Why is it nonetheless excellent to respect people's rights? The most plausible answer, I believe, will take the form of claiming (as in Scanlon's theory) that respecting people's rights is important for relating well to them.

---

[24] Scanlon, *What We Owe to Each Other*, p. 162. My view of the nature of duty is different from Scanlon's, but not in a way that matters decisively to the point made here.

[25] Ibid.

[26] Ibid., p. 154.

This is not to say that justice is enough to make a person virtuous on the whole in the absence of altruistic motivation. Like the cultural goods of philosophy, literature, and music, the values supported by the just person as such cannot exist except as aspects of the life of persons. As in the case of interests in those cultural goods (as discussed in the last section of chapter 3), so also caring about justice without also caring about the good or well-being of the persons would constitute a bizarrely distorted pattern of interests in human life. Justice and the rights it respects are doubtless more central objects of interest in human life than those cultural goods are. There is something misshapen even about caring for the well-being of persons without caring about justice. But I think the value of justice is equally compromised if one does not generally care, for its own sake, about the good of persons with whom one has to do. There may surely be cases in which commitment to justice sustains right action when one is too angry or too worried about one's own good to care about the other person's good; and such a commitment is an admirable moral strength. But a commitment to justice that is not normally combined with benevolence is something unattractively chilling, lacking one of the best parts of a normal motivation for justice.

## 4. SELF-SACRIFICE

In arguing that an ideal of altruism should not *exclude* fundamentally self-regarding motives, I do not mean to claim that altruistic motives never *compete* with self-regarding motives, and particularly with the desire for one's own well-being. Should altruistic motives have priority in such competition? It seems absurd to assign the most extreme priority to them, claiming that an ideally virtuous person would always prefer the slightest benefit for another person to the greatest benefit for herself. As noted in chapter 2, section 2, seriously endangering one's life to rescue a child's favorite toy is not an act of virtue but of folly. But there are some cases in which most of us think it admirable to make a significant sacrifice of one's own good for another person's benefit. How and why self-sacrifice may be intrinsically excellent, and virtuous, is the chief remaining topic of this chapter.

It is relatively easy to explain the excellence of sacrificing oneself (perhaps one's life) for goods that plausibly must indeed be regarded as more important than one's own good. This is a view that is commonly held (in some cases rightly, I suppose) of soldiers who "give their lives for their country" in warfare. And it is easy to take this view of martyrs of the American civil rights movement of the 1960s. But those are not the only cases to explain. We also admire people who give up some good of their own to save or achieve a merely equivalent good for someone else. Preferring one's own equivalent good in such a case may not be blameworthy, but does not seem as admirable as preferring the other person's good. Why?

Consider a pair of cases. In Case 1 a person *B* is killed, being helpless to prevent it. *B*'s death is unmitigated loss. (Here I ignore issues about an afterlife.) In Case 2 another person *A* succeeds in saving *B*'s life by sacrificing his own life. *A*'s death is a loss, but not unmitigated, we may think, because *A* has accomplished something very good thereby (namely, saving *B*'s life). And accomplishing something very good, as I have argued, is also a way of participating in the good. So in losing what is lost by death *A* also gets something very good (that is, a sort of participation in something very good). In this way we may plausibly think that *A*'s death in saving *B* is objectively a better outcome than *B*'s dying helplessly. That might tempt us to conclude that *A*'s self-sacrifice is excellent, and admirable, *because* *A* thus prefers the objectively better outcome. The line of thought is suggestive, but I do not think that what is excellent in self-sacrifice is a preference for better outcomes as such.

Perhaps the assumption of success in my choice of example misleads. We probably think *A*'s self-sacrifice might be no less admirable if *A* had lost his life in an unsuccessful attempt to save *B*'s life (assuming *A*'s hope of saving *B*'s life was not foolish). Here it is important to say that it is not just through success in causing the intended outcome that the self-sacrificer participates in a good. Regardless of the success or failure of one's efforts, one may participate in a good of relationship by giving oneself to or for another person.

In goods of relationship self-sacrificers may gain something for themselves, an enrichment of meaning if not of experience. And they may be conscious of this, as is Sidney Carton as Dickens imagines him at the end of *A Tale of Two Cities*, saying, of his giving his life to save another man's, "It is a far, far better thing that I do than I have ever done," and evoking a rich relational significance of his sacrifice.[27] Thus self-sacrificers may be, simultaneously, *for* the other persons and goods for which they give themselves and also for the significance of their own lives. They may see a richer texture of values in their lives inasmuch as they appreciate, not only the subjective satisfactions that any of us can hardly help caring about, but also the relational meanings that can more easily be overlooked.

The relational good that is constituted by the self-sacrifice is not undermined but enhanced by the excellence it constitutes for the self-sacrificer. For, as I remarked with reference to the New Testament, the relational significance of self-sacrifice is not that the self is destroyed but that the self is given; and it is enhanced by the excellence of the self that is given. It is possible, of course, to sacrifice oneself without thinking any of these thoughts, thinking only of the good one seeks to secure for another, but it is not necessarily less excellent to be conscious of them. People who are reflective in certain ways may be unable to avoid thinking of such things, and I don't think such reflectiveness detracts from altruistic excellence.

[27] Dickens, *A Tale of Two Cities*, p. 390. The quoted words, among the most famous Dickens wrote, are not something Carton actually says in the story, but part of what Dickens imagines Carton would have said if he had uttered "the thoughts that were inspiring" him (ibid., p. 389).

Such consciousness of self-sacrifice as both costly and enriching to the self of the giver is a feature of the primal image of self-sacrifice seen as excellent in Western culture, which is that of the self-sacrifice of Christ. The New Testament portrays Jesus as laying down his life for his friends, out of love for them, and as thinking of himself as "glorified" in doing so.[28] If Christ gave himself up for the Church out of love for her, it was also "so that he himself might present the Church to himself as glorious,"[29] and thus with a relational good in view.

Christ has been seen as a model of *generosity*, and one of the ways in which self-sacrifice can be seen as excellent, and virtuous, is certainly as a manifestation of generosity. As the use of 'liberality' as a synonym of 'generosity' suggests, generosity has been seen as a form or manifestation of *freedom*—freedom in relation to needs and constraints that might hold one back from giving. If the richness from which such freedom springs is inner and psychic rather than external and material, it is an excellent strength of character.

There are ways in which the freedom of generosity may be lacking in self-sacrifice. I do not think the generosity of a sacrifice is compromised by every sort of sense that one *must* make it. One's conception of one's duty can be generous too. But if one thinks one must sacrifice oneself because one devalues oneself or fears social disapproval, the sacrifice will not be an act of freedom or generosity, though it may require a certain courage.

These reflections suggest, I believe, the right answer to the suspicion, sometimes voiced by feminists, among others, that admiration of self-sacrifice devalues self-respect. The most admirable self-sacrificers are not people who think they are less important, or worth less, than other people, but people who have better, richer ways of valuing themselves as well as other people—ways that take fuller account of values of relationship. My argument for admiring such acts and their motives depends on the premise that they constitute really excellent features of interpersonal relationship, *and* that there is no comparably great excellence of *intra*personal relationship that would be constituted by holding back more for one's own good. And the second conjunct of this premise may not be satisfied in cases in which one's motivation or thinking in sacrificing oneself expresses servility or a serious lack of self-respect.[30]

In the end, therefore, my praise of altruism does not amount to praise of selflessness. Unselfishness, yes, but not exactly selflessness. Because so many moral faults involve some vice of self-preference, we are tempted to go to the other extreme and speak as if we idealized a motivational pattern totally free of self-regard. But that, I believe, is a sentimentality incompatible with accurate perception in these matters. Like falsehood in general, it is probably unhelpful morally in the long run.

---

[28] John 15:12–14; 12:27–33; 17:1–5.     [29] Ephesians 5:25–7.
[30] The argument of this paragraph draws inspiration from Hill, "Servility and Self-Respect."

# 6

## Common Projects

### 1. A MORAL PHENOMENON TO BE EXPLAINED

We speak of someone being a "good colleague" in a philosophy department, in a sense that has less to do with philosophical, pedagogical, or administrative talent than with motives and traits of character.[1] A good colleague in this sense is considerate of students and co-workers, sensitive to their needs and concerns, conscientious in carrying out responsibilities to them, and cares about them as individuals. These qualities are forms of benevolence and conscientiousness, and it is relatively uncontroversial that they are morally virtuous.

There are other qualities of a good colleague, however, which do not seem to be forms of benevolence and conscientiousness. A good philosophical colleague cares about philosophy for its own sake. She wants to do it well herself, and she wants other people, specifically including her students and colleagues, to do it well. She wants them to do it well, not only for their sake, but also for philosophy's sake. And she cares about her department for its own sake, in a way that is not simply reducible to caring about the welfare of the individuals involved in it. She wants it to be the best philosophy department it can be. She labors to build and improve the department and strengthen its position in the university and in the discipline. She shows a consistent loyalty to this project, and a willingness to make personal sacrifices for it. If she has shown this devotion for many years, her colleagues owe her a great debt of gratitude. Members of other departments (which may compete with hers) do not owe her the same debt of gratitude, but they ought certainly to admire her for being such a good colleague. And I think this is *moral* admiration, not only insofar as it is admiration for her benevolence and conscientiousness, but also insofar as it is admiration for her devotion to the project of making a certain philosophy department the best it can be.

Similar judgments can be made on the side of deficiency. Suppose that after fifteen years as a member of a fine philosophy department, having been generally well treated by my colleagues and the university, I were conscientious and benevolent toward my students and colleagues as individuals, but cared not at all about the department's collective aspiration to be exceptionally

---

[1] This chapter is adapted from Adams, "Common Projects and Moral Virtue." In that earlier work, however, I placed more weight on broadly trait-consequentialist criteria of virtue than now seems right to me

good philosophically. This lack would appropriately elicit some anger from my colleagues, and disapproval from others. And I think the disapproval would have a strongly moral flavor.

Being a good or bad philosophical colleague is not an isolated case. Someone who plays on a serious athletic team without caring about winning,[2] or in an orchestra without caring about the musical quality of the performance, is apt to be perceived as "letting the side down." This is a morally tinged criticism, and it applies even if the offender is attentive to the interests of her associates as individuals. (What would be more likely to blunt the criticism would be the discovery that she was distracted with some personal grief or worry.) Conversely, one who "puts her heart into" the game or the music is perceived as exhibiting a moral or quasi-moral virtue. Similar considerations apply to a large proportion of situations in which one cooperates with other people to make a product or perform a service. One is expected to care about the product or the service in a way that is not easily or obviously reducible to caring about the welfare of the individuals affected.

At work and at play we are involved in a great variety of common projects, projects that we share with other people. They make up an enormous part of the fabric of our lives. And in most cases the project will go better if participants care about it for its own sake. A capacity for investing emotionally in common projects is a quality much to be desired in an associate in almost any area of life. I think it is largely because they are believed to contribute to the development of that capacity that team sports are widely regarded as useful for moral education.

It may be suggested that the sort of devotion or caring or commitment of which I am speaking enters the purview of morality as a kind of *loyalty*. I have no objection to the use of that term; but if what I am speaking of is a loyalty, it is a loyalty to a project as such, rather than to a group of people as such. If I join a choir, I ought to care about the quality of its singing; but there need not be any reason why I should be committed to the group in such a way as to want it to continue to exist as a group, and want to belong to it myself, if it ceased to be a choir. Perhaps it will be said that the loyalty one ought to have as a choir member is to the choir as an institution, though not to a group of individuals as such. Again I need not disagree; for I count institutions, or their development, maintenance, and flourishing, as common projects.

In this I have focused on the common projects of groups of people that are associated for a specific purpose, or for a limited range of purposes. Such associations play a dominant role in our pluralistic, technological society. Their projects are a good starting point for our reflections. The discussion will be

[2] Winning is not everything, of course. Parents may well want a school's coach to give all members of a team roughly equal time in the game, rather than maximizing chances of victory by playing only the best athletes (Marc Lange's example, for which I thank him). That may be demanded by a project that is excellent in its own way.

extended, in due course, to projects characteristic of associations, such as family and friendship, that are not for special purposes but for a more comprehensive sharing of life. The main thesis of this chapter is that *caring, in an appropriate way, about good common projects for their own sake is morally virtuous.* My aim is to explain why it is virtuous, and thus to give a rationale for the thesis.

The conditions noted in my thesis, that the project be good and the caring appropriate, are not idle, and must be emphasized from the start. Not that a common project must be especially noble or exalted if moral virtue is to be manifest in devotion to it; but devotion to a common project is not always virtuous. Devotion to an evil project is bad, and a vast amount of human involvement in evil is involvement in bad common projects. Probably the majority of the most horrendously evil projects are common projects of groups. In a bad common project, people will often perpetrate evils that few if any of them would choose if it were solely up to them. Conversely, in a good common project goods may be achieved that few if any of the participants would have the nerve to attempt without a shared enthusiasm. But even devotion to a good project can be a morally ugly thing if it is too ruthless, or absorbing out of proportion to the project's importance, or is not seasoned with a lively concern for the rights and welfare of other people.

Given that we are concerned specifically with investing oneself in *good* common projects, the first point in my rationale for thinking such investment virtuous follows obviously from my conception of virtue as excellence in being for the good. For investing oneself in a good project is a way of being for something good. What remains to be explored here is why investing specifically in good *common projects* for their own sake should be thought an excellent way of being for what is good.

## 2. COMMON PROJECTS AND HUMAN GOOD

In arguing for the virtuousness of such investment in common projects I shall assume that altruism, caring for the good of other persons for its own sake, is excellent and a virtue, as I argued in chapter 5. I think it reasonable to assume this in the present argument, not only because I have argued for it and believe it to be true, but also because I think it is apt to be believed by those who are likeliest to have serious misgivings about regarding it as a virtue to care for good common projects for their own sake.

We may therefore begin our exploration by noting that good common projects, and caring about them for their own sakes, play a huge part in the constitution of human well-being. For that reason a readiness for investment in good common projects can surely be considered a generally beneficial trait. That alone might be a decisive reason for trait consequentialists to count it a virtue. For reasons explained in chapter 4, I am not a trait consequentialist; but I will certainly agree that the involvement of common projects in human well-being has something to do with the importance we normally assign to being a good partner in such projects. Moreover, as we examine the interrelations between human well-being and the ends of common projects, we may be better able to appreciate the diversity of motives that can play a part in being *for* other people and being good *to* them.

Here we may usefully return to a topic that came up in chapter 5. In much of ethical theory, as I noted there, there is an emphasis on aspects of human good that can be thought of in terms of *commodities*, an emphasis that forms part of what might be called an *economic* model of beneficence. Being good to people is widely understood in terms of conferring benefits on them, and that in turn is conceived on the model of giving them commodities or money. This model captures what is most important in some contexts. Commodities provide an indispensable physical basis for human good, and economic issues are among the most important topics of public morality.

In other contexts, however, the economic model of beneficence is very misleading. Human good is not itself a commodity. A person's life does not consist in abundance of possessions.[3] A person's good, I believe, is best understood as consisting chiefly in enjoyment of excellence. In relation to human good, so understood, commodities are generally only means or raw materials. It follows from this conception of human good that opportunities for human good will generally involve opportunities for excellence, and our opportunities for excellence may at the same time be opportunities for human well-being (as I think in fact they usually are).

Aristotle thought that human good or well-being (*eudaimonia*) consists in excellent *activity*.[4] While that formulation seems to me to undervalue the possibilities of enjoyment of excellence in which it is something other than one's own activity that is excellent, I don't doubt that activity that is excellent and enjoyed must make up at least a large part of human good. Must human good therefore involve *caring* about some activities *for their own sake*? A life without such interests, at any rate, would be barely recognizable as human. We surely would not desire it. Where would all activity be valued only for the satisfaction of physical needs? Even in a subsistence economy people typically develop activities of play, conversation, ritual, and art that are carried on largely, if not solely, for their own sake. And even in economically necessary activities, such as farming and cooking, people learn to find satisfaction in the activity itself, and come to care for its own sake about the *way* in which it is done. It is clear, at a minimum, that such interest in activities for their own sake is in fact a major contributor to human good. The disappearance of such interest would be a loss for which there could be no adequate compensation in any human life that is likely to exist in this world.

[3] Luke 12:15.     [4] Aristotle, *Nicomachean Ethics*, I.vii (1097a 22–1098b 20).

This much about the importance of activities and the interest we have in them for their own sake would be accepted by most moralists, I think. Many writers in ethics have made use of it, John Rawls being an obvious example.[5] What is less often emphasized in moral philosophy is the extent to which the activities in which we find so much of our good are shared or *common* projects. Conversations, for example, essentially require the participation of more than one person. So do concerts and dances and most games and rituals. Political activity is by its very nature situated in the context of some common project of social organization. The only possible exceptions would be acts of rebellion so isolated and so alienated as to be at most marginally political. Science and philosophy could to some extent be carried on in isolation, but we would not get very far with them as purely private projects. Some forms of work could in principle be solitary, while others could not, but almost all work is in fact done in the context of some common project.

Except for the most rudimentary activities of satisfying physical needs, moreover, all our activities depend on abilities and interests that are acquired only through participation in shared projects. Education is an induction into common projects. Educationally the most fundamental of common projects is conversation. Almost all distinctively human activities depend in one way or another on language, and language is acquired by children in conversation with their elders—mainly, I suspect, in conversations that are ends in themselves for both the child and the elders. As we acquire language, so also we acquire a culture, anthropologically speaking. We are inducted into a culture as we grow up. And a culture depends for its existence on common projects which very largely determine what activities will make sense to people who participate in the culture.

Thus human good is found very largely in activities whose point and value depend on the participation of other people in a common project. And the value of these activities depends on more than one person's caring about the common projects. Common projects are not mindless biological processes like digestion and metabolism. They exist only because people care about them. And if too many of the participants do not care enough about them, the activities connected with them are apt to lose value for all the participants.

There are other goods to be prized for their own sake besides the well-being of particular persons. And many of these goods are found in shared activities and projects. Their goodness is intimately related to the well-being of particular persons. But insofar as their goodness is excellence, it is commonly a ground of personal well-being rather than grounded in it, and can appropriately be prized for its own sake, and is not likely to make its best contribution to human well-being unless it is so prized. This is true, for example, of the goodness of a philosophical discussion, a musical performance, or a game of basketball. Metaphysically,

---

[5] See Rawls, *A Theory of Justice*, section 65.

no doubt, those joint performances consist of actions and experiences of individual persons, related to each other. But I believe that the joint performance can also have an intrinsic value as a whole which is not a sum of the values *for* individual persons and is an appropriate object of intense interest. Something similar is true of longer-term common projects such as the performance over time of a philosophy department.

This helps to explain why one must often be more than an economic benefactor, and more than altruistic in the usual sense, if one is to be humanly good to one's associates. Commodities are vitally important as means to human good, but a very full realization of human good also requires benefits of another kind. In particular, it typically requires the opportunity to participate actively in common projects that engage the interest, in some cases even the enthusiasm or devotion, of other people. That opportunity is a great benefit that we derive from other people's interested participation in the common projects. It is a benefit to which their motivation, their interest in the project, is essential and not external. And as that interest in the project is distinct from a benevolent interest in the good of those who may be benefited by the project, this benefit is one that cannot be given solely out of such benevolence.

It is worth dwelling on this point in relation to *friendship*. The richest of excellent personal relationships are embraced as ends in themselves in such a way as to be themselves common projects, or complexes of common projects. In such relationships, devotion to the common project is not merely one way of being for something good, but the only possible way of participating fully in one of the central excellences of human life.

Moral virtue is shown in being a good friend, as well as in less intimate relationships. This can be understood partly on the basis of the fact that a good friend is conscientious, committed to do her duty to her friend, and benevolent, wanting her friend to flourish. The importance of conscientiousness and benevolence in ethical theory (and in popular moral thinking) may tempt us to think these are the only qualities that are morally virtuous in being a good friend. Even such an eloquent apostle of the moral value of friendship as Lawrence Blum appeals only to the benevolent aspect of friendship in arguing for its moral worth.[6]

But being a good friend involves more than conscientiousness and benevolence, as Blum would surely agree.[7] Another characteristic of a good friend is that she values the friendship for its own sake; she is glad to be this particular person's

---

[6] Lawrence Blum, *Friendship, Altruism, and Morality*, ch. 4. See, e.g., p. 67f.: "[O]ther things being equal, acts of friendship are morally good insofar as they involve acting from regard for another person for his own sake.... [T]he deeper and stronger the concern for the friend... the greater the degree of moral worth (again, other things being equal)."

[7] Cf. Blum, op. cit., p. 82, where he expresses a desire to avoid "an overmoralized view of friendship" that "sees the concern for the friend's good as the central element in friendship, downplaying or neglecting the liking of the friend, the desire to be with him, the enjoyment of shared activities, etc."

friend, and she wants very much to continue and enhance the relationship. Why shouldn't this aspect of being a good friend also be regarded as virtuous in its own right? I think in fact it is. My reasoning about common projects supports this view.

A friendship is, in a broad sense, a project shared by the friends; and as such it is a particularly important type of common project. Few of us would want to be without friendships, and having good friends is generally acknowledged to be important to human happiness. The value of a friendship, moreover, depends very much on both parties caring about the common project (their relationship) for its own sake. An ostensible friend who does not value the relationship in this way is apt to be perceived as spoiling the common project—"letting the side down," so to speak. It may even be doubted whether a friendship really exists unless both parties care about the relationship for its own sake, no matter how great their benevolence and conscientiousness toward each other. What is usually understood (and desired) as "the gift of friendship" is therefore one of those goods that no one can give you solely out of a desire to benefit you.

For such reasons a lively interest in common projects for their own sakes is a normal part of being humanly good to one's associates. It is a normal part of being a good colleague, a good teammate, a good citizen, a good mentor, a good friend, a good spouse, a good parent, child, or sibling. And being a good occupant of these relational roles is morally praiseworthy. It is normally counted as morally virtuous. Being a colleague, friend, or parent, but not a good one, on the other hand, is a moral shortcoming, or in extreme cases a moral failure. Not caring appropriately about common projects can constitute such a shortcoming or failure.

## 3. COMMON PROJECTS AND ALTRUISM

I am now in a position to complete an argument for the thesis that a readiness to embrace good common projects for their own sake, and to participate in them loyally and well, is a virtue. The first premise, as already noted, is that it is a way of being for something good. The second premise is that it is an *excellent* way of being for something good. From these premises it follows that it satisfies the two main requirements I have laid down (in the last section of chapter 2) for being a virtue.

The part of this argument that requires further defense here is the second premise. Whether a persistent motivational quality that aims at something good is a virtue depends on its excellence. The excellence of the quality depends at least in part on the modality of the motivation: for instance, whether it is persistent; whether it is sensitive to values involved in a project, and to conflicting values; whether it engages the object at a depth appropriate to its significance. I see no reason to doubt that in many cases the modality of a readiness for devotion to common projects is excellent in such ways.

We are concerned here, however, with a quality that would be a motivational rather than a structural virtue (in the classification introduced in chapter 2, section 4). That being so, the excellence of the quality depends not only on the modality of the motivation but also on its object. If a quality is a motivational virtue, it is so principally because of what it is for, what it favors. There are many goods that could be objects of our concern, and some of them it does not seem a matter of virtue to love. Whether one is fond of ice cream is neither here nor there so far as virtue is concerned.

A readiness to embrace good common projects matters more for assessment of virtue, in view of the pervasive importance of such projects in human life. The good of human persons consists very largely, I have argued, in enjoying the flourishing of common projects that are rightly valued for their own sake. The flourishing of such projects is related to the good of persons not merely as a means, but as a constituent. Indeed it is a large part of what is excellent in human life. I argued in chapters 3 and 5 that concern for the good of persons is such a prominent and pervasive part of the fabric of human life that it would be bizarre, and not excellent, to care about such cultural goods as literature and philosophy, or even about justice, without caring for its own sake about the well-being of persons. Similarly in the present context we can argue that interest in the goods of common projects is such a pervasively important constituent of human good that there would be something bizarre, and not excellent, about caring about the well-being of persons without caring about any of their common projects as ends in themselves. We will not be valuing human flourishing as we should if we do not care about excellent projects for their own sake.

To this argument one might be tempted to object that the excellence of altruism is not just in caring for the good of persons, and whatever goods that consists in. There is an excellence of being *for* the *persons*, which the objector sees as part of altruism but not of caring for good common projects as such. It would, of course, be open to us to argue that caring for excellent common projects has the sort of excellence required of a virtue even if it does not have the particular excellence of concern for persons. In fact, however, I believe that being for a common project for its own sake is commonly also a way of being for persons who are one's associates in the project.

One piece of evidence for this is that we not only *admire* a person's devotion to a good common project, but are also *grateful* for it if we are among the participants in the project. And we think we ought to be grateful for it. This suggests that we feel, at least in some contexts, that things done for a project that is also a project of ours are also done for us. That will seem strange if we have too narrow a conception of what it is for something to be done for us—in particular, if we suppose that you can do something *for me* only if (1) it is good for me, or makes my life go better for me. In practice, however, we normally and rightly assume that something can be done (at least partly) for me if it is done (at least partly) because it is (2) something I have reason to want or wish for, and to be glad of if actual, or (3) something I have actually asked for, or (4) something expressive of friendship or esteem for me.[8] The idea of doing something *for* a person is naturally connected with that of treating the person as intrinsically valuable or an end in herself. Such treatment has commonly been understood in ethical theory in terms of promoting the person's well-being and respecting her rights and especially her freedom to make choices for herself. But I think it has at least the four dimensions that I have indicated for doing something for a person.

Goods that our associates promote, in their devotion to a common project, are often constituents of our well-being, as I have argued, because they are often excellences that we enjoy. That being a fact that makes some impression on the consciousness of most people, what our partners do for the project may be motivated in part by regard for our well-being, and in that way may be done for us. But that is certainly not the only basis on which one may be grateful to associates for their support of a common project; and not everything that is done for us is done for the sake of our well-being.

Consider how we are grateful to people who give money or service to a common project that is also a project of ours. If you are involved in the fund-raising, you may have occasion to thank the generous donor *on behalf of the charity*, but it will often be appropriate for you to be *personally* grateful too. Personal gratitude will be especially appropriate if you participated in asking for the gift, because doing something because you asked is a way of doing it *for you*, as we regularly put it. When we say that it was done for you, we need not suppose that it was done with any thought that it would contribute to your well-being or that you would be better off for it. You may indeed hope that it was not your well-being, but the ends of the charity—the relief of poverty, the advancement of learning, or the flourishing of the arts, as the case may be—that the donor meant to promote. Still you may think that she did it partly for you—because the ends of the charity are also ends of yours, ends that you care about and seek to promote, or simply because you were one of those who asked for the contribution.

This sort of distinction among ways of doing something for another person is particularly clear in cases in which you have occasion (as surely you can) to thank someone for assisting you in doing something that involves, or may involve, a considerable sacrifice of your well-being. Such assistance is still something that may have been done for you, because you asked, or because it was in aid of a project of yours. In such cases saying that something was done for you is apt to be a comment less about the ends the agent sought to promote than about a motivating attitude *out of which* she acted.[9]

Suppose what I do for you is make a financial contribution that you have requested in support of a humanitarian mission that seems very likely to result

---

[8] Here I am developing further a point introduced in chapter 5. The thought that it is important to distinguish between (1) and (2) is familiar from discussions of rational choice.

[9] On the latter, less teleological aspect of motivation, see Stocker, "Values and Purposes."

in your death. In that case it will be much less plausible to suppose that I am moved by the prospect of an outcome that I desire for your sake, than that I act *out of respect for you*. Or perhaps I act out of sympathetic response to you in your enthusiasm for a worthy project. To the extent that there are *ends* that I am pursuing for their own sake in making such a contribution, we will think they should mainly be humanitarian ends of the mission, rather than anything to do with you personally. Even apart from such an extreme case, in devotion to a common project one normally pursues for their own sake the ends that define the project. At the same time one may act both out of respect for one's own choices and commitments, and out of regard for one's associates in the project. These are commonly not competing motives, and none of them always aims at well-being as such.

These considerations give reason to regard devotion to good common projects not only as a virtue, but as an *important* one. To one's associates, devotion to such a project is apt to be an occasion not only for admiration as virtuous, but also for gratitude, because what one does for the project is done also *for them*, though not necessarily for the sake of their well-being. Similarly, the special place that altruistic benevolence has in our moral sentiments is due, in no small part, to the gratitude that it occasions because it is a motive of doing things *for* other people. It is not only as occasions of gratitude, however, that altruism and devotion to common projects have a special claim on our moral affections. They are special also in the possibilities of *alliance* that they afford. People who are devoted to the same common project are thereby obviously in a sort of alliance. Likewise, if other people care altruistically for your well-being, you may count them as allies of yours if you care for your own well-being as most people do for theirs (and if their conception of your well-being is not too different from yours). Indeed, your well-being may be a common project of yours and theirs.

To be allied with other people is in some measure to embrace their ends; and embracing their ends is also, as I have argued, a way of being *for them*. The importance we assign to virtues in our lives depends not only on the objective excellence that marks them as virtues, but also on other factors such as their benefits, as noted in chapter 4, section 2. Much of our practical interest in other people's virtue is an interest in them as potential, or at least imagined, friends and allies—allies in good projects. And the *good* friend and ally is an appropriate object of gratitude. If altruistic benevolence and devotion to good common projects are objects of especially warm approbation, that may be due in large part to their fitting a person to be embraced in alliance that is friendly as well as virtuous.

Why do I think common projects deserve a chapter in a book about the nature of virtue? Largely because they are an essential part of strongly *cooperative* social contexts. Social contexts characterized by competition may have special importance for thinking about some aspects of justice. But cooperation provides a more essential context for excellence in human living (and for appreciating moral excellence, as I suggested at the end of the first section of chapter 5). Personal traits and states of mind that respond well to cooperation and possibilities of cooperation have a corresponding importance for virtue. A focus on competitive contexts has supported a tendency in modern ethical theory to dichotomize motives as altruistic or self-interested. A focus on cooperation tends to break down that dichotomy. In this way our reflections on common projects may support the conclusion that *self-love* can be virtuous and can cohere very well with being *for* other people. That is one of the themes that will engage our attention in chapter 7, particularly in its final section.

# 7

# Self-Love and the Vices of Self-Preference

An account of virtue in terms of excellence in being for the good suggests that self-love, in some forms, may be a virtue. For caring for one's own good is obviously a way of being for something good. And it seems quite possible to do it with excellence—for instance, with courage, moderation, and prudence. Those are virtues independently of self-love, but I believe that one's caring for one's own good can itself be more or less excellent, depending on such factors as what goods one wants for oneself, and how one conceives of one's own good.

If we doubt that caring for one's own good can be excellent enough to constitute a virtue, that will probably be because we imagine or suspect that moral excellence or virtue must be altruistic in such a way that there cannot be any place in it for self-love. The main question for this chapter, accordingly, is whether self-love is necessarily in conflict with a wider and more excellent sort of love. Or is there a possible harmony of self-interest with altruism, and a place for self-love in virtue?

## 1. BUTLER AND THE HARMONY OF SELF-LOVE WITH BENEVOLENCE

Discussion of this topic in English finds a natural starting point in the work of Joseph Butler, and especially in his famous Sermon XI, "Upon the Love of Our Neighbor." He argues there that it cannot be to our advantage for self-love to absorb us so totally as to leave no room for the love of our neighbor. Butler conceives of self-love as "a regard to [one's] own interest, happiness, and private good" (XI.8),[1] by which he means one's good in the long run, comprehensively considered. Butler distinguishes self-love from "particular appetites and passions," which are desires for objects "distinct from the pleasure arising from them." Indeed the object gives pleasure only because there is a prior "affection or appetite" for it, according to Butler (XI.6). He argues that therefore:

if self-love wholly engrosses us, and leaves no room for any other principle, there can be absolutely no such thing at all as happiness, or enjoyment of any kind whatever; since

---

[1] References in this form, in this chapter, are to a sermon, and a paragraph thereof, in Butler, *Fifteen Sermons*.

happiness consists in the gratification of particular passions, which supposes the having of them (XI.9).

It is therefore advantageous to our happiness to have particular passions or desires for objects quite distinct from our happiness. Without them we would have nothing to be happy about.

From the point of view of self-love, Butler argues, benevolence toward another person has this advantage just as much as a desire to be loved or esteemed by the other person—though the latter is commonly seen as a more self-interested desire than the former. He treats benevolence in this context (though not always) as one of the particular passions, having another person's happiness as its object.[2] The other person's happiness can be a source of pleasure or happiness to me, if I desire it and learn of its reality in the other person. "Is desire of and delight in the happiness of another any more a diminution of self-love, than desire of and delight in the esteem of another?" Butler asks. "They are both equally desire of and delight in somewhat external to ourselves: either both or neither are so" (XI.11).

It is not my purpose to examine this justly celebrated argument. Butler's treatment of the nature and sources of pleasure requires some amendment,[3] which need not be attempted here; and any adequate amendment may well affect the force of the argument. But I do not doubt the correctness of two Butlerian theses. The first is that one can hardly live a happy life without strong and more than merely instrumental desires for ends distinct from one's own happiness. And the second is that the happiness or good of other persons is among the ends best suited to play this part in a happy person's life.

We must be clear that such considerations cannot establish an automatic harmony of self-love and benevolence for everyone. At most they provide grounds to believe in the desirability, and to hope in the possibility, of people becoming such that self-love and benevolence are in harmony for them. An attractive story about Butler may help to make this point vivid. It is said that once, being asked for a charitable contribution, and learning from his steward, upon inquiry, that he had £500 on hand, Butler replied, "Five hundred pounds! What a shame for a bishop to have so much money! Give it away; give it all to this gentleman for his

---

[2] Cf. Penelhum, *Butler*, p. 79f. Butler sometimes (e.g., in I. 7) treats benevolence as distinct from "the several passions and affections," and more parallel to self-love, though no less distinct from it. Among Butler's notable admirers, C. D. Broad regards the position suggested by I.7 as Butler's real or characteristic view, one in which benevolence is seen as a "general principle" and "a rational calculating principle," while Henry Sidgwick reads the dominant tendency of Butler's thought (more accurately, in my opinion) as one in which benevolence is less parallel to self-love. Benevolence, according to Sidgwick's Butler, "is not definitely a desire for general good as such, but rather kind affection for particular individuals." See Broad, *Five Types of Ethical Theory*, pp. 61, 71–3; and Sidgwick, *Outlines of the History of Ethics*, p. 195.

[3] Some indication of what is needed may be found in Broad's critique in *Five Types of Ethical Theory*, pp. 66–7.

charitable plan."[4] One imagines that Butler enjoyed doing this—perhaps more than he would have enjoyed any other use of the money. But it is obvious that someone with different interests might not have enjoyed it. The harmony of self-love with benevolence, as Butler conceives of it, depends on having, and perhaps cultivating, generous interests.

To some extent it may also depend on a relatively unalienated membership in some social group—an advantage sadly inaccessible to some people. Bishop Butler was in many ways at home in his social context, and his main personal projects seem to have been at the same time social or even public projects. He was fortunate to be able to find his own happiness in seeking the good of his church and his people. To a far greater extent than one would gather from Butler, the possible harmony of self-love with benevolence rests on social as well as individual foundations.[5] This is true even where the harmony involves a deeper altruism than can be expected to result from rewarding egoistic individuals for socially useful behavior.

We shall find Butler helpful at several points in the present investigation. Throughout it I shall use the term 'self-love', as he did, to signify the desire for one's own long-term happiness or good on the whole (though the term certainly has other uses). But my aim here is not properly historical and I offer no systematic exposition or critique of Butler's moral theory. My focus indeed is rather different from his.

Much of Butler's argument was directed against the egoistic moral theory of Thomas Hobbes. It was meant to commend a life of conscientiousness and benevolence to an audience for whom self-love was "the favourite passion," as he put it (XI.3). In this paper, however, I shall be addressing concerns that come from the opposite direction. I want particularly to ask how far self-love can be cleared of the suspicion under which it lies in ordinary moral opinion. Karl Barth surely speaks for many when he says of self-love, "God will never think of blowing on this fire, which is bright enough already."[6] So does Iris Murdoch when she declares that "In the moral life the enemy is the fat relentless ego."[7] Even Butler says that "vice in general consists in having an unreasonable and too great regard to ourselves, in comparison of others" (X.6), though he also holds that "self-love in its due degree is as just and morally good, as any affection whatever" (Preface, §39).[8]

Vices of self-preference, such as selfishness and pride, are rightly among the chief objects of moral censure. Our understanding of them is not enhanced,

---

[4] Mossner, *Bishop Butler and the Age of Reason*, p. 11.
[5] A similar point is made by Broad, *Five Types of Ethical Theory*, pp. 75–6. Cf. also Nagel, *The View from Nowhere*, pp. 204–7. Nagel, less complacent than Butler, rightly stresses the need for political changes to which such considerations point.
[6] Barth, *Church Dogmatics*, vol. I/2, p. 388.
[7] Murdoch, *The Sovereignty of Good*, p. 52.
[8] References in this form too, in the present chapter, are to Butler, *Fifteen Sermons*.

however, by an oversimple dichotomization of morally relevant motivation into desire for one's own good and desire for other people's good. The complexity that belies this dichotomy, I shall argue, does support a possible harmony of self-love with altruistic virtue.

## 2. SELFISHNESS

One of Butler's insights is that the role of self-love in actual human motivation has been exaggerated. So far as I can see, the main vices of self-preference do not necessarily involve self-love. *Selfishness* is the one we are probably most tempted to identify with a degree of self-love that is too great, either absolutely or in proportion to the strength of one's altruistic and conscientious motivation. This identification cannot be right, however, for selfishness is clearly possible without any degree of self-love at all.

One of the virtues of Butler's account of self-love is that it makes clear that self-love is a rational achievement. One cannot desire one's long-term happiness or good on the whole without having a concept of that good. And that is not an easy concept. This is not the place to expound a full conception, Butler's or mine, of a person's good; and I would not necessarily wish to defend all of Butler's views on the subject. One feature of Butler's conception of a person's good that seems to me clearly right particularly concerns us here. It is that the conception is an instrument of rational self-government, and can play that role because it is a rather comprehensive conception in which many interests, and the person's whole future, are taken into account.

We are not born with such a concept. It is not even among the first concepts we learned. I had the concept of "*my* toy" some time before I had the concept of "*my* life," let alone the concept of "*my* long-term good on the whole," and thus before I had the conceptual resources necessary for self-love in Butler's sense. But by the time I had the concept of "*my* toy" I was certainly capable of being selfish in various ways. That selfishness cannot have been an excess of the self-love of which I was as yet incapable.

What was it then? Or more broadly, what would selfishness be where it is not an excess of self-love (as I will not deny that it can be)? The obvious Butlerian answer is that selfishness can consist in some disorder of the "particular passions"—some lack or weakness of benevolent passions, or some excess of self-regarding passions, or both. These ideas are nicely combined, though without the use of the word 'selfishness', in Butler's statement that:

The thing to be lamented, is not that men have so great regard to their own good or interest in the present world, for they have not enough; but that they have so little to the good of others. And this seems plainly owing to their being so much engaged in the gratification of particular passions unfriendly to benevolence, and which happen to be prevalent in them, much more than to self-love (Preface, §40).

The idea of "particular passions unfriendly to benevolence" invites further elaboration. A charge of selfishness implies some lack of due regard to something other than oneself, and this will commonly involve a lack of benevolence. What is benevolence here? A "regard. . . to the good of others" is easily construed as a concern for the comprehensive, long-term good of at least one other person, if not the even more comprehensive utilitarian "greatest good of the greatest number." It is true that a lack of regard to the comprehensive good of others is apt to be censured as selfish in adults, but that cannot exactly be what constitutes selfishness in very young children. For, if their selfishness is a lack, it must surely be a lack of something that is not utterly beyond their conceptual capacities. And they are not capable of regard to the long-term good of other people as such, having no more conception of it than of their own long-term good. If selfishness is a lack in very young children, it must be a lack of some passion more particular than a comprehensive regard to the good of another person. Which unselfish passions of this more particular sort ought not to be lacking in very young children? We might look for concern about the pleasure or pain, satisfaction or frustration experienced at present by another person.[9]

There is more to be said about the "particular passions unfriendly to benevolence" whose excessive prevalence would constitute selfishness, and which we have yet to identify. I speak of the *excessive* prevalence of the passions in question, for I think there are few desires or interests that are inherently or necessarily selfish. Selfishness lies not in caring about one's own comfort or one's stamp collection, but in letting oneself be governed inappropriately or too strongly by such interests. That seems to be the typical relation of selfishness to its motives, though there are doubtless exceptions to the general rule—desires that are inherently selfish. W. H. Auden wrote of the "crude," but in his opinion "normal," wish that "craves. . . not universal love, but to be loved alone."[10] That certainly seems to be an essentially selfish desire.

Which of the passions that may oppose benevolence can ground a charge of selfishness if one is too much governed by them? Not all, I think. 'Malicious' rather than 'selfish' seems the word for sheer ill-will toward another person, from which, as Butler notes, one may "rush upon certain ruin for the destruction of an enemy" (XI.11), desiring the other person's pain or loss regardless of what happens to oneself. The motives of selfishness involve wanting something *for oneself.*

In what way must it be for oneself? It seems safe to say at a minimum that motives of selfishness must be *self-regarding* in the sense of having an object involving oneself that is desired or intended at least partly for its own sake, and

[9] Butler may have meant to comprehend such passions under the heading of "benevolence" here. He may sometimes have thought of benevolence as a pre-rational "affection" (XII.2) manifested in particular passions, and needing further "to be directed by. . . reason" (XII.27) rather than as itself a principle of rational self-government. (Cf. also Sermon V.) This is one way in which benevolence may not be fully parallel to ("cool" or rational) self-love; cf. n. 2 above.
[10] Auden, "September 1, 1939," in his *Collected Poetry*, p. 58f.

not merely as a means to some other end. But this is not a terribly restrict-ive condition. The class of self-regarding motives is very wide—so wide that they are probably involved in almost all our actions. Desiring a relationship for its own sake—whether one desires the continuance of one's marriage, or to be a good parent or friend to so-and-so—is always a self-regarding motive, inas-much as the relationship essentially involves oneself. Likewise conscientiousness is a self-regarding motive, inasmuch as it is a commitment to act rightly *oneself*.

A more difficult question is whether motives of selfishness have some necessary connection with the idea of a good for oneself. Let us say that a *narrowly self-interested* motive is one in which one desires or intends something at least partly for the sake of one's own comprehensive, long-term good. It is an expression of self-love in Butler's sense. Even if motives of selfishness must be self-regarding, I have argued that they are not always narrowly self-interested. But it is harder to refute the hypothesis that they must be, if not narrowly, then *broadly self-interested*, in the sense that they must aim at something that is (or is taken to be) *good* for oneself, in the short term or in some respect, if not in the long term and comprehensively.

This hypothesis might be suggested by thinking of *greed*, which is probably the motive most frequently branded as selfish. The child behaving selfishly may be dominated by a desire to control a particular toy, or to eat the whole of a particular piece of cake. Adults are capable of a more comprehensive greed, for money or wealth in general. The object of greed, particular or general, is not one's own good as such. But it is generally seen as a good, in some way, for its possessor, and as a good that exists in limited supply and is desired by or for other people as well as oneself. The phenomena of greed present us with many cases of selfishness from motives that are broadly but not narrowly self-interested, as when someone who knows he is eating more than is good for him takes more than his fair share of food in order to have the pleasure of eating it.

The hypothesis that in selfishness one always aims at some *good* for oneself requires at least some qualifications. Your judgment that someone acts selfishly from a certain desire does not necessarily commit *you* to the view that the object desired is truly good for the desirer even in the short run or in any respect. If you think someone is selfishly controlled by a desire for posthumous fame, it does not follow that you hold the controversial opinion that posthumous fame can be in some way good for a person. If the question is whether *my* quest for posthumous glory is selfish, probably my opinion as to whether it would be a good for me is more relevant than yours. But my opinion is not decisive either, in such a case. Clearly one can be selfishly moved by a desire without having any opinion as to whether the object of the desire would be a good of any sort for oneself. For children can be selfish before they have the concept of something being good for a person in any way (though probably not before they have, at least in rudimentary form, related concepts such as those of pleasure and pain).

We count it as selfish to be overly dominated by a desire for such objects as pleasure, convenience, wealth, or reputation. In so classifying such motives, we need not presuppose any opinion of our own, or of the possessor of the motive, as to whether the object is truly good for anyone in any way, even in the short term. Of course all these objects are indeed regarded by many as good for a person, at least in the short run or in some respect. So our readiness to accept them as figuring in motives of selfishness might be explained as deference to public opinion, and thus as not shaking the connection of selfishness with the idea of a good for oneself.

One reason for the difficulty of shaking it is that so few self-regarding motives are clearly not broadly self-interested. Perhaps self-destructive motives, such as self-hatred, provide the most plausible case of self-regarding motives that do not aim at anything that is good for oneself from any point of view. Consider, then, the question of selfishness in the following pair of examples. It is often thought selfish to abandon certain responsibilities by committing suicide in order to avoid a situation painful to oneself. Avoiding the pain is a good for oneself, at least in the short run. Would it be thought selfish to abandon the same responsibilities by committing suicide out of sheer self-hatred, desiring nothing that anyone would call a good for oneself? Certainly such action can be subject to moral censure—for instance, as irresponsible. Moreover, it manifests an excessive concern with oneself; it is probably self-centered. In trying to talk the self-hater out of suicide, one might perhaps argue that it would be selfish to abandon the responsibilities in order to act on one's feelings about oneself. Yet in a cooler hour I might hesitate to call it *selfish*, precisely because the motive is hostile rather than friendly toward oneself. Perhaps it does not matter much whether we avoid the label 'selfish' here. Self-destructive behavior is commonly very harmful to other people, and it seems no better morally to engage in it from sheer self-hatred than from desire for some short-term good for oneself.[11]

So I am not sure that selfishness *necessarily* involves a desire for anything regarded by anyone as a good for oneself. But in *some* of our judgments of selfishness it does seem to matter whether the offending motive aims at a good for its possessor. For example, consider someone who always insists on assuming the most burdensome role in any situation, even when there are others who are willing to do it and it is clear that it would be better for all concerned if one of them did it. 'Selfish' does not seem the right word for such a person, but it does seem the right word for someone who is too *un*willing to assume burdensome roles; and this contrast applies even when the two attitudes are equally inconvenient for others. The most salient difference between the two cases is that the selfish person is seeking an obvious good for himself, and the other person is not.

---

[11] I am indebted to Marilyn McCord Adams for particularly helpful discussion of the topics of this paragraph, as well as for comments on this chapter in general.

One further point is particularly important for the relation between selfishness and self-love. Whether we think people selfish or unselfish often depends less on the strength of their self-love than on the character of the interests or "particular passions" in which they seek their happiness. There are interests in which people find happiness, and whose pursuit therefore is typically both broadly and narrowly self-interested, but which are regarded as *unselfish interests*. One example is the desire to be a parent, when it is embraced with sufficient maturity. Conversely, people who take no delight in any but the most narrowly self-regarding interests do not have an exemplary unselfish character even if they are willing to sacrifice those interests when duty or the common good demands it. And people with strong enough interests in other people and in public or ideal ends may be notably unselfish even if almost everything they do contributes also to their own happiness, as seems to have been the case in Bishop Butler's life. In this connection one might speak of a selfish or unselfish conception of one's own good.

## 3. SELF-CENTEREDNESS AND VICES OF COGNITIVE SELF-PREFERENCE

A particularly important self-regarding desire which it usually is not exactly selfish to carry to excess, even at others' expense, is the desire to be a morally good person, the desire for virtue. It is possible to be overly concerned, or concerned in an objectionable way, with one's own virtue. This is the case in the vices of self-righteousness and moral priggishness. People who refuse to do something morally questionable in order to attain some great good or avoid some great evil are often accused of selfishness in their desire for "clean hands." I doubt the correctness of the charge of selfishness in such cases, unless the agent is moved by mere delicacy of feeling, rather than by a belief that it would be wrong to do what he refuses to do. It is never selfish, I think, to refuse conscientiously to do something that really is wrong. Even where a misguided conscientiousness leads one to abstain from an action that really is morally required, 'selfish' does not seem quite the right word for one's motivation.

In some cases 'idolatrous' would be a better description. The desire to be a morally good person is in principle an excellent desire for something unquestionably good. Yet it does seem that this motive can be distorted, and its value compromised, by various sorts of excessive consideration of self. It can be an idolatry if one is not prepared to set aside projects of moral self-improvement in some contexts for the sake of urgent concerns that are more directly other-regarding.

In other cases 'self-centered' may be a better description. In these cases the difference between a wholesome and a self-centered desire for virtue is not primarily in the ends that are desired. What is desired in both cases may be the same: to be a morally good person. The difference is rather in emphasis, or in the place that one's wanting to be good has in a larger pattern of thinking and feeling. If one's desire for virtue is self-centered, one is likely to be thinking often about how good one is, or filled with anxiety about one's moral shortcomings, or comparing one's moral qualities to other people's. A purer love of virtue might be manifested in thinking more about virtue in general, and admiring the good qualities of other people, without reference or comparison to oneself.

This difference in one's thinking, in one's attention,[12] is virtually certain to affect one's judgment on moral issues. The self-centered interest in one's own virtue, we think, is apt to distort judgment, making it likelier that one will be mistaken in one's beliefs about what virtue involves. In this way the difference between a self-centered and a purer desire for virtue is likely to issue in differences in the detail of what one wants for oneself. These differences in the object of desire are not primary, however, but derive from a more fundamental difference in focus.

Self-centeredness is a vice of self-preference that is distinguishable from selfishness. The feature of self-centeredness that most interests me here is that it is not in general to be understood in terms of what one wants. The simplistic dichotomy of egoism and altruism commonly carries with it the assumption that any vice of self-preference is a matter of what one wants. Self-centeredness is a counterexample to this assumption. There may be desires that are essentially self-centered; perhaps the desire to be the center of attention is one such. But most good relationships between oneself and other people, or between oneself and values or ideal ends, can be desired, for their own sake, in both more and less self-centered ways.

A homelier example may help to confirm this point. Suppose Daddy is planning to shoot baskets with Susie. Daddy desires the following state of affairs, and desires it at least partly for its own sake: Daddy and Susie shoot baskets together; both have fun; both take the activity seriously; and both do their best. Daddy will be disappointed if either of them fails to enjoy it, and if either of them does badly. This characterizes Daddy's desire in both of the following versions of the example:

Case (1): As Daddy contemplates the planned recreation, his mind runs to thoughts such as "I'm really being a very good father," "I'm still very good at this, considering my age," "I wish my dad had done this with me," "Susie will get a kick out of this because I'm spending time with her." He forgets to ask her what she did in school today.

Case (2): As Daddy contemplates the planned recreation, his mind runs to thoughts such as "Susie has so much fun shooting baskets," "She's getting really good at it," "Susie's a neat kid." He remembers to ask what she did in school today.

---

[12] In using this word I am mindful of Murdoch, *The Sovereignty of Good*, pp. 17–42, 55f. I refer, however, to something which is commonly less intentional than the "attention" of which Murdoch wrote.

Other things being equal, these descriptions give reason for saying that Daddy's interest in shooting baskets with Susie is more self-centered in Case (1) than in Case (2). And this does not seem to be primarily a difference in the ends that Daddy desires. Though Daddy desires this recreational activity at least partly for its own sake, it is likely that in both cases he has a number of ulterior ends in wanting it. We may plausibly assume that in both cases these include his being a good father, his getting some exercise, Susie's physical and social development, and their having a good relationship. The difference between the two cases is rather a difference in focus. In wanting a largely relational complex of ends essentially involving oneself it is possible for one's interest to be centered overwhelmingly on one's own role in the complex, or much more on other persons, or other features, involved in it. Self-centeredness, as its name suggests, is typically a perversion in this sort of centering.

My account of self-centeredness has emphasized the thoughts one has. In many cases, I think, self-centeredness is a perversion of cognition as much as of the will. And certainly there are vices of cognitive self-preference, such as pride, conceit, or egotism.[13] One of Butler's sermons is largely devoted to the distortions of moral perception and judgment that arise from cognitive "self-partiality" (X.7), particularly as it is manifested in a disposition not to recognize one's own moral faults. Still more offensive than such blindness to one's own sins is the arrogance of thinking of oneself as more important than other people. I don't mean merely caring more about one's own good, and one's own projects, than about those of other people. The arrogance to which I refer is that of seeing oneself as objectively more important than others, thinking one's own problems and goals more urgent morally than theirs.

In speaking of *moral vices* of cognitive self-preference in such cases, we think of them as engaging the will, as I put it in chapter 2, section 1. They could be motivated by one's desire for one's own good, or by more particular self-regarding desires. One may not recognize one's faults because one does not *want* to think of oneself as wrong, or perhaps because one fears that guilt would deprive one of the long-term happiness one desires.

But it is not obvious that vices of cognitive self-preference always have such an explanation in terms of desire; and they are not themselves forms of any desire. They are not defined by ends at which one aims, but rather by ways in which one's thinking shapes one's aims. They may themselves be rooted in identifiable bad desires; but it may often be clearer that certain judgments or views are arrogant, conceited, or egotistic, than that any desires that may motivate them are morally objectionable. If I tend to think of myself more highly than I ought, that vice may well have among its causes a desire to *have* the excellences that I fondly imagine myself as having—a desire that makes it painful to face the sad truth of

---

[13] The 't' in 'egotism' marks an important difference: egotism is primarily a matter of one's opinion of oneself; egoism, a matter of one's aims.

how far short of them I fall. But that desire seems morally innocent, perhaps even laudable. The vice may have to be located in the way my thinking is shaped by the desire.[14] There is more than one way in which self can loom too large in one's life. It can loom too large in one's desires, but it can also loom too large in one's thoughts. And neither of these two forms of vice is merely a form of the other.

For this reason it seems to me somewhat strained to characterize these vices as forms of selfishness.[15] The word 'selfish' ordinarily signifies something about one's desires, something about the ends one is going for. The vices of cognitive self-preference seem rather to be forms of the sin of pride, or perhaps in some cases of self-centeredness—if indeed they can be reduced at all to a small number of categories.

Since they are not forms of any desire, it follows that these vices are not forms of self-love, if by 'self-love' we mean the desire for one's own long-term good. Indeed some of them do not presuppose a conception of one's own good, and hence can in principle exist without self-love—though they may involve in their own way too much cognitive sophistication to exist in very young children.

## 4. UNSELFISH SELF-LOVE

We have now seen two or three types of case in which vices of self-preference cannot be identified with an excess of that desire for one's own long-term good which Butler called self-love. There are cases—indeed quite typical cases—of selfishness in which the excessively dominant desire is one of what Butler called the "particular passions." The aims of the particular passion may not agree, in the particular case, with those of a rational self-love. And there are vices of self-centeredness and cognitive self-preference which are not to be defined by an end desired. So is self-love innocent, or perhaps even virtuous?

Sometimes, but not always, is the short answer. A somewhat longer answer may begin by noting that easily recognizable excellence in caring for one's own good is often overlooked because moral perception is distracted by worries about selfishness. Being rightly suspicious of self-preference in ourselves and in others, we are ready to see self-love in competition with altruistic benevolence, and forget the other factors with which self-love must contend. In comparison with the highest flights of generosity, public-spiritedness, and devotion to others, we may well think no form of self-love comes in better than second. But no human life is lived entirely in the highest flights. Suppose the question is whether care for one's own long-term good is strong enough to overcome temptations of immediate comfort and pleasure, of frivolity and excitement, of carelessness

---

[14] Some would argue that the vice, if any, should be sought rather in a voluntary failure to make sufficient efforts at self-criticism. I argue against that view in Adams, "Involuntary Sins," especially pp. 11–14, 17–21; the whole article is relevant to issues discussed in this paragraph.
[15] Though Butler seems to do this (X.6).

and ease, of weariness and frustration, of boredom and depression, of self-hatred and self-destructive impulse. In such contests we can see something genuinely admirable in rational self-love.

We admire (though perhaps not extravagantly) people who are enterprising, whether in providing for their economic needs or in developing friendships and hobbies that they enjoy. We admire more intensely those whose commitment to their own well-being sustains them through a long and painful struggle to recover from a potentially disabling injury, or to make the best of some other hard situation. Old age can set a context in which caring for oneself necessarily looms larger in one's concerns, and we do admire people whose loyalty to their own good helps them to care for it sensibly and gives them the will to go on in that context.

If one lives to become very frail, caring for oneself may become not only a very large part of what one can do, but also a large part of what other people desire of one. This is something that old age has in common with childhood. Reflection on children's learning of self-love may help us to appreciate that a healthy concern for one's own good can hardly develop without a social context, and can be admired as a broadly social motive. We have noted that very young children are incapable of desiring their own long-term good because they have no conception of such a good. Much ethical thought has proceeded on the assumption that self-love is "natural," or even an instinct in human beings. I suppose it is natural, in the rather minimal sense that we have a natural propensity to it; but it is not an instinct. Self-love is something a child is normally *taught* by its elders. None of us invented for ourselves the concept of our own happiness or good, which plays an essential part in self-love. I believe there are objective facts of human good; but the *concept* of one's own good is a product of human culture and socially transmitted—something we acquired from those who came before us.

Nor did we get it merely by observing their deliberations about their own good. Unless we were very unfortunate in our childhood circumstances, we were brought up by adults who had our long-term good as a project of theirs before it was a project of ours—indeed, before we had any conception of it. They recognized it as a project that could not get very far unless it became our project too. Therefore they taught us the concept of our own good with the intention that we should desire that good, explaining, for instance, that certain things were good for us and others bad for us. Teaching children to conceive of, and care for, their own good is one of the main ways in which one cares for their good. Conversely, children who are undervalued by those who bring them up may find it harder to adopt their own good with clarity and firmness as a project of their own.

In happier circumstances children's acquisition of self-love is an initiation into a common project, a project they share with adults who love them. Like morally correct behavior, my own long-term good was not something *I* wanted to begin with. I came to want both, with some ambivalence, as I learned about them from people about whom I cared who cared about both, and as I sensed the place of both in a whole network of common projects into which I was being initiated. What was good for me—cod liver oil, for example—was about as likely to be unpleasant as what was morally required. I cannot recall that the appeal to enlightened self-interest enlisted a readier or more enthusiastic cooperation from me than the appeal to righteousness. Both of these appeals had to struggle against what Butler called "particular passions," many of which I had long before I possessed the relatively complex conceptual apparatus necessary for self-love and conscientiousness.

The concept of my own good is related to my caregivers not only as one that I learned from them. I believe it is a concept most precisely adapted to the perspective of my caregivers as such, and to my own perspective only insofar as I am one of my own caregivers. What is best *for me* is not necessarily what is best *from my point of view*—that is, from the point of view defined by *all* my aims, taken together as systematically as possible. For I can and do aim at ends distinct from my own good. For Butlerian reasons, indeed, as discussed in section 1, it would be bad for me if I didn't. The concept of my good is not plausibly designed to characterize the inclusive end of any person's whole system of aims. It signifies rather a more modestly inclusive end one will have insofar as one cares wisely and well for me. I think it remains in a way a more important concept for others who care for me than it is for me, precisely because my greater ownership of my own good entitles me to let it keep a joint account with my other aims, and to be less careful in marking out its boundaries.

Against this background it should not surprise us that a good deal of self-love, in Butler's sense, is regularly treated as a moral virtue in children. 'Be a good boy and take your medicine; it's good for you.' 'Be a good girl and do your homework; it's important to your future success.' In these injunctions an appraisal that certainly feels moral rides on a response to the motive of the agent's own long-term good. In many contexts children who take an effective interest in their own good are "being good," and children who don't are letting the side down, damaging a project in which others have invested much.

Similar things can be said about adults. Butler remarks:

that there are as few persons who attain the greatest satisfaction and enjoyment which they might attain in the present world; as who do the greatest good to others which they might do: nay, that there are as few who can be said really and in earnest to aim at one, as at the other (I.14).

For it so often happens that "cool self-love is prevailed over by passion and appetite" (I.14), whereas "self-love. . . is, of the two, a much better guide than passion" (Preface, §41). A failure to pursue one's own good may be less apt to be subjected to moral censure in adults than in children. But there is commonly a distinctly moral flavor to criticism of adults who neglect their own good through indiscipline or indolence.

Differences in our attitudes toward a lack of self-love in adults and in children are connected with issues of responsibility and ownership. Part of what I learned about my own good as a child was that it was a project that was to belong to me in a special way. I learned that as I got older I would have more and more responsibility for it, and others would take less and less responsibility for it. Linked with this was the fact that the form the project would take would be increasingly up to me. Likewise it would be more my own business if I neglected the project. Taking my own good as a project that is mine in a special way was part of my learning and accepting my moral position in a complex web of rights and responsibilities. At least in a broadly liberal Western society, one acquires more ownership of one's good, and it becomes less of a common project, as one grows to adulthood.[16]

But it never ceases entirely to be a common project in any society that is not completely heartless. If I am found near death in the street, I will be taken to a hospital. If I am starving and there is food around, an effort will probably be made to provide me with some. If I am threatening to throw myself off a tall building, those responsible for public safety will try to talk me out of it. And if I am fortunate enough to have other people who are close to me, they will normally concern themselves more comprehensively and more deeply with my welfare. It goes with this that other people who count my good to some extent among their projects may be angry or reproachful if I neglect it too much. In a religious perspective one might say in the same vein that believing that God loves you (though not *only* you) means, among other things, seeing your own good as a project (though not an exclusive project) shared with God. A certain sense of responsibility to God for doing your part in the project may go with that view of the matter.

As these remarks suggest, caring for your own good is something you may do *for other people*, or at least partly so. This is not to say that your caring in such a case has the other people's *good* as its *end*, instead of your own, or even in

---

[16] The considerations under discussion have an obvious relevance to ethical issues about *paternalism*, about which I will say here only the following. Suppose I do or should accept that my life is enough of a particular project of yours for my caring for my good to be something that I do for you as well as for myself. In that case I can reasonably feel to some extent that I *owe* it to you to care for my good in some ways, and it will be reasonable for you to make some demands on me in that regard which may be described as paternalistic. In more general terms, and to a rough approximation, the degree to which I am reasonably entitled to demand that you stay out of my life seems to vary inversely with the degree to which I reasonably can and do expect you to make some sacrifice to benefit me. And the latter varies directly with the degree to which community blurs the separateness of our lives. Suppose there is the maximum degree of separateness compatible with our being in a position to interact. In that case, it will normally be more reasonable to demand (1) that you stay out of my life than to expect you to intervene to benefit me at significant cost to yourself (even if that sacrifice would still leave you better off than me). It will also be reasonable for me to demand (2) that in any intervention in my life you allow my preferences regarding my life, and my opinion about what is best for me, to override your opinion on the subject (even if your opinion is right, and rationally preferable). At intermediate degrees of separation, matters can become too complex to be handled in a brief discussion such as this.

addition to your own. It may in some cases, but not in the cases that seem to me most interesting and important here. There it is more accurate to say that the intended end of your caring as well as the other people's is your good, but it is partly for them (not for their good but for them) that you care for it, because you are moved by the fact that it is an end of theirs as well as yours.[17] I believe that the most excellent ideals for human community involve patterns of social relationship in which the good of each person is a common project shared with others, and in principle a project of the community as such. Such relationships are characterized by caring for one another's good, and gratefully accepting the care of others for one's own good as a reason to care for it too. In that way, caring for one's own good can be involved in the most excellent ways of being for the most excellent sorts of community.

My good was a common project when I first learned about it. It was also not a completely autonomous project. As my parents' project, my good was not neatly isolated from all their other projects—from the good of the family, from the common good of the human race, or from their commitment to Christianity. My good was for them a part of God's will, a part of the common good, and a part of the family's good. Making my good a project of theirs was not clearly distinct from accepting me as part of the family and part of the community. In one sense of community, one becomes part of a community precisely by such a blending of projects. One's good is accepted by the other members of the community as a project—a project not totally separate from the common good; and one comes to see one's own good in that way. One also accepts the good of the community and of each other member as, to some degree, a project of one's own (if one is competent to form such projects).

Still, making my good a project is not just a matter of factoring something about me into one's conception of the common good. It involves regarding me also as a somewhat independent focus of value. An individual's good is always a project or sub-project that can come into competition with other projects. There are contexts in which it is important to consider my good (or your good) separately. This is obviously the case where issues of distributive fairness arise, and where parents want to take each of their children's good "equally" into account (perhaps not simply or exactly as a matter of fairness).

It is possible for this separateness to be carried to an extreme, by others or more likely by the person in question. I could make it my project that *I* have a good life—and let the rest of the world go hang. That would be an alienated way of taking my own good as a project of mine. It would also be a form of selfishness, which clearly can in this way consist in a corruption of self-love. (As Butler argued, of course, it would be an unpromising project too, unlikely to result in a very good life for me, by any plausible standard.)

---

[17] That doing or wanting something *for your good* is not the only way of doing or wanting it *for you* is argued in chapter 6, section 3.

I need not make my own good such a separate project, however. It can be for me rather the project that I have a good life in a flourishing human community. That is much more like the project into which I was initiated by my elders when I first learned to care for my own good. The tendency of much moral philosophy is to insist on distinguishing two separate projects here: my flourishing and the flourishing of the community. But we might do better to see two foci in a single project—or perhaps two projects, but each having the other as a part.

This is not to deny that there are heroic forms of altruism that involve self-sacrifice, and situations in which it would be selfish not to make some self-sacrifice. Circumstances can certainly place my desire for my own good in conflict with my desire for the common good. Such a conflict will arise in most circumstances, indeed, if the two projects are conceived as absolutely maximizing my own good, as in strict egoism, and absolutely maximizing some common or general good, as in strict utilitarianism. However, such maximizing projects do not seem to me the most excellent ways of being for goods. I think it is healthier to pursue important *goods* without worrying whether they are the *best*. In such an approach it will often be unnecessary to break down one's desire for a good life in a flourishing community into separate self-interested and altruistic desires.

Self-love can be positively rather than negatively related to community. Fully accepting my own membership in a good community involves accepting my own good as a project, both as a common project of the community and as part of the common good. At the same time my good is a project that a good community regards, and expects me to regard, as mine to care about in a special way (though not necessarily *more* than about the good of others or in isolation from the good of others). Being willing to be special to myself in this way is appropriately responsive to my place in communities (not to mention my place in the universe). This is a relatively unalienated and unselfish way of taking my own good as a project. Are you tempted to feel guilty (as some people do) about *ever* pursuing your own good when it competes *at all* with the good of others? Then ask yourself whether you really think a society that did not have your good too as part of a common project would be an excellent society. Are you being for the good as excellently as you should want to be if you treat yourself as such a society would?[18]

Looking back on the themes and arguments of chapters 5, 6, and 7, we may view not only self-love but also altruism in a different light. Altruism, in the sense of regard and care for the good of other persons, is a crucially important aspect, but only one aspect, of the sort of regard for the goods of human life that is characteristic of the kinds of social and personal relationships it is best and most excellent to have. An ideal of altruism as antithetical to self-love, to be realized in a community in which each person would care for the good of all the others

---

[18] I am much indebted to Lisa Halko for suggesting this argument, in conversation with me, twenty or so years ago.

but not at all for her own good, is bizarre. It is as bizarre and inhuman as an egoistic ideal to be realized in a society in which each would be moved only by prudent self-interest. A more excellent sort of altruism will be one in which one enters sympathetically into a concern that one hopes, and in most cases believes, that the other person has for her own well-being. It will also not exclude a concern for the excellence of human lives, and human relationships, for their own sake. The relatively abstract notions of altruism, benevolence, and self-interest may bring a useful precision to our thought in certain contexts. I suspect, however, that the totality of an excellent concern, admiring as well as nurturing, for human good, relational and shared as well as individual, is better summed up in the richer biblical terminology of *loving* other people as oneself.

# PART III

# ARE THERE REALLY ANY VIRTUES?

# 8

# Moral Inconsistency

Part III of this book is concerned with the relation of virtue to human frailty and imperfection. We begin with a look at a vigorous contemporary challenge to the reality of virtue, and at the empirical evidence to which the challenge appeals. I believe virtue is real. But the evidence does support the conclusion that such virtue as is found in human beings is fragmentary and frail in various ways. It is also dependent, in part, on conditions beyond the voluntary control of the individual whose character is in question. A theory of virtue needs to take account of such facts.

## 1. TRAITS AND SITUATIONS: A CHALLENGE

Virtues and vices are typically classified as traits of character. Recently several philosophers have argued that developments in empirical psychology suggest serious doubts about the reality of traits of character, and therefore about the reality of virtues and vices.[1] In the strongest formulation, proposed by Gilbert Harman, the suggestion is that "despite appearances, there is no empirical support for the existence of character traits." Harman infers that "it may even be the case that there is no such thing as character, no ordinary character traits of the sort people think there are, none of the usual moral virtues and vices."[2]

This is an arresting claim. It is bolder, in my opinion, than the evidence supports. That is partly because it rests on an excessively narrow conception of traits of character. It has the merit, however, of calling the attention of philosophers to a very interesting experimental literature in social psychology, which does indeed have important implications for thinking about virtue. This literature is a product of a school of thought sometimes called "situationism," which emphasizes the contribution that differences in social situation make to the explanation of human behavior, in comparison with the contribution made by differences in personal qualities. Harman's challenge can serve as a starting point for trying to

[1] In discussing this subject I am particularly indebted to Jesse Couenhoven and Dana Nelkin, for helpful discussion and for directing my attention to relevant literature.

[2] Harman, "Moral Philosophy Meets Social Psychology," pp. 330, 316. Similar claims, though somewhat more carefully qualified, have been made by other philosophers. See Doris, "Persons, Situations, and Virtue Ethics," and *Lack of Character*; and Campbell, "Can Philosophical Accounts of Altruism Accommodate Experimental Data on Helping Behavior?"

find an empirically defensible conception of the sorts of traits of character among which virtues might be found.

The situationist argument can be introduced by way of one of the oldest of the experimental studies to which it appeals. It is still one of the most important studies in the field. In the 1920s several organizations interested in religious and moral education sponsored a study of the moral views and behavior of thousands of children in the fifth to eighth grades of schools in several American communities. It was led by Hugh Hartshorne and Mark A. May. The part of their work most discussed today consisted of a large set of controlled experiments on honesty and deception. They were designed to test frequencies of lying, cheating, and stealing and correlate them with a variety of other variables.[3] Honesty was tested in many different situations: cheating or not on different tests or tasks or games; lying or not; stealing or not; doing these things at school, at a party, or at home. The experimenters found that individual children were fairly consistent, or stable, over time in repeated tests of their honesty or dishonesty in the *same* type of situation. But they also found, to their surprise, that individual results in *different* types of situation showed low correlations, and thus little cross-situational consistency.[4]

We should be clear about certain features of the results of these experiments, and of similar results of more recent experiments. Their measures of "consistency" are statistical correlations across populations of some size (hundreds or thousands in the case of Hartshorne and May). It is *not* claimed that *no* individuals are consistent across situations. "At one extreme of a normal distribution," say the experimenters, "there are a few children who cheat as often as they get a chance, and at the other extreme there are a few children who do not cheat on any opportunity presented."[5] *How* few are the consistently honest and consistently dishonest children? On ten tests of 2,443 children *measurable cheating* on *all* the tests was found in less than 4 percent of the cases, and on *none* of the tests in only 7 percent of the cases. Analyzing these data, Hartshorne and May's associate Frank Shuttleworth argues that "we may be certain that a large proportion of this 7% actually did cheat on one or more of the tests." That is because the measurement techniques were strongly biased in favor of classifying behavior as honest.[6] The experiments are taken, however, to support at least the conclusion that a few children were *rarely* dishonest in any situation, cheating much less often than most children, while a few others cheated virtually any time they could.

---

[3] Hartshorne and May, *Studies in the Nature of Character*, vol. 1.

[4] Hartshorne, May, and Shuttleworth, *Studies in the Nature of Character*, vol. 3, especially pp. 1–2, 287–93, 373–6.

[5] Ibid., p. 143. "No one thinks the correlation from one situation to another is zero," as Sabini and Silver remark ("Lack of Character?" p. 540). Their discussion of the consistency problem (pp. 540–4) is illuminating.

[6] Hartshorne, May, and Shuttleworth, *Studies in the Nature of Character*, vol. 3, p. 317.

Hartshorne and May and other social psychologists have not concentrated on these "extreme" cases, because they are looking for causal factors that have a social and not merely individual explanatory and predictive power. They are particularly interested in identifying factors with respect to which most members of large groups are relatively consistent across a fairly wide range of diverse types of situation. If $F$ is to be a factor of the relevant sort, then in the absence of other relevant information, the fact that an individual's behavior has manifested $F$ in one situation should establish a very significant probability it will manifest $F$ in the next relevant situation that arises.

Even on a social rather than individual scale, it is *not* claimed that there is *no* positive correlation of honest behavior (for example) in one situation with honest behavior in other types of situation. What is claimed is rather that such positive correlations are *low*. What this means concretely is illuminated in *The Person and the Situation*, an admirable situationist psychological textbook by Lee Ross and Richard Nisbett, which is a major source for philosophical situationists.[7] It reports that experimental psychologists have found "the average correlation between different behavioral measures specifically designed to tap the same personality trait" to fall "typically in the range between .10 and .20, and often . . . even lower." Ross and Nisbett explain the implications as follows. Suppose "the correlation . . . between friendliness in any two situations" is .16 (near the middle of the typical range). "This means that knowing that Jane was friendlier than Ellen in situation 1 increases the likelihood that she will be friendlier in situation 2 only to 55 percent" from the 50 percent probability that would be assigned in total ignorance.[8] The indicated conclusion, we might think, is not that the traits under study don't exist,[9] but rather that they have only *weak* explanatory and predictive power.

Situationists particularly emphasize a comparative point. The explanatory and predictive power of such traits is commonly much weaker than that of certain features of situations in which agents find themselves. And some of the influential features of situations seem (in advance) quite trivial. Here is a dramatic and surprising example. Accidentally on purpose, a member of a team of experimenters drops a folder-full of papers in a shopping plaza, in front of a stranger who is emerging from a phone booth. Will the stranger stop to help pick up the papers? The stranger did help in fourteen of sixteen cases in which he or she found a dime planted by the experimenters in the phone's coin return, but in only one

[7] It is cited prominently in Harman, "Moral Philosophy Meets Social Psychology," and Doris, *Lack of Character*, whose index contains more citations of Ross and Nisbett than of any other psychological authors.

[8] Ross and Nisbett, *The Person and the Situation*, p. 95.

[9] The claim that "there are no traits of character corresponding to the virtues and vices of ordinary language" can be found in the psychological literature (Kohlberg, *Essays On Moral Development*, vol. 1, p. 35). See also the more cautious statement in the same volume, p. 79, and nuanced statements in Hartshorne, May, and Shuttleworth, *Studies in the Nature of Character*, vol. 3, p. 143 and vol. 1, book 1, p. 385.

of twenty-five cases in which no coin was there.[10] This correlation of helpful and unhelpful behavior with presence and absence of the dime is much higher than any general, cross-situational correlation that has been found experimentally for helpful behavior as a trait of individuals.

I have no inclination to contest the situationist claims about low and high correlations, which seem based in many cases on experiments of great elegance.[11] We must take such data into account in our thinking about virtue. The largest question to be discussed is whether such data justify anything like Harman's extreme suggestion that "there is no such thing as character" and that "no ordinary character traits" and "none of the usual moral virtues" really exist. Or can we articulate a conception of traits of character, and of virtues in particular, on which their existence is compatible with the empirical evidence? The situationist challenge to virtue theory received its first widely cited philosophical treatment in 1991,[12] and most philosophical discussions of it are much more recent than that. Three main ways of responding to it without giving up the language of virtue and vice are already discernible in the literature, and can be sketched here.

(1) At one extreme, those who are ready to concede the most to the situationist challenge would free the terminology of virtue and vice from commitment to traits of character by applying it primarily to actions and attitudes and mental states occurring at a particular time. Thomas Hurka takes this line in his important study, *Virtue, Vice, and Value*. He holds that "the concept of virtue is essentially that of a desirable state," and suggests that in typical areas of moral concern "virtue should be found in occurrent attitudes." He is willing to "find some value and virtue in appropriate dispositions," but his theory is not heavily committed to the reality or robustness of such dispositions.[13]

I think we should not be so ready to give up a commitment to enduring traits or qualities of character as a central object of moral evaluation. Are we really to give up all aspiration for improvement of our own character? Even harder to give up, probably, is the project of moral education of the young. But how are we to understand that project if it does not aim at enduring moral dispositions of some sorts?

(2) At the opposite extreme, offering the least accommodation to the situationist critique, is the strategy of arguing that a classical conception of virtue is untouched by situationist experimental evidence. At least two reasons may be given for this conclusion. In the first place, the classical conception envisaged

[10] Isen and Levin, "Effect of Feeling Good on Helping," cited in Doris, *Lack of Character*, pp. 30–2.

[11] I should note, however, that my reading in the situationist literature has turned up no experimental studies of *adult* behavior comparable in scope and scale to the Hartshorne and May study of *children's* behavior, which was "still the most ambitious study of behavioral consistency" according to Ross and Nisbett, *The Person and the Situation* (1991), p. 98.

[12] Flanagan, *Varieties of Moral Personality*, chapters 12–14.

[13] Hurka, *Virtue, Vice, and Value*, pp. 43–4.

in this response does not suppose that true virtue is common enough to leave a statistically significant footprint in social psychologists' studies. It views virtue as an integrated condition by which one reliably responds appropriately to all sorts of situation. Without that integrated condition morally desirable dispositions are not counted as virtues. If virtue so conceived is rare, that is hardly surprising and does not show that virtue is not an ideal to which we should aspire. And, in the second place, the question whether anyone has such a comprehensive disposition to respond *appropriately* is heavily laden with evaluation. The evaluation will be controversial at some points, and is not likely to be convincingly operationalized in the sorts of behavioral test used by social psychologists.

A strategy of this sort is presented in Rachana Kamtekar's perceptive essay on "Situationism and Virtue Ethics on the Content of Our Character." In her view virtue finds its integration in practical wisdom, as a firm and reliable disposition to respond rightly or appropriately to all sorts of situations on the basis of wise deliberation and right reason. Particular virtues are specifications or manifestations of this one comprehensive disposition in relation to particular domains or types of situation. For instance, courage relates to dangers, and justice to certain kinds of social situations.[14] I believe that Kamtekar's account is substantially faithful to views shared by Plato, Aristotle, and the Stoics, and that she is right in arguing that it has not been refuted by the situationist experiments. If I do not adopt a strategy of this type, that is because I believe it is important to find moral excellence in imperfect human lives, and because I disagree with ancient views about the kind of integration human virtue can and should have. The development of these disagreements will occupy us through much of the rest of this book.

(3) The third strategy, which I favor, is to argue that there are real moral virtues that are not extremely rare and that play a part in a wide variety of human lives. I will grant that this requires a conception of virtues that allows for virtues that are frail and fragmentary in various ways. Maria Merritt presents an interesting version of this strategy in a recent paper on "Virtue Ethics and Situationist Personality Psychology." The "motivational self-sufficiency of character" which seems to be part of the Aristotelian conception of virtue conflicts with the dependence of individual traits on social conditions, for which situationists have argued. Is there an alternative to self-sufficiency as a basis for the stability of character that virtue is thought to require? Merritt seeks such a basis in Hume, in whom she sees a conception of the virtues as "socially or personally beneficial qualities of mind," which "should be relatively stable over time somehow or other," but not necessarily through motivational self-sufficiency. She argues that on such a conception we can find real virtues in people whose character depends for its stability on social conditions that are in fact relatively stable.[15]

---

[14] Kamtekar, "Situationism and Virtue Ethics," pp. 479–81.
[15] Merritt, "Virtue Ethics and Situationist Personality Psychology," pp. 374–81.

That certainly seems to be a coherent line of thought. For reasons indicated in chapter 4, however, I do not believe that it is enough for qualities of mind to be socially or personally *beneficial* if they are to be virtues. Virtues must be intrinsically *excellent* qualities. I need therefore to confront the question whether personal qualities can be excellent enough to be virtues if they are as fragmentary and socially dependent, and as frail in some situations, as I will grant that morally desirable qualities generally are in human life.

In relation to the situationist challenge, this question may be divided in two. The *frailty problem* is whether all the otherwise desirable traits of character there may be are too frail or fragile or too dependent on social and situational factors to have the excellence required of a virtue. That problem is the subject of chapter 9. The *inconsistency problem* is whether any personal qualities we might regard as virtues have, in actual fact, sufficient generality and consistency across situations to count as traits of character. Reflecting on this problem will lead to questions about the types of mental and social properties among which virtues are likeliest to be found. This set of issues will engage our attention in the present chapter. What I will try to show is that there are qualities with respect to which it is empirically allowable to suppose that people are commonly consistent over time, and which are promising candidates for recognition as virtues or potential parts of virtues. I will not argue that any human being is consistently virtuous in *all* respects, or has all virtues.

## 2. DIRECT BEHAVIORAL DISPOSITIONS

I consider it a weakness of situationist writing about traits of character, both in philosophy and in psychology, that it tends to assume that all traits of character must be what I shall call *direct behavioral dispositions*. My use of this phrase is inspired by terminology in Richard Brandt's classic analysis of the concept of traits of character. Brandt thinks the main alternative to his own view is what he calls "the Direct Disposition Theory" of traits of character. It:

proposes that *for various trait-names a form of behavior typical of that trait can be identified* (as talking for talkativeness), and that what it is for a person to have a certain trait is primarily for him to be *disposed to behave in the correlated typical way, in certain conditions, relatively frequently.*[16]

If some dispositions of this sort are virtues and vices, they will presumably be dispositions to morally good and bad types of behavior, respectively. Indeed the direct behavioral dispositions most likely to be identified as virtues and vices are those whose correlated type of behavior is defined in ethical terms. The obvious examples in the present context are "honest" and "dishonest" behavior. To

---

[16] Brandt, "Traits of Character," p. 31; Brandt's italics.

conceive of honesty as a direct behavioral disposition is to suppose that an honest person is simply one who is disposed to *behave* honestly. She will be disposed to tell the truth and not to engage in cheating or deceptive behavior, under normal circumstances.

Situationist claims of the explanatory unimportance or non-existence of traits of personality or character generally seem to presuppose a direct disposition conception of traits. How do Ross and Nisbett, for instance, understand the "traditional personality traits" that they suggest may not capture very well such consistencies as are found in persons' behavior? They equate them with "enduring predispositions to be friendly, dependent, aggressive, or the like." Harman says that character traits "are relatively long-term stable dispositions to act in distinctive ways. An honest person is disposed to act honestly. A kind person is disposed to act kindly."[17] I take John Doris's book, *Lack of Character*, published in 2002, to be the fullest and most balanced current philosophical presentation of situationism. It presents a similar though slightly more nuanced conception of traits. Doris says that "to attribute a character or personality trait is to say, among other things, that someone is disposed to behave in a certain way in certain eliciting conditions."[18] Despite the qualification, "among other things," Doris seems to me to have little to say about the "other things," focusing overwhelmingly on behavioral dispositions.

It is very doubtful that a direct behavioral disposition is sufficient to constitute a virtue. At a minimum, we may think, one must have a good motive for the behavior in question if the disposition is to count as a virtue. It seems possible to have a direct disposition to behave honestly out of fear of social consequences of dishonest behavior without caring much at all about honesty and other people's rights for their own sake. Such a disposition, badly motivated though it be, will still be socially *useful*, if the alternative is no disposition at all to honest behavior; but few will think it is *excellent* enough to be a virtue. This is a difficulty, independent of situationist research, in identifying virtues with direct behavioral dispositions. The connection of virtue with motivation will be a recurring theme in our investigation.

However, no such difficulty totally undermines the situationists' strategy for showing the rareness of thoroughgoing honesty. For surely a disposition to honest behavior is at least necessary, if not sufficient, for a virtue of honesty. A person who is not strongly disposed to behave honestly in a wide variety of situations is not thoroughly honest. If it turns out, in the empirical study of behavior, to be hard to find a person who almost never cheats or lies, that will be evidence that honesty, as a virtue, is at best very rare. Conceptually simple, straightforwardly behavioral tests can in principle give strong evidence of the absence of some virtues. Not, I think, of all virtues; in section 3 we will come to

---

[17] Harman, "Moral Philosophy Meets Social Psychology," p. 317.
[18] Doris, *Lack of Character*, p. 15.

virtues less closely tied than honesty is to types of behavior that the situationists' experimental strategies are adapted to measure. But there is still a question for the moral psychologist to ask about behavioral dispositions as such.

Do the situationist arguments show that there are no direct dispositions to good and bad types of behavior? No. The experimental evidence admits, in particular, dispositions that are (1) probabilistic and (2) modular. It will be worth considering to what extent such dispositions might qualify as virtues.

## 2.1 Probabilistic Virtues

An important qualification of situationist claims in the psychological literature has received surprisingly little attention in philosophical commentary.[19] It concerns the statistical significance of low but positive correlations in "a great number of trait-relevant responses for each individual" in different situations. Such aggregation of observations still does not make it possible to predict individual behavior with confidence in each single situation. But it does make possible fairly reliable predictions about "the mean [i.e., average] response that each individual will exhibit over a great number of future observations" and "about each individual's entire *distribution* of responses."[20] The predictions about distribution of responses will be particularly important.

Suppose we had an extremely large number of past observations of a population of a hundred individuals in a great variety of situations. Suppose that on that basis the individuals have been accurately ranked with regard to a set of behavioral characteristics including aggressiveness and generosity. And suppose the positive correlation measuring cross-situational consistency in the population with regard to each of those traits is .16 (significant but low).[21] Suppose further that in this population Bob has the second highest average aggressiveness ranking, and Ted the second lowest, while Carol has the second highest average generosity ranking and Alice the second lowest. This grounds no confident prediction about how any of them will act on the next occasion for more or less aggressive or more or less generous behavior. That's the *negative* finding of situationist research.

In a typical population the behavior of all individuals will vary quite a lot as to the degree in which it manifests such traits. With regard to behavior on the next single occasion, the highest probability for any of our four individuals is that he or she will be pretty close to the average of the population with regard to aggressiveness or generosity. Almost all of us are pretty "normal" or ordinary in our behavior most of the time.

---

[19] It gets excellent and very interesting attention, however, from philosophically sensitive psychologists in Sabini and Silver, "Lack of Character? Situationism Critiqued," pp. 540–4.

[20] Ross and Nisbett, *The Person and the Situation*, p. 110.

[21] Treated by Ross and Nisbett as typical for this type of correlation (*The Person and the Situation*, pp. 111–15).

Indeed, this ordinariness combines with situational factors to ground a large proportion of our most confident behavioral predictions. There are situations in which social norms define normal expectations quite precisely—with respect to non-violence or truthfulness, for example. In such situations I may be virtually certain how an acquaintance will behave, but will commonly have a similar confidence about perfect strangers, if their behavior has given no contrary cue. (If not, how often would it be rational for me to step into the crosswalk as a pedestrian?) This in itself need not be disturbing to virtue theorists. Some of our very ordinary reliableness may actually be virtue that most of us share, as is suggested by the concept of an ordinarily "decent" person.[22]

This is a point at which it is especially important to have a *non*-elitist conception of moral excellence and allow that there are excellences, and in moral contexts virtues, that people ordinarily have. Statistical studies can hardly give the lie to our belief in exceptional cases of goodness. We may draw inspiration from saints and heroes, from individuals who are much better than average in some broadly ethical respects, though they generally also have faults. But it would be a serious mistake (and the opposite of inspiring) to suppose that there is no point in attaining or maintaining this or that good disposition if it won't put us in a position where we can look around and conclude that most people are worse than we are. Virtue is not a competitive sport. If we are morally serious about it, we compete, if at all, mainly with ourselves, as many golfers do in trying to improve their scores.

We do have reason to be concerned about "extreme" behavior, however. The predictive power of past experience looks quite different with respect to such behavior. Suppose we want to know for each of Bob and Ted and Carol and Alice what is the likelihood that he or she will be one of the two most aggressive or one of the two most generous individuals in the population at least once in the next ten observations. Then, on the basis of our extremely large database of past observations, the probability of Bob being one of the two most aggressive, and Carol one of the two most generous, at least one of the next ten times is about 60 percent for each of them. On the other hand, the likelihood of Ted being one of the two most aggressive, or Alice one of two most generous, at least one of the next ten times, is less than 1 percent for each of them.[23]

These are hugely significant differences for pragmatic purposes, and I believe also for the theory of virtues and vices. If we ask, 'Is she a generous person?' we do not mean, 'Does she show notable generosity on every occasion?' Nobody has the personal resources for that. It will be worth asking her help, and appropriate to praise her character in this respect, if she is disposed to act with notable generosity as much as 10 percent of the time. Similarly, 'Is he a violent person?'

[22] Cf. Risse, "The Morally Decent Person."
[23] In this, as in everything I have said so far in this section about statistical implications, I am relying on the discussion in Ross and Nisbett, *The Person and the Situation*, pp. 107–18.

does not mean, 'Does he *always* act violently?' No one can get away with that. But if acting more aggressively than almost everyone else often means acting violently, then a disposition that amounts to a 60 percent probability of being one of the most aggressive 10 percent of the time is cause for concern, and a serious moral deficiency. These considerations suggest that direct behavioral dispositions may play a major part in constituting cross-situational virtues and vices if they are understood in probabilistic terms. Behavioral dispositions involved in constituting a virtue of generosity or a vice of violence need not predict with certainty; it is enough for them to amount to significant probabilities of relevant behavior.

Of course being likely to exhibit a particular type of behavior that normally is morally appropriate will not constitute a virtue if it is badly motivated. If Ted's gentleness is most plausibly explained as a result of great timidity, and Carol's apparent generosity is coolly calculated to win her popularity, we probably will not count either as a virtue. But this is a problem in the relation of virtue to behavioral dispositions in general (as we have already noted), and is not specific to probabilistic dispositions. If behavioral dispositions can have good motives at all, so can probabilistic ones. Ted's high probability of gentleness and Carol's relatively high probability of generosity may be due to his wanting not to hurt people and her liking to help people, even if these good motives are not certain to control them in every situation.

More serious worries about a probabilistic account of virtuous dispositions may arise from another fact. Even gentle Ted's very low probability of being one of the most aggressive, and perhaps acting violently, some of the time, must be supposed to be greater than zero. Virtues of "imperfect" obligation can be probabilistic more comfortably than virtues of strict or "perfect" obligation. A perfect obligation is one that is violated if one does not perform (or refrain from performing) a particular type of action in every relevant case. An imperfect obligation is satisfied if one "does enough"—typically, if one performs the relevant sort of action in a sufficient proportion of cases. And it is usually hard to say precisely how much is "enough." Generosity, and more broadly beneficence, are virtues of imperfect obligation. We are not required, and probably not able, to do good on every possible occasion. But non-violence, like truthfulness, and more broadly conscientiousness, looks like a virtue of perfect obligation. With the exception of a debated minority of cases in which violence, arguably, is justified, we are morally required to refrain from violence toward each other *all* of the time. And likewise with regard to truthfulness.

Shall we conclude that the behavioral dispositions involved in virtues of perfect obligation cannot have a merely probabilistic character? Here conceptions of virtues as ideals and as dimensions of actual moral character pull in opposite directions. Both types of conception have their uses, and I see no harm in operating with both, provided we are clear about what we are doing. If we are framing ideals of non-violence and truthfulness which we may hope to approximate, it is reasonable for them to include never lashing out at others, and never telling a lie, when it is wrong to do so. But it is hardly reasonable to treat the assessment of actual character in these respects as the proverbial "night in which all cows are black." It seems that even gentle Ted and truthful Sam will have dispositions amounting to a non-zero probability of Ted's occasionally lashing out, and Sam's occasionally telling a lie, when they should not. But that need not keep us from counting it as excellences and as virtues in them—probabilistic ones—that Ted is unusually gentle and Sam is unusually honest.

## 2.2 Modules of Virtue

In one of the first philosophical works to focus seriously on situationist psychology, Owen Flanagan speaks of the "modularity" of virtue.[24] Let us see what we can make of the idea that dispositions to respond well to particular types of situation may be *modules* of virtue. In its current predominant sense the word 'module' means "a more or less independent component part," most often in reference to manufactured objects, signifying "each of a series of standardized parts or units from which a complex structure . . . is or can be assembled."[25]

The word has come to be used in a similar sense, or senses, in various contexts in the biological and social sciences, and related fields of philosophy. In those contexts it can signify not only material parts of a body or physical system, but also subprocesses that are or can be components of more complex or more inclusive processes. Modularity is a hot topic in some of these fields. Surveying the use of the concept in biology, Gerhard Schlosser and Günther P. Wagner have recently stated that "a generally accepted definition of modularity does not exist and different authors use the concept in quite different ways."[26] That is hardly surprising, given the great diversity of phenomena under discussion. I must therefore say what I take to be included in the idea that some behavioral dispositions are "modules of virtue." And I should state at the outset that I am not concerned here with questions about innateness and neurological bases of psychological phenomena, which have figured prominently in discussions of modularity in biology and psychology and the philosophy thereof.

The idea as it concerns me includes four claims, two of them causal and two evaluative. (1) The first causal claim is that direct behavioral dispositions commonly are mutually *independent* in a way that is *domain-specific*. That is, a person will often acquire and exercise a disposition to act in a certain way in one domain without being disposed to act similarly in somewhat different domains. The domains may be types of situation quite narrowly defined, as in

---

[24] Flanagan, *Varieties of Moral Personality*, pp. 268–75.
[25] *Shorter Oxford English Dictionary*, s.v. 'module'. According to the OED this usage dates only from the middle of the twentieth century.
[26] Schlosser and Wagner, eds., in the introduction to *Modularity in Development and Evolution*, p. 4.

the Hartshorne and May experiments, or they may be as widely defined as social roles, such as those of a parent, a stockbroker, or a committee member.

To classify a disposition as domain-specific is not to say that it is not affected in any way by a larger causal nexus. As noted by Hartshorne and May, the correlation between similar dispositions in different situations is rarely zero.[27] Moreover, I take it to be a fact of ordinary moral experience that we have holistic and relatively domain-neutral (and to that extent non-modular) capacities of moral and other practical thinking that we more or less often apply in and to a wide variety of situations. It is plausible to suppose that we can in principle apply such thinking in and to most situations in which we may find ourselves. I take it further to be an empirical fact that the behavioral output of behavioral dispositions specific to a domain can sometimes be inhibited or otherwise overridden by the output of such general and relatively domain-neutral intellectual capacities.

This does not, however, imply any particular conclusion about how often we do successfully exert such "central" control.[28] The rate at which we actually do so might turn out to be depressingly low, even though we have, in principle, the ability to do it. In particular, I do not mean to deny that some domain-specific dispositions are relatively unlikely to be overridden by "central" thinking, especially in situations of stress or temptation.[29] That is perhaps particularly likely to be true of domain-specific dispositions amounting to stereotypical "habits." Moreover, I do not mean to deny that some situations might be so terrifying or so confusingly or inscrutably unfamiliar that in them many or perhaps all of us would be quite unable to exercise our more general capacities for practical thinking. That is one way in which those capacities may be only *relatively* domain-neutral.

(2) The second causal claim I take to be implied in speaking of behavioral dispositions as "modules" is that they can be added together to form a more inclusive composite disposition. This is a main point of analogy between the role of modularity in behavioral development and its more widely familiar role in manufacturing processes. Behavioral modules of a single virtue will be dispositions whose behavioral manifestation is similar (being characteristic of the single virtue), but specific to different domains of behavior, and acquired separately.

---

[27] Hartshorne and May, *Studies in the Nature of Character*, vol. 1, book 1, p. 385. Similarly, in a biological context, Schlosser and Wagner remark that "conceptualizing modules as strictly autonomous units is a simplification that is easy to attack. It appears to be more fruitful to acknowledge that modularity comes in degrees" (*Modularity in Development and Evolution*, p. 3).

[28] The term 'central' is borrowed from Fodor, *The Modularity of Mind*; and what I am saying here about central control of voluntary behavior is analogous to things that Fodor says about human capacities for central, non-modular control of cognition. I doubt very much, however, that the domain-specific behavioral dispositions of most interest to a theory of virtue are ever as thoroughly independent or "encapsulated" as Fodor argues that some cognitive processes are.

[29] My use of 'temptation' in this context is probably not very informative. For we may often mean by 'temptation' nothing more than a situation where we have dispositions (often domain-specific) that are quite resistant to being overridden by "central" moral dispositions that are in fact opposed to them.

And combining them is to yield a more general, and more consistent, disposition to behave in the relevant way in a wide variety of situations.

(3) The first of the evaluative claims that I promised is that, at least in some cases, where a disposition to behave in accordance with a particular virtue is a module in the ways indicated in the two causal claims, it is a good disposition, having a certain positive moral value, even before dispositions to behave in accordance with the virtue in other situations are added to it. (4) The second evaluative claim is that the result of adding such dispositions together to form a cross-situationally consistent composite disposition can rightly be regarded, in some cases, as constituting a genuine and more complete case of the particular virtue. These two evaluative claims are implicit in speaking of a behavioral module as a *part* of a *virtue*.

I take it as a working hypothesis that the causal claims (1) and (2) are correct. I doubt that enough is known about moral development to sustain certainty about that, but I believe that ordinary experience of behavioral learning joins with situationist experimental data to provide considerable support for the hypothesis. The case for the evaluative claims (3) and (4) will be explored in several portions of this book, particularly in the present section and in parts of chapters 10 and 12.

There is at least one of the traditional cardinal virtues that we are routinely willing to divide into modules in moral discourse. That is courage. Our ordinary ethical vocabulary distinguishes between "physical courage," which deals well with physical dangers, and "moral courage," which deals well with social dangers.[30] Honesty also invites treatment in terms of modules. Even for people who cheat on their spouses, it is good to be honest in business, and vice versa. If we regarded you as honest in business, and law-abiding, but dishonest in many other areas of life, we probably would not call you "an honest person" without qualification; but we might think you had a start on honesty.

Whether that is good enough to constitute a micro-virtue, or a first installment of a virtue, will depend on more than the behavior in which the person is disposed to engage. Motivation matters, as we have already observed. Honest behavior in one area of life (or even in many) that is motivated merely by fear of formal or informal punishment is arguably not a virtue. But what about honesty in a single area of life (perhaps one's professional life) that is motivated by appreciation of values of that realm, and strong commitment to them? Why wouldn't that be a virtue, as far as it goes?

In thinking about the possible modularity of incomplete virtue we should also consider to what extent impressions of inconsistency may be an artifact of our nomenclature of virtues. Whether a particular term that has been thought to name a virtue really picks out a trait that has psychological reality is one question. It needs to be clearly distinguished from the more fundamental questions

[30] The modularity of courage will be explored more fully in chapter 10, section 2.2.

whether there are any psychologically real and ethically significant traits in the neighborhood, and whether some such traits might qualify as virtues.

Honesty is a case in point. As Rachana Kamtekar points out, "although we use a single word, 'honest'," for them, "it does not seem obvious that not lying, not cheating, and not stealing are the same sort of thing, or even that they are deeply connected." Suppose honesty is not a single psychological trait, but a group of "distinct and unrelated dispositions" that we have packaged together conceptually for non-psychological reasons. We use the name 'honesty' to cover both "a disposition not to lie, supported by the thought that respecting others requires one to tell them the truth," and "a disposition not to cheat, on the grounds that in cheating one exploits a system that one should uphold." But this does not show that those are not separable psychological traits that we might have reason to count as virtues independently of each other.[31] I don't mean to suggest that we will find no phenomena of inconsistency with respect to these more narrowly defined dispositions. But we should be wary of reading too much significance for ethical theory into evidence of cross-situational "inconsistency" with regard to supposed traits that are really rather heterogeneous groups of dispositions.

The results of the Hartshorne and May experiments might be explained in part by the hypothesis that we have grouped together under the label 'honesty' a variety of different traits that are commended by rather different reasons and have quite different psychological structures and roles. What in fact do we mean by 'honesty'? Perhaps we can best capture the full breadth of the term if we begin by defining *dis*honesty as doing something morally wrong that involves deception or concealment. Then honesty, in its behavioral aspect, will be a disposition not to do wrong things that involve deception or concealment. This covers such a miscellaneous class of abstentions that it seems very doubtful that it should be considered a single trait of character. Not lying is often largely a matter of respect for truthful communication and truthful relationships. Not stealing is typically much less a matter of respect for truthfulness than for other people's property rights, even where theft would involve concealment. These motives seem quite separable, and we should not be surprised if the corresponding behavioral dispositions are separable too.

Even if we restrict our attention to misdeeds whose main morally objectionable feature is *deception*, why should believers in virtue expect children of ages 10 to 14 to be uniformly attuned to their wrongness and uniformly motivated to abstain from them? Consider a child who usually won't lie to a close friend or relative, but cheats on tests of the sort used in the Hartshorne and May experiments. Are those actions so obviously similar that she should be expected to see some inconsistency in her own behavior? Perhaps she sees and appreciates the point of abstaining in the one case but not in the other.

---

[31] The quoted material in this paragraph is from Kamtekar, "Situationism and Virtue Ethics," pp. 468–9.

It may be said that both the cheating and the lying involve deception. But the "cheating" involves no lie. What it involves is more precisely doing something the child believes an adult (the experimenter) doesn't want done, and not letting the adult know of that fact. None of us thinks that concealing facts unwelcome to others is always morally equivalent to lying. Do we think we are obliged to reveal facts about our personal lives to everyone who might be offended by them? Perhaps the child also knows that her test behavior is something adults classify (and condemn) as "cheating," and that they classify both it and lying as "dishonest." That this is not a consistently motivating consideration for the child may show that she is not consistently *conscientious* (if she in some sense believes that what the adults say is wrong is indeed wrong). But we should not let our broad use of the term *honesty* keep us from taking seriously the hypothesis that she manifests in familiar conversation a virtuous behavioral module that can legitimately be distinguished from the kind of honesty that she is seen to lack in the test situation.

It is quite possible that the child appreciates why people would object to being lied to by someone they know, and that is why she is moved not to lie to people she knows. If she is so moved reliably, that seems morally good, and may be a virtue, and as such perhaps a module of a virtue of truthfulness. Why shouldn't such a narrow-scope trait be counted as a virtue if it is appropriately responsive to reasons that commend the behavior involved in it? How wide a sweep must a well-motivated disposition to truthful behavior have if it is to constitute a virtue?

Few think it a virtue to be disposed to disclose the truth in *every* situation. For truthfulness is not an unrivaled value in human communication; discretion and tact, for example, can compete with it. Secrets are important. Most of us believe it is occasionally right even to tell a lie, and often imperative to avoid mentioning secrets or facts whose utterance would give offense or affect inappropriately the social dynamics of a situation. Perhaps it will be suggested that truthfulness is not a virtue unless it involves a reliable tendency to say what is true *whenever, and only when,* one ought to do so. We should not need the situationists' experiments, however, to tell us that perfect possession of that sweeping tendency would be extraordinary, perhaps impossible, in a human adult, let alone a child.

For reliable possession of such a tendency obviously depends not only on the will or commitment to do what is right in this area of life, but also on understanding of what is right. And rightness or appropriateness in these matters is highly conditioned by situational and cultural factors. In order to appreciate all the factors affecting rightness and wrongness of truthful disclosure and concealment, one would have to have immense knowledge of human life and of various cultures and subcultures. There are quite different things one needs to understand about disclosure and concealment as a parent, as a lawyer, and as a physician, for instance. Such knowledge could hardly be attained without much more experience of life than the children in the Hartshorne and May experiments (for example) could have had.

For reasons of this sort, we should expect that much learning to be virtuous will come in situational or domain-specific modules, as we learn to understand and appreciate relevant considerations only after some exposure to relevant situations. What reason is there to think that such modules could not be virtues? Will it be claimed that their narrowness of scope keeps them from being *important* enough? That can hardly be right as a general rule, though it may be true of some cases. Dealing well with disclosure and concealment in family life or in professional life is surely important even if one does not deal as well with corresponding issues in other domains.[32] Is there reason to think that even if the modules are important, they still could not be *excellent* enough? I don't think it is in general right to deny that excellence can come in small packages. But some influential theorists of virtue have denied that virtue, or virtues, can come in fragments. Their thesis of "the unity of the virtues" raises large issues which will be the subject of chapters 10 and 11. Here we may try to state provisionally what moral psychology should learn from the empirical evidence of cross-situational inconsistency in behavioral dispositions, ethically defined. The lesson, I believe, is not that no such dispositions manifest virtues, but rather that it will typically be as probabilistic or modular traits that they manifest virtues, if they do.[33]

### 3. TRAITS OF MOTIVATION AND THOUGHT

There is no doubt that virtues have often been conceived, both in philosophy and in ordinary life, as behavioral dispositions. Julia Annas, for example, in an unusually comprehensive study of ancient moral philosophy, states that "all ancient theories understand a virtue to be, at least, a disposition to do the morally right thing."[34] The qualification, "at least," is significant. It suggests, correctly, awareness that simply identifying a virtue with a direct behavioral disposition, even a disposition to do the right thing, may be too simple. Reasons for thinking that it is too simple do not all depend on situationism. One that does not is that motivation is important for virtue, as we have already noted. A disposition to do the morally right thing for wrong reasons, or from exclusively selfish motives, should generally not be counted as a virtue. It is a *well-motivated* disposition to do what is right that constitutes a virtue, and it takes the motivation as well as the behavioral disposition to constitute the virtue.

There is another problem about identifying virtues, or more broadly traits of character, with direct behavioral dispositions. Both psychological theories and theories of virtue seek to identify traits that are factors in explanations that are illuminating and not too superficial. It is a feature of Harman's situationist

---

[32] Cf. Badhwar, "The Limited Unity of Virtue."

[33] These conclusions do not seem to me to be seriously called in question by the criticism of some aspects of situationism in Krueger and Funder, "Towards a Balanced Social Psychology."

[34] Annas, *The Morality of Happiness*, p. 9.

argument, for example, that "character traits are *broad based* dispositions that help to explain what they are dispositions to do."[35] These aspirations are not likely to be satisfied by the behavioral dispositions that are likeliest to be regarded as virtues. This is something else we should be able to see without situationist psychological experiments.

Suppose, for instance, you have a reliable, well-motivated disposition to say what is true whenever, and only when, it is right to do so. We can say that you tell the truth in such cases because you are so disposed, but that is a superficial explanation. We want to know how you manage to behave so well in this aspect of life. Your motivation—your desire or commitment—to tell the truth when you should is an explanatory factor of the sort we are looking for; but it is not a direct behavioral disposition. It will not produce morally right behavior by itself, but only in conjunction with whatever factors lead you to a correct judgment about what is right in a given situation. Those factors are likely to be multiple, and to differ from situation to situation. Some might say it is your general good judgment about issues of truthfulness, combined with your moral motivation, that explains your correct behavior. But that will be relatively unexplanatory, in comparison with an account that specifies the experiences, sensitivities, and disciplines of reasoning that produce your good judgment.

Human behavior, except the most routinely habitual, is a product of multiple psychological factors which differ in different situations.[36] A theory of virtue will have more explanatory power to the extent that the excellent qualities it identifies as virtues are found among these factors that lie behind behavior, rather than in direct behavioral dispositions. And in fact situationist psychologists have generally acknowledged some types of personal quality as relatively enduring and as more useful than direct behavioral dispositions for explaining individual differences in behavior. Some of these qualities are motives. These are facts of great significance for the relation of situationist research to the study of the virtues.

Ross and Nisbett propose that "enduring motivational concerns and cognitive schemes" provide "a more powerful conception of individual differences" than is provided by "traditional personality traits. That is, individuals may behave in consistent ways that distinguish them from their peers ... because they are pursuing consistent goals, using consistent strategies, in the light of consistent ways of interpreting their world."[37] Walter Mischel, another leading figure in the development of situationist thought, writes of individual differences that he calls "person variables" instead of "traits." He classifies them in five types: (1) "competencies" to generate cognitions and behaviors; (2) "strategies" for "encoding" or categorizing situations and other information; (3) "expectancies" regarding

[35] Harman, "Moral Philosophy Meets Social Psychology," p. 318.
[36] As is emphasized by situationist psychologists. See Ross and Nisbett, *The Person and the Situation*, pp. 11–13, 59–89.
[37] Ross and Nisbett, *The Person and the Situation*, p. 20; cf. pp. 96, 163. This is echoed by Harman, "Moral Philosophy Meets Social Psychology," pp. 320–1, 326.

"outcomes" of actual situations or possible behavior; (4) "subjective values"; (5) "self-regulatory systems and plans," rules, and goals.[38]

Why shouldn't "person variables" of some or all of these types be counted as traits of character, if they play a sufficiently prominent and enduring part in the life of a person? Indeed, properties of these types play a central part in the constitution of virtues and vices according to most theories of virtue. That is most obviously true of motives, though I think it is true of all or most of the other mentioned types of quality as well.

Mischel insists that person variables shape behavior, not independently of situations, but in interaction with situations; but that is no obstacle to counting such properties as moral virtues. Virtues are not supposed to lead us to ignore the characteristics of situations in which we find ourselves. They are supposed to enable us to respond appropriately to situations. Virtues and vices operate largely by determining what an individual will see or feel as reasons, and weighty reasons, for action and emotion in different situations. Such determination is obviously affected by individual differences in "motivational concerns and cognitive schemes." Theorists of virtue should not be disturbed by the suggestion that many of the virtues are not to be identified simply in terms of their behavioral output, as direct behavioral dispositions, but rather in terms of the way they enter into complex psychological interactions in which many factors jointly shape behavior. This is not to say that such traits do not involve dispositions at all. As enduring causal factors that can be present even when there is no occasion for their actual operation, they do have a dispositional aspect. But the dispositions involved in them will typically be dispositions, first of all, to types of psychological processing, rather than directly to types of observable physical behavior.

### 3.1. Motives and Commitments

Among the factors shaping what will weigh with us as a reason for action or emotion are our motives, variously described as loves and hates, desires and aversions—or "consistent goals," in Ross and Nisbett's phrase. I see no reason why such appetitive states, or a large class of them, should not count as traits of character. Brandt goes further, endorsing a "motivational theory of character traits" according to which a trait of character is always a "state of the person's *system of wants/aversions*."[39] That's going *too* far, I think. Such a theory seems a procrustean bed, too simple and too uniform a logical and explanatory structure to fit all our concepts of traits of character, and of virtues and vices. Courage, for example, is not, as Brandt proposes, simply "the absence . . . of an all-absorbing attachment to personal safety and position."[40] Proneness to fear, and ability to

---

[38] Mischel, *Introduction to Personality*, pp. 500–5.
[39] Brandt, "Traits of Character," pp. 27, 30; Brandt's italics.
[40] Ibid., p. 35.

handle it, are not simply functions of deep-seated attachments. Deep attachments are specific to objects of interest, fears to situations of danger. One may have learned to deal well only with some types of danger. It seems likely the dangers one handles well will in some cases be those one is practiced in facing rather than those that do not engage one's deepest attachments. Different forms of courage arguably are apt to involve different *competencies* (in Mischel's terms), and are nonetheless traits of character for that.

In arguing that not all virtues are simply, or even chiefly, motives, I don't mean to exclude the hypothesis that all of them necessarily involve some sort of fact about motivation. Even if courage, for instance, is not constituted chiefly by motives of a particular sort, or by lack of them, running a significant risk to achieve nothing that one really cares about can hardly be understood as an act of courage. Moreover, it seems extremely plausible to suppose that some traits of character, and some virtues and vices, are constituted *chiefly* by motives. We can hardly avoid this conclusion, indeed, if we think of the virtue of a whole character, as I do, as excellence in *being for the good*, which surely depends heavily on one's motives, on what one loves and what one wants.

*Benevolence*, desiring or aiming at the good of other people for its own sake, is a prime example of a motive that is widely regarded as a virtue—and rightly so, if it is relatively enduring. Benevolence is not worth much, we may think, if it never leads one actually to do good to others. Nevertheless the benevolence as such is a motive, defined by an end desired, and is thus a disposition to a type of psychological processing rather than directly to a type of behavior. It shapes behavior only in interaction with other appetitive states, and with cognitive states, as well as with situations. In a more sinister vein, *avarice*, an excessive desire for wealth, is a motive plausibly regarded as a vice. There is doubtless behavior that is avaricious, but it is characterized as such on the basis of its motive. The conceptual priority is on the other side in the case of a direct behavioral disposition: it is defined in terms of a type of behavior it tends to produce.

*Policies* and *principles* (principles to which one is committed) are a type of reason-shaping state worth discussing separately, though one might think of classing them under wants or desires. I suppose they are examples of the type of person variable that Mischel calls "self-regulatory systems and plans." Having a stable personal policy of not acting out of a desire to get even, so far as one is able to control oneself, is a way of being non-vindictive. I would call it a trait of character and a virtue. Being conscientious is largely a matter of being committed to moral principles. So understood, conscientiousness is not simply a behavioral disposition, though it surely involves at least an indirect behavioral disposition to be guided in action by the principles to which one is committed.

Treating commitment to a principle as a trait of character is not merely a possibility. For Kant the notion of character (in a sense in which it is possible not to have character) was specially connected to such commitment. To have character, according to him, "signifies that property of the will according to which the subject binds himself to certain practical principles which he has unalterably prescribed to himself through his own reason."[41] This too we may regard as too narrow a conception of character, but it would be bizarre to deny that it indicates at least one way of having a trait of character.

## 3.2. Cognitive States and Traits

Being committed to act on a principle is closely connected, in many cases, with the *belief* that the principle is right, or ethically sound. One could hold that belief without being really committed to act on the principle, but loss of the belief would typically lead to (or even amount to) loss of the commitment. It is doubtless in some sense correct to say that beliefs are *cognitive* rather than appetitive states. But it would be wrong to infer that they do not play a part in motivating behavior, for they help determine what we regard as reasons for action. Behavior is normally produced through the interaction of beliefs and other cognitive states with more straightforwardly appetitive states. In that sense we "act on" beliefs, and it would be questionable to ascribe a belief to someone who has no disposition to act on it, if it is relevant to action at all.

Some contemporary philosophers have argued that normal motivation of voluntary action in human adults can be understood entirely or almost entirely in terms of judgments and beliefs about reasons for action. I think that's going too far, in the opposite direction from Brandt; but I agree that action can often be explained in terms of such judgments and beliefs without invoking any special desire. In learning the language of evaluation and normativity part of what we normally learn is to use it in making decisions and governing our behavior. In learning this use of it we acquire a strong and quite general disposition to conformity between our behavior and our evaluative and normative judgments. When strong, I believe, this disposition can reasonably be counted as a virtue—a structural virtue, an excellent strength of rational self-government. It is distinct from any judgment, and can reasonably be classed as an appetitive rather than cognitive state; but it is not a "special desire."

It would be a mistake, however, to conclude that special desires play no morally important role in our motivation. Especially significant for the theory of virtues and vices are persistent, deep-seated desires. Suppose it appears that some person almost always does what he or she believes will most enhance his or her wealth. We are surely warranted in concluding, or at least strongly suspecting, that this person's behavior is largely controlled by a powerful desire for wealth. In so concluding we need not necessarily suppose that *beliefs* about the value of wealth, or about a desire for wealth, function as reasons in the person's practical thinking. The conclusion is not about a process of deliberation or practical

---

[41] Kant, *Anthropology*, Ak VII. 292.

reasoning, but about a desire that shapes such processes, and that may do so without being conscious.[42]

It is a part of popular wisdom that people's behavior is commonly more profoundly influenced by what they want than by what they think—more, that is, by desires and kindred affective and conative states than by their evaluative opinions. I think the popular wisdom is right on this point. Sometimes this is a matter of judgment being overridden by passion. But sometimes it is rather a matter of a deep desire or "passion" controlling the larger pattern of one's life, including one's choices and also what reasons one will see as salient. The deep desire may be for money or control, for instance. The passion may be infatuation or love for a particular person. Deep conative and affective states of this sort are quite resistant to change by rational persuasion; and I think they probably should be, even though evil as well as good can come of such resistance. We rightly rely on them as predictors of behavior. If we are focused on deep states of this sort, we are typically not wrong to care more about what people want than about what they think. It is largely for such reasons as this that it is plausible to define some of the most important virtues chiefly in terms of what one *loves*.

For comparable reasons, however, virtue and vice can also be found very plausibly in beliefs, outlooks, sensitivities, and other broadly cognitive dispositions regarding questions of value and normativity. They may shape our behavior without needing any particular desire to explain how they do so, beyond the general disposition to conform our behavior to our judgment. One may have beliefs that are humane or inhumane, enlightened or bigoted, deep or shallow, reasonable or unreasonable, fair- or unfair-minded. One's characteristic ways of looking at things, or "consistent ways of interpreting [one's] world," as Ross and Nisbett might call them, can be good or bad in similar respects.

These broadly cognitive states play a major part in constituting a person's character. If someone holds white-supremacist or other racist views, that is not a fact external to his character. Such features of a person's way of thinking clearly have great influence on action and feeling, and are often themselves ways in which one is for or against something good or bad. They can also be quite persistent. As Ross and Nisbett observe, "it is notoriously difficult to change someone's political views."[43] If morally significant beliefs and outlooks are relatively enduring, and sufficiently prominent in the economy of a person's life, it is reasonable to count them as traits of character, and often, certainly, as virtues and vices. Surely much of what is horrifying about Hitler, for example, was constituted by aspects of the ways in which he *viewed* the world, and people in it.

---

[42] This paragraph and the next are adapted from Adams, "Scanlon's Contractualism," p. 574. Of that paper, pp. 572–8 contain more extensive discussion of the roles of desire and cognitive states in motivation.

[43] Ross and Nisbett, *The Person and the Situation*, p. 35.

### 3.3. Must Virtues Be Direct Behavioral Dispositions After All?

The suggestion that virtues may be constituted in large part by motives and cognitive states and traits will not pass unchallenged. Doris is "happy to allow that people manifest considerable reliability with regard to variables like beliefs, goals, values, and attitudes; at any rate, more so than they do with overt behaviors." He claims, however, that empirical evidence indicates that consistent attitudes, goals, and values often fail to produce behavioral consistency. "And consistency with regard to more overt behavior is," he insists, "central to our thinking on moral character."[44] Readers might take this as suggesting that the "consistent attitudes, goals, and values" do not have the role that virtues and vices must have. Doris does not make it unambiguously explicit that he is arguing for this conclusion. But he is evidently arguing against the thought that the relative stability of some personal variables other than direct behavioral dispositions might provide a reason for resisting situationist skepticism about character.

I will resist the temptation to dismiss this argument on the ground that it slights the intrinsic moral significance of motives and attitudes. Though I will resist it, I do want to dwell for a while on some of the reasons that give rise to the temptation. While overt behavior has an undoubted moral importance, I believe it is by no means all that counts morally. Officially, Doris does not disagree; he claims to have "been at pains to acknowledge that the importance of personal variables is not limited to their contribution to overt behavior."[45] But this acknowledgment seems to me largely ignored in his argument. If persistent personal variables have a non-instrumental goodness or badness beyond their influence on overt behavior, why should we think only about behavioral consistency in judging whether they are virtues or vices?

This point is hugely important for the place of virtue in ethical theory. If enduring personal qualities are morally important and valuable only for the value of actions to which they contribute, then a theory of virtues and vices can hardly be more than a pendant to the ethics of actions. I am as interested as I am in the ethics of virtues and vices because I believe that the value of what we *are* morally is important independently, to some extent, of the value of what we *do*.

Indeed, I believe that the value of what we do often depends in large part on the value of our attitudes and enduring traits. This view will be rejected by any who believe that the value of the material or physical consequences of our acts virtually always swamps any competitors in the grounding of moral value. But while I grant that the latter view is humanly understandable and even intellectually respectable, it seems to me at bottom insane and dehumanizing. Surely the most important good we can do in relation to each other lies often in the expression of love, respect, honor, solidarity, and the like. And such expression is not worth much if it is not sincere—that is, if the valuable attitude expressed

---

[44] Doris, *Lack of Character*, pp. 87–8.     [45] Ibid., p. 87.

is not really present. In many cases, moreover, an expression that may be sincere at the moment is still devalued if the affection, concern, or respect expressed is unreliable, unstable, or inconsistent with attitudes that emerge in other contexts.

Why resist the temptation to dismiss, for such reasons, Doris's comments? Because it is also true that motives, principles, moral views, and other attitudes, enduring or transitory, can be devalued by behavior that is inconsistent with them. If they are to have the excellence that qualifies them as virtues, they should not be impotent in the shaping of behavior. Hence even virtues that are not simply behavioral dispositions, and that are centered in causally or explanatorily deeper features of a person's psychology, should normally involve behavioral dispositions of some sort.

It is therefore important, in rejecting the argument suggested by Doris's comments, to be clear that motives, beliefs, and commitments do contribute to shaping behavior in ways that accord with them. This is not to say that any attitude a person holds will always shape her behavior in accordance with it. The psychic processing that produces behavior is too complex for that.[46] In addition, hypocrisy, self-deception, and just plain thoughtlessness and weakness of will are common enough and familiar enough to make it unsurprising that attitudes of broad scope have been found to be quite "tenuously" correlated with "single behavioral measures." On the other hand, as Doris acknowledges, "aggregated behavioral measures correlate more impressively with attitudes . . . than do single behavioral measures." And "more specific attitudes, such as attitudes toward particular behaviors, may be strongly associated with specific behaviors."[47]

It is also relevant that overt behavior is significantly likelier to be consistent with attitudes, goals, and values if they are consciously held, and if the behavior issues from well-informed planning and deliberation.[48] This is not surprising at all, but is ethically significant, as the more deliberated decisions are commonly regarded as the more defining personal decisions, morally (and indeed legally). They have not always been treated as more important by social psychologists. Much of the situationist evidence of morally inconsistent behavior comes from contexts of relatively unreflective behavior. Sometimes, indeed, it comes from contexts in which experimenters have set up what I would call a moral ambush, taking subjects by surprise or even deceiving them. This may be reasonable in terms of the explanatory projects of the psychologists, but it does not follow that the more deliberated decisions do not have a special moral significance.

The idea that "deliberate" sins are more serious than "inadvertent" sins has a very long history, and wide influence. This is a point at which the intrinsic value of motives and attitudes seems relevant. I doubt that deliberate sins are viewed with more gravity because they are thought to have worse consequences

---

[46] Eagly and Chaiken, *The Psychology of Attitudes*, pp. 155, 159.
[47] Doris, *Lack of Character*, p. 87.
[48] Eagly and Chaiken, *The Psychology of Attitudes*, pp. 168–92, 216.

than inadvertent sins. It would be very hard to prove (and indeed is not clearly true) that they do. Rather the deliberate sins are thought to have a greater non-instrumental badness, as expressions of what the agent is for and against in a more personally authenticated way.

## 4. AFFILIATIONS AND SOCIAL ROLES

In sections 2 and 3 I have argued that people actually have enduring personal qualities that are candidates for moral evaluation. These are of quite a variety of psychological and relational types: motives, principled policies, beliefs, as well as modular and probabilistic behavioral dispositions. They are enduring in the sense that people commonly are pretty consistent over time with regard to them. It is hard to deny that at least some of these qualities are morally preferable to others. I believe that we have not found, and will not find, any compelling objection to regarding some of them as virtues.

These are not the only types of property that characterize persons in enduring and morally significant ways. In most human lives there are actual social relationships that are persistent features of the moral structure of those lives. People often characterize themselves, and others, in terms of their affiliations and social roles. Statements like 'I'm a Christian' or 'I'm a life-long Democrat' may be used as part of a way of saying what kind of person the speaker is, at least partly in an ethical dimension. And 'He's a good father,' or ' . . . a good citizen,' is ethical praise, and praise of character inasmuch as it ascribes an enduring property to the person. I believe that affiliations and social roles play an important part in constituting moral character, and virtues and vices. This will doubtless be a controversial view. It is obvious that social roles and affiliations are often very persistent attributes of human individuals, and often are morally significant. But it will be debated whether their social and relational character excludes them from the class of moral virtues. Treating them as traits of character blurs the line between situational and personal or character variables. I think that line deserves to be blurred, but some may disagree.

Consider first *affiliations*. Religious and political affiliations are closely connected with ethically relevant beliefs. If we say that someone is a Christian or a Muslim, we may mean only to characterize the individual's religious beliefs. Alternatively, we may mean only to ascribe membership in a religious community or institution. More often, I suppose, we mean both, and more, and what we mean is freighted with ethical significance. An analogous array of *political* meanings would have been available, in Europe in the 1930s, for saying that someone was a Nazi or a Communist or a Socialist or a Liberal. In all these cases what is said about an individual is expressed in terms of a relation to a concrete, historically contingent institution, organization, or movement. If you identify *yourself* in terms of such an affiliation, however, it probably will not come naturally to you to think of that identity as something external to your moral character. Or perhaps you will think of your moral character as internal to your religious identity rather than the other way around.

Such affiliations are commonly as durable as most traits of character. They contribute, often strongly and pervasively, to the shaping of action and attitude. I suppose we do not usually classify being a Christian or being a Socialist as a trait of character or a virtue or vice, but why shouldn't we, at least if it is a matter of being a "good" or committed one? In general, affiliation with a good cause does seem virtuous, and affiliation with a bad cause seems antithetical to virtue. This makes perfectly good sense if we think of virtue as a matter of excellence in being for the good. Willing participation in something good is good. Willing participation in something bad is bad. Both the goodness and the badness are broadly moral. Most human lives participate in both.

We can be for the good together in ways in which we cannot be for the good by ourselves, by being for the good in projects that are essentially common projects (as discussed in chapter 6). Not only in religion and politics, but also in more broadly cultural matters such as science and music, there are excellent ways of being for the good that are essentially collaborative projects. One of the interesting possibilities of being for the good together is that a group can be more firmly and unconditionally committed to a cause or project than most of its members can be individually. You may know that you will manage to be very active for a certain cause only during a fairly limited period of your life. But as a member of the group, if it is strong enough, you may still be able to say, '*We* are committed to see this through to the end, however long it takes.' Religious and political identities provide a way of sharing in the (real or supposed) excellence of a larger way of being for the good than could be sustained by one's own individual resources alone. That is undoubtedly part of the appeal of such identities. In such contexts the value of what *we* are for affects, though it does not totally determine, the value of what *I* am for.

This may puzzle or disturb because it implies that the determinants of a person's virtue and vice do not always lie entirely within the actions and internal states of the individual. Some of them may lie elsewhere in a community or movement of which the individual is a member. Is your loyalty to your church or political party a virtue and a way of being for the good? That may reasonably depend in part on what that group's projects actually are, and what their ethical and human significance is, and not just on what you think the group stands for. Indeed, you may even *intend* to be understood in a general way as being for what your church is for, or for what your party is for. And your cognitive grasp of the supposed goods that you are for may be much less than the grasp you assume the leaders of your church or party have of them.[49]

---

[49] I am indebted to Richard Boyd for encouraging me to develop this line of thought. He suggested, in conversation, that there may be a defensible externalism about moral character,

It may be impossible to avoid ambivalent assessments in such matters. When Hans Delmotte arrived at Auschwitz as a young SS doctor and first witnessed its horror, he was nauseated and refused to participate in selecting prisoners for the gas chambers. He is reported, instead, to have "said he requested either to be sent to the Front or he himself should be gassed," and that "he would never have joined the SS if he had 'known that there was such a thing as Auschwitz'."[50] He may well have felt that he had been deceived, and his ideals betrayed, by those responsible for the camp; and one might have thought him justified in that complaint. However, in evaluating his character as he arrived at the camp—to what extent, if at all, he was for the good—we probably won't be willing just to abstract from the actual malignity of the organization to which he had committed himself. And we probably shouldn't be willing to abstract from it if we believe that moral qualities can depend on luck at all.[51] I do think the moral significance of a negligent action can depend in part on its innocuous or disastrous consequences. So also the moral significance of affiliations and allegiances which may be stable and structuring features of one's moral stance in life can depend in part on the actual character of the communities, movements, and projects to which one is committed. There is a partly external dimension of moral evaluation, and it has its own validity.

But an internal dimension of moral evaluation also has its own validity. Rightly uneasy about "guilt by association," we cannot wholly abandon the effort to abstract from external factors in evaluating character. In such evaluation we think it quite relevant to wonder about Delmotte's previous naïveté or complicity. Was he self-deceived or negligent, too complacent? Did he already have some degree of conscious partnership in the evils that now shocked him? He is said to have held an anti-Semitic belief in combating "Jewish influence," though with less inhumane measures.[52] On the other hand, it is only right to give full weight to the honorableness of his initial reaction to Auschwitz, in its contrast with the moral corruption of the organization to which he belonged.

---

analogous to the "externalism about the mental" that has been influential in recent philosophy of language and philosophy of mind. Without entering into the debate about the merits of the latter externalism, I would say that my view about moral character does have some analogy with it—for instance, in the roles that deference to expert understanding plays in the two views. There is a significant disanalogy, however, in that the widely discussed externalism about the mental is grounded largely in the role of social convention in language, and I do not think that moral character is conventional in the way that language is.

[50] Lifton, *The Nazi Doctors*, p. 309.

[51] Moral luck, as it has been called, will be discussed in chapter 9, sections 4 to 6. In view of what we will see in chapter 9 about "the power of the situation," I am inclined, in thinking about Delmotte's character as he arrived at Auschwitz, largely to abstract from the appalling end of his story. After two weeks of Josef Mengele's persuasion, Delmotte consented to do selections, and did them until they ceased at Auschwitz. At the end of the war he killed himself (Lifton, *The Nazi Doctors*, pp. 310–11).

[52] Ibid., p. 310.

This is a rather extreme example of the relation between affiliation and moral character. Human institutions, organizations, and movements rarely are wholly good or wholly evil. It is virtually inevitable that knowledgeable and morally clear-sighted individuals who play a significant part in such collective projects accept a degree of complicity in some evils while they seek to correct others and help achieve the goods of the project. They may well be justified in doing so, but it doesn't follow that they are morally untainted by their complicity. They can reasonably claim as their own a share in excellences of the common project that do not depend entirely on them. And while they may think and do things that distance them in some ways from its less savory features, it does not follow that their complicity in those features is not also an aspect of what they are like ethically.

The purely internal and the more external dimensions of evaluation may cohabit uneasily in our minds. There may be no unified perspective in which they fit seamlessly together. The moral facts may be more adequately appreciated by a certain ambivalence than by any summary verdict. That is not to deny that we should have high admiration for some lives that are lived in contexts of disturbing moral ambiguity.

Granting that character may not be purely internal to the individual is a way of softening the dichotomy between personal and situational factors in explaining behavior. Psychologists who emphasize the influence of situational factors on the behavior of individuals also point out that the influence goes both ways. The situational factors have often been shaped in part by the individual. "People in everyday circumstances do not just 'happen' to face the particular situations that compel and constrain their behavior. They actively choose many of the situations to which they expose themselves," and "they transform situations by their presence, their demeanor, and their behavior."[53]

The behavior of the priest and the playboy may predictably fit persistent patterns in a variety of social contexts, and be predictably different from each other's behavior and the behavior of other people in the same contexts. The situationist will point out that the priest and the playboy will differ quite noticeably in the types of contexts in which they are likely to be found. Moreover, they are not in the same *situation* as others even in the same *contexts*. For the expectations and attitudes directed at them in those contexts, which may affect their behavior profoundly, are quite different from those directed at others in the same contexts. But where individuals have such differences in their typical contexts and in the attitudes of others toward them, those differences are apt to be rooted largely in differences in their own individual choices, commitments, preferences, styles, and social history.

---

[53] Ross and Nisbett, *The Person and the Situation*, pp. 154–5; cf. Mischel, *Introduction to Personality*, pp. 510–11.

This brings us to the topic of *social roles*. The types of social contexts in which individuals are likely to be found, and the roles they are likely to play in those contexts, are relatively durable, and often morally significant, characteristics of the individuals. They are shaped by morally significant, though not always consciously voluntary, choices and qualities of the individuals themselves, as well as by more external features of their situations, including the actions and attitudes of other people. In setting the aims of moral education, parents and teachers are concerned about these factors in something like the same way as about motives, and rightly so. One of the commoner, and probably more commonly successful, ways of trying to learn to be good is by learning to inhabit well a good social role. One can learn to be a good parent, a good friend, a good teacher, a good supervisor, a good citizen. This is not the only, nor probably the most admirable, way of being virtuous. But I believe it can and sometimes does issue in a sort of genuine excellence in being for the good, which may constitute a genuine virtue.

Such a virtue (or module of virtue) is apt to be profoundly dependent on social context. The virtue of being a good citizen of a democratic state, for example, cannot be fully learned or practiced except in the context of a more or less democratic state. Moreover, your disposition to act in ways that sustain a role is likely to be materially strengthened by your perception that people around you view you as occupying the role. A morally good response in certain situations may be sustained in large part by a role you have chosen, or at least accepted, and the attitudes toward you that your role has engendered in others. But your disposition to act well, morally, in role-sustaining ways is still a feature of what you are like morally. And it can have a good motive in appreciation of the value of so acting, even if it is also encouraged by others' acceptance of your role. If it is in fact well motivated, and a relatively enduring disposition, then I think it may reasonably be regarded as a virtue or a module of virtue.

The excellence of being good at a social role will not be neatly separable from the moral value of the role itself and of the institutions and common projects that provide its indispensable context. In particular, if collective projects that shape the role of an *R* are bad enough, it seems that being "a good *R*" will be no virtue. It may still be possible to manifest virtue in occupying the role of an *R*, but that is likely to involve subverting the role rather than being, in the usual sense, "a good *R*."

Because social roles are so easily and often formed or coopted by unsavory collective projects, the idea that being good at a social role can be a virtue may arouse suspicion. Over the centuries people have committed terrible wrongs telling themselves they were being "good soldiers." And being a "good worker" in the wrong bureaucratic context might conceivably lead to doing as Adolf Eichmann did. Even when a social role is not defined by thoroughly vicious projects, we should consider the possibility that inhabiting it in a truly virtuous way would involve being sensitive to values that are in tension with those that guide one's society in defining the role. Such critical distance in relation to one's social context can be very important for avoiding serious evils. It is plausible to hold at least that any social role can be inhabited more virtuously with it than without it. The moral importance of this point will be underlined in chapter 9.

We should not underestimate the pervasiveness of our dependence on social roles. It seems unlikely that any child makes much progress in virtue, or even in life, without learning to be reasonably good at a number of social roles, before becoming capable of very much critical distance. We are social animals, and arguably even more dependent on collaboration than our distant ancestors whose economies involved less elaborate division of labor. We can hardly live without social roles, and individuals cannot create their social roles by themselves. What social roles we can occupy and learn to be good at depends largely on the culture, institutions, and common projects of the people among whom we live. What possibilities of virtue are available to human individuals depends to some extent on what roles are available in their societies. Many who are interested in virtue may find this dependence disturbing. Individual virtue's dependence on social context and social support will be a major topic of chapter 9.

# 9

# Moral Frailty and Moral Luck

In chapter 8 I identified two problems, one about moral inconsistency and one about frailty, that situationist arguments have presented as objections to belief in the reality of virtues. My arguments in chapter 8 addressed the inconsistency problem, trying to identify morally significant traits of character with respect to which individuals are acknowledged to be relatively consistent over time. Some of the traits with respect to which this consistency is found, however, are of rather narrow scope. I have only begun to address the question whether the traits that are psychologically and socially real and persistent are too fragmentary to constitute virtues. That is a question that opens into much older issues connected with the ancient thesis of "the unity of the virtues." They will be discussed in chapters 10 and 11.

Before taking up that ancient theme, however, we must address the situationists' other problem about the reality of virtue. That is the *frailty* they see in supposed virtues in relation to what they have called "the power of the situation."[1] From it arise the themes of the present chapter. It is claimed that much experimental evidence shows that the influence of personal qualities or traits on overt behavior can be swamped, in morally significant contexts, by the influence of situational variables. This may be thought to imply that personal qualities and traits lack a *robustness*, as John Doris puts it, that virtues must have, and that in that way they are not *excellent* enough to be virtues. This is in my opinion the most disturbing of situationist objections to the reality of virtue.

## 1. SITUATIONIST EXPERIMENTS AND THE FRAILTY OF VIRTUE

The principal foundation of situationist claims about the frailty of supposed virtues is found in experiments intended to identify factors that explain variations in human behavior. It is claimed that such experiments have shown that situational factors that seem to have little moral significance have more explanatory power than the personal qualities we are likeliest to regard as virtues. And this is taken as evidence that those personal qualities are too weak to qualify as virtues.

---

[1] This is the title of the second chapter of Ross and Nisbett, *The Person and the Situation*.

## 1.1. Helpfulness and Imperfect Obligation

Care is required in using situational variability in behavior as evidence of weakness of a supposed virtue. Response to situations is much affected by the ways in which individuals perceive the situations, as situationist psychologists emphasize. And many factors may shape such perceptions. One consideration that will commonly need to be taken into account in using behavioral evidence to judge the strength of virtuous motivation is whether a strict and perfect obligation is at stake in the behavior in question. A perfect obligation (as explained in chapter 8, section 2.1) is one that is violated if one fails in any single case to behave in a particular way. An imperfect obligation is satisfied if one "does enough" of the relevant sort of thing.

This consideration is important for thinking about the significance of helping behavior, which is a recurrent topic of situationist experimental work. Helpfulness is in general a virtue of imperfect obligation (or of supererogatory or non-obligatory action). We do not expect anyone to help on every occasion that presents itself. It is acceptable, and normal even in helpful people, that one sometimes does not help. So perhaps we should not find it shocking that not helping can often be explained in large part by situational variables, and even by an apparently trivial situational variable, as in the case of the payphone with and without a dime.

That experimental situation, mentioned in chapter 8, section 1, is one in which a woman who had dropped a folder-full of papers was helped by fourteen of sixteen people who had just found a dime in a payphone, and was not helped by twenty-four of twenty-five who had not found a dime. Some have argued that motives of helpfulness must be appallingly weak if they are so strongly affected by such a trivial situational variable, but I am not convinced. Both helpers and non-helpers probably regarded helping in such a situation as a non-obligatory kindness rather than a matter of strict and perfect obligation. As Doris remarks in presenting the case, "Scattered papers are a less-than-dire predicament, so the omission is not serious."[2] And it is not clearly a moral fault to regard oneself as free to allow oneself to be influenced by trivial factors, including whims and moods, in deciding when and how to perform what are at most imperfect obligations. The experimenters' explanation of the influence of the dime is that it put subjects in a better mood, and "feeling good leads to helping."[3] No doubt all of us are aware that we are likelier to do some good things when we are in a good mood, but it hardly seems reasonable to refuse to count as a virtue any trait whose

[2] Doris, *Lack of Character*, p. 31.
[3] Ibid., p. 30. Referring to this experiment, Sabini and Silver ("Lack of Character?" p. 540) note that "one of the ways that. . . mood effects are thought to operate is via attention. Good moods are thought to broaden attention, bad moods to violate it." So, if finding the dime puts you in a good mood, you may be likelier to notice the dropped papers than if you emerge from the phone booth in a bad mood.

manifestation is influenced by moods. Conceptions of human virtue should be apt for characterizing human beings, not ethical computers.

It is worth emphasizing that the dime is the salient variable, but not the only factor in the situation that must be supposed relevant to explanation of the observed behavior. That is underlined by the fact that variants of the dime-finding experiment have not always yielded the same result.[4] Other factors might be (and I suspect were) that the incidents occurred at a suburban American shopping center, and that it was a respectable-looking woman who dropped the folder-full of papers. The dime by itself surely would not be enough to assure or explain helping behavior. It's thinkable that someone finding a dime might just say to himself, "Wow! It's my lucky day. She dropped a pile of papers but I found a dime"—and walk right on by her, singing, "Oh what a beautiful morning! Oh, what a beautiful day!" Why didn't most of the dime-finders do that? Surely because they had some predisposition to helpfulness (probably having been socialized to it). What the experiment shows is one factor that turns out to affect whether such a predisposition is activated on a particular occasion.

But there are forms of helping toward which people in the same culture are not so uniformly predisposed. Suppose what the subjects found on stepping out of the phone booth was a shabby but unthreatening-looking person asking for money. I imagine the percentage of non-dime-finders who would help in that context would remain low, but the percentage of dime-finders who would help would be significantly lower than in the paper-dropping example. One reason for that is that people in the suburban American culture have different personal policies as to whether they will give to mendicants in public places. Some will never do so, as a matter of policy. (Remember that policies easily find a place, as "self-regulatory systems and plans," among the "person variables" situationists agree influence behavior, as argued in chapter 8, section 3.)

I once had the policy of never giving in the street because it's inefficient giving. Some years ago I changed my policy. I still think it's inefficient giving, as regards what the money will do, but my policy is now to give sometimes, for the sake of the respectful human interaction that it facilitates. Since I don't always give, however, I'm quite conscious that various more or less trivial contingencies strongly affect my decision to give or not in a particular case. I am less likely to give, not only if the mendicant seems too aggressive or threatening, but also if I'm in a hurry or have my hands (literally) full. I'm more likely to give if I have the right sort of coin in an outside pocket than if I'd have to unbutton three raincoat buttons and dig it out of my wallet. And those are just some of the *conscious* factors in my case.

Still I do have the policy of sometimes giving to mendicants, and it does affect my behavior. Some people I respect don't have it, and I can remember not having it myself. It makes me significantly more likely than I was before to respond to

[4] See Doris, *Lack of Character*, p. 180 (n. 4).

an instance of mendicancy by giving. I don't see why I shouldn't think of having that policy as a module of benevolence, one which can be, and was, acquired independently, to some extent, of other modules of benevolence.

There are cases, of course, in which there is a strict and perfect obligation to help another person. An experiment much cited in the literature under consideration here is discussed by some philosophers as well as psychologists in terms that suggest they see it as concerned with such a case. The "subjects" of the experiment were on their way to an appointment, during which they would give a brief talk. Slumped in a doorway along their route lay a collaborator of the experimenters who feigned distress, coughing and groaning. Whether the subjects offered help was found to vary chiefly with the extent to which they were in a hurry. Of those who were told they were already late for their appointment, only 10 percent paused to offer any assistance to the apparent sufferer, or to tell anyone about him.[5] It has been argued that the fact of being in a hurry in this situation is "pretty trivial," and that its determinative power therefore tells against there being "powerful altruistic forces in [the] psychological makeup" of the subjects.[6] Since there is no reason to think the subjects (seminarians in the original experiment) were less altruistic than most of us, this has also been taken as a reason for a rather general doubt of the reality of altruistic motives strong enough to constitute a virtue.

I believe that the assumptions of a strict obligation and of the triviality of the situational variable are both highly questionable in this case. As to the former, we should not overlook a feature of the experiment (in its original and most cited version) that often goes unmentioned in the philosophical commentary. The experimenters state that it was part of the plan of the experiment that "the victim should appear somewhat ambiguous—ill-dressed, possibly in need of help, but also possibly drunk or even potentially dangerous."[7] Do we really believe there is *always* a *strict* obligation to offer help in "somewhat ambiguous" cases like that?[8]

As to the supposed triviality of the situational variable, we are concerned here with something more momentous than a mood effect. The fact of thinking oneself late for an appointment engages the motive of wanting to fulfill the demands of one's social roles. People want not to disappoint certain kinds of social expectations, especially the expectations of persons in the sort of authoritative positions assumed by the experimenters in this and other similar cases. More broadly we want to seem, and to be, in tune with our social surroundings. For better *and* for worse, this is a powerful motive in virtually all humans. We shall shortly be dealing with much more troubling evidence of its power. It is not hard to think

---

[5] Darley and Batson, " 'From Jerusalem to Jericho'."

[6] Campbell, "Can Philosophical Accounts of Altruism Accommodate Experimental Data on Helping Behavior?" p. 41.

[7] Darley and Batson, " 'From Jerusalem to Jericho'," p. 102. This point receives appropriate emphasis in Sabini and Silver, "Lack of Character?" p. 558.

[8] This point is perceptively noted in Kamtekar, "Situationism and Virtue Ethics," pp. 472–6.

of Darwinian reasons why its power should not surprise us, and why we might not think it wholly a misfortune that it is so strong in us.[9] A motive that can be swamped by it is not necessarily a weak motive. We might well think better of subjects if they stopped to help, but their not stopping, when late for an appointment, hardly tends to show they had no strong altruistic tendencies.

## 1.2. Milgram's Experiments and Perfect Obligation

Unfortunately it is hardly in doubt that apparently virtuous dispositions are sometimes overcome by the power of social situations even in contexts of strict and perfect obligation. Empirical evidence of this, and at the same time of the strength of the motive of social conformity, is dramatically presented in Stanley Milgram's famous experiments on obedience.[10] Milgram and his associates found that, under the pretense of experimenting on the role of punishment in learning, they could get subjects to administer what they falsely believed to be electrical shocks of increasing (and alarming) strength to another person. As the supposed intensity of the shocks increased, subjects often evinced distress at what they were doing, and objected verbally. But even after verbally refusing to continue beyond a certain point, many did in fact continue when the experimenter refused permission to stop. In most versions of the experiments a substantial proportion of the subjects (as many as 65 percent in some versions) continued their (supposed) shocking all the way to the maximum. The subjects were put under no pressure beyond that of an experimenter telling them that they "must" go on. And as the "shocks" intensified, the supposed victim put on a convincing show of severe distress and possibly serious injury. The behavior of these subjects has seemed morally unjustifiable to virtually all reflective commentators.

Harman claims that the number and proportion of subjects in these experiments who went to high levels of shock is so large that we cannot plausibly attribute their behavior to "a character defect."[11] That hardly follows. Is it really so implausible to suppose that almost everyone has a certain character defect? Is it a tautology that character must be worse than average to be defective? Has it not at least historically been a widely held belief that most or all of us have traits of character in some ways sinful?

A more moderate version of Harman's claim surely is plausible, however. It is not credible to attribute the behavior of most of Milgram's subjects to notable wickedness. It is highly probable that most of them were people who would generally be regarded as of pretty good character. It seems we must conclude that it is possible, by manipulation of situational variables involving social authority, to get many normally decent people to inflict harm (as they suppose) on others, to a

---

[9] Cf. Milgram, *Obedience to Authority*, pp. 123–5; and Krueger and Funder, "Towards a Balanced Social Psychology."

[10] In my account here I summarize the results reported in Milgram, *Obedience to Authority*.

[11] Harman, "Moral Philosophy Meets Social Psychology," p. 322.

degree that is morally wrong. And that does strongly suggest that personal dispositions that normally sustain moral decency can be overcome in some cases by the power of the situation.[12]

Milgram's experiments involved a highly artificial situation, involving staged and pretended harms rather than real ones. Unfortunately, history leaves little doubt that situational factors can lead normally decent people to inflict real harm on real people in obedience to grossly immoral orders. Nazi crimes against humanity provide an obvious example, cited repeatedly in Milgram's work; and the history of warfare indicates that the Nazi context is not unique in this respect.[13]

Milgram's findings clearly and explicitly leave room for the hypothesis that there are personal traits that enable and dispose people to resist authoritative pressures to do harm. In none of the versions of the experiment reported in his book did more than 65 percent of subjects go on administering "shocks" to the maximum level. At same point 35 percent, or more in some versions, refused and withdrew from the experiment. The latter were classified by Milgram as "defiant" subjects.

We may also want to know at what point the "defiant" subjects refused to go on punishing. Typical responses to the Milgram experiments assume, plausibly, that we are dealing here with a matter of strict or perfect obligation. It seems that the subjects had a strict or perfect moral duty to refuse cooperation with the experimenter, given their belief that the apparatus of the experiment really delivered very painful shocks to another person. At what point did it become a strict or perfect duty? In typical versions of the experiment the subject was led to believe that the victim (the "learner") had voluntarily agreed to his part in the procedure. But at a certain point in the process, at a level of "strong shock," the subject heard the learner, who had been strapped in his chair, begin to demand to be released from the experiment. That withdrawal of consent may plausibly be taken as marking the point at which the subject begins to have a strict obligation to desist. Interestingly, in most of the versions of the experiment that proceeded more or less as I've just described, the proportion of subjects that desisted at or (less commonly) before that point was 15 percent or more.

Can we identify traits of character or personal qualities that distinguish the defiant subjects from those that obeyed all the way to the end? Milgram tried. He found statistically significant correlations of defiant or obedient behavior in the experiment with one aspect of ethical thinking, which I will mention presently. He found such correlations also with some types of religious affiliation, educational level, and professional and military background, though not with political affiliation. He concludes, however,

---

[12] Milgram draws a similar conclusion in *Obedience to Authority*, p. 205.
[13] Cf. Milgram, *Obedience to Authority*, pp. 179–89, on the My Lai massacre in Vietnam.

My over-all reaction was to wonder at how few correlates there were of obedience and disobedience and how weakly they were related to the observed behavior. I am certain that there is a complex personality basis to obedience and disobedience. But I know we have not found it.[14]

Based on interviews, rather than their behavior, a relatively small number of undergraduates[15] who participated in a version of the experiment were also rated on Lawrence Kohlberg's scale of moral reasoning development. This is a scale on which, roughly, those whose ethical reasoning is more principled are rated higher. A majority of the defiant subjects were rated higher on this scale than almost any of the obedient ones. Kohlberg makes quite a bit of this finding. However, the numbers are small (including only eight defiant subjects), and the content and use of Kohlberg's scale are not free of controversy. Milgram's more cautious verdict seems to me justified: "the findings are suggestive, though not very strong."[16]

The dimension of ethical thinking that Milgram himself found most interestingly correlated with obedience and defiance is assignment of responsibility. He found that among sixty-one defiant and fifty-seven obedient subjects, the defiant assigned significantly more of the responsibility for the punishment to themselves than the obedient subjects did, and significantly less to the victim (only half as much).[17] The two groups did not differ significantly in the proportion of responsibility assigned to the experimenter. The experimental finding therefore relates only suggestively to Milgram's own theory of "the process of obedience," in which a principal mechanism in producing the shockingly high rates of compliance in his experiments is a transfer of responsibility from the subject to the authority figure. "The most far-reaching consequence of [regarding oneself as an agent of an authority] is that a man feels responsible *to* the authority directing him but feels no responsibility *for* the content of the actions that the authority prescribes."[18]

That such a shift of responsibility is a factor in producing compliance seems very plausible, though Milgram evidently regards it as less than the "complex personality basis" he thinks the phenomena must have. It may be significant that the strongest form of pressure the authority figure in Milgram's experiments was allowed to apply was saying, "You *must* go on." The compliant subjects seem to have allowed the authority figure to define what they *had* to do. This contrasts in an interesting way with a feature of some of the most studied phenomena of actual resistance to powerful social or situational pressure to do wrong.

---

[14] Milgram, *Obedience to Authority*, pp. 203–5.

[15] Thirty four of them according to Milgram, *Obedience to Authority*, p. 205; twenty-six or twenty-seven according to Kohlberg, *Essays on Moral Development*, vol. 2, pp. 546–8.

[16] Ibid., p. 205. For even stronger reservations about the value of Kohlberg's results, see Doris, *Lack of Character*, p. 48, and references there.

[17] Milgram, *Obedience to Authority*, pp. 203–4.

[18] Ibid., pp. 145–6.

In the appalling history of the genocidal Nazi persecution of Jews there are some inspiring cases (though far fewer than we should wish) of individuals who did resist the pressures of the Nazi system by trying, sometimes successfully, to rescue Jews. This was a risky, and often costly, thing to do. Some rescuers lost their lives; others suffered imprisonment or great financial loss. And some were reviled by neighbors even after the war as well as during it. There have been a number of attempts to illuminate this phenomenon of exceptional altruism through interviews with surviving rescuers. To my mind the clearest and most convincing common thread of motivation to emerge from these interviews is that very many of the rescuers said that helping Jews who came to them was something they "had" to do.[19] The interviews do not suggest any shared metaethical understanding of "having to do" in this context. It's pretty clear that the affirmation was typically not exactly one of moral duty. 'I have to' is used in many different ways. I think the one thing it always signifies is that alternatives to the indicated course of action are judged unworthy of further consideration.[20] The reasons for the judgment may be moral or may be rooted in relatively trivial personal projects. So perhaps what the rescuers have most clearly indicated about their motivation is that when Jews appeared on their doorstep they judged that not helping them was not an alternative worthy of consideration. Without such an attitude, as Lawrence Blum suggests,[21] it would probably have been more difficult to accept, for months on end, the risks of sheltering Jews from the Nazis.

What Milgram's experimenter was telling his subjects was structurally very similar. "You *must* go on" means there is no alternative worthy of consideration, in view of your participation in the experiment. Typically, indeed, the experimenter said, "You have no other choice, you *must* go on." Justification offered for this claim would not have gone beyond "The experiment requires that you continue."[22] Compliant subjects allowed the experimenter to structure their perception of what they *had* to do. "One way the experimenter induced obedience was this: he interpreted for the subject what the appropriate way to act was in

[19] This is true both of rescuers whose rescuing was part of a shared effort of a close-knit community (Hallie, *Lest Innocent Blood Be Shed*; Blum, "Community and Virtue") and those who acted alone (Monroe, "John Donne's People," especially p. 428; Monroe *et al.*, "Altruism and the Theory of Rational Action"). Blum (pp. 242–50) offers particularly illuminating comments on the significance of such statements, without giving a metaethical account of their content.

[20] In a very interesting discussion in Zagzebski, *Divine Motivation Theory*, pp. 151–9, the nature of moral obligation is explained in terms of "seeing an act as admitting of no alternative" (p. 152). That is plausibly part of the phenomenology of obligation. But I think that seeing an act as admitting of no alternative need not be grounded in anything we would call an obligation. For example, I may think "I have to" go downstairs now to "rescue" my wash-and-wear shirts from the dryer, just because I regard it as personally unacceptable for them to be wrinkled. Zagzebski is particularly interested in explaining the sense of obligation in terms of seeing alternative actions as involving a loss of identity or selfhood; cf. also Monroe, "John Donne's People," and Monroe *et al.*, "Altruism and the Theory of Rational Action." That is a possible motivation. But I doubt that it comes close to explaining all altruistic cases of "I have to."

[21] Blum, "Community and Virtue," pp. 242–3.

[22] Milgram, *Obedience to Authority*, p. 21.

this circumstance."[23] Similarly, researchers quote non-rescuers in the holocaust context as saying, "What could I do, one individual alone against the Nazis?"[24] They allowed the Nazis to structure their alternatives for choice in this matter. We should not doubt that it was hard not to let that happen.

The rescuers did not let that happen. Instead they allowed their judgment of choiceworthy alternatives to be shaped by their awareness of another human being's need—not that of a faceless person far away, but of a person they actually saw, perhaps on their doorstep. There is evidence that some of the rescuers showed a readiness to respond in that way to the need of other human beings not only during the period of Nazi domination, but before and after it.[25] That looks like a persistent trait of character, and a virtue of the first magnitude. It may be a rare one, however, and may not have been possessed over so many years by all who rescued Jews from the Nazis. I know of no basis for thinking that the deservedly celebrated rescuer Oskar Schindler, for example, manifested such a trait before or after the war (see chapter 10, section 4.2).

## 2. SOCIAL TEMPTATIONS

The behavior of Milgram's subjects remains harder to understand than that of non-rescuers in the extremely threatening Holocaust situation. Few would have expected most of the subjects to allow the experimenter to define for them, so inhumanely, what they must do. Milgram himself calls the outcome of his experiment "unanticipated."[26] The experiment was also described to people who did not already know the outcome, and they were asked what outcome they would expect, and what they would predict they themselves would do in the experimental situation. Milgram tabulated the answers of 110 individuals: 39 psychiatrists, 31 college students, and 40 middle-class adults. Not one predicted that he or she would go more than two-thirds of the way to the highest level of supposed shock. Less than a quarter of the respondents expected they themselves would continue shocking after the "victim" requested release. The psychiatrists predicted that only "about one subject in a thousand would administer the highest shock on the board."[27] The experiment seems to reveal an area of usually unsuspected moral weakness in all or most of us. What is the nature of this deeply rooted vulnerability to moral temptation?

What Milgram's research reveals, according to Ross and Nisbett, is not a general disposition people have "to obey authority figures unquestioningly—even

[23] Sabini and Silver, "Lack of Character?" p. 550.
[24] Monroe *et al.*, "Altruism and the Theory of Rational Action," p. 119.
[25] Monroe, "John Donne's People," pp. 414–15; Monroe *et al.*, "Altruism and the Theory of Rational Action," p. 112; Hallie, *Lest Innocent Blood Be Shed*.
[26] Milgram, *Obedience to Authority*, pp. 193–4.
[27] Ibid., pp. 27–31.

to the point of committing harmful and dangerous acts." They rightly point out that dispositions to disobedience are commonly manifested in many contexts. Rather, they claim, Milgram reminds us "about the capacity of particular, relatively subtle situational forces to overcome people's kinder dispositions." They think "it was certain subtle features of Milgram's situation—whose influence tends to be unrecognized or underappreciated . . .—that prompted ordinary members of our society to behave so extraordinarily." They don't claim to know all these features, but they emphasize, as Milgram himself does, "the gradual, stepwise character of the shift from relatively unobjectionable behavior to complicity in a pointless, cruel, and dangerous ordeal." They point to extensive experimental evidence that manipulation can be potent when it "induc[es] people to take initial small, seemingly inconsequential steps along a path that will ultimately lead them to take much larger and more consequential actions."[28]

The psychologists John Sabini and Maury Silver have argued that situationists have wrongly supposed that the situational factors that can overcome people's better dispositions "are numerous and. . . do not form a coherent class from the point of view of folk psychology."[29] Sabini and Silver see a relatively small number of factors as accounting for virtually all the phenomena of social influence in the situationist experiments. One such factor is the slippery slope. Once the subject has administered a mild shock, it's harder to think that the next one, "a mere 15 volts" stronger must not be administered—and so on. As Sabini and Silver remark, however, "the fact that people are trapped by slippery slopes is not news." So if there has been a shocking discovery that would upset established notions of character, we must seek it elsewhere.[30]

Sabini and Silver "suggest. . . that there is a single thread that runs through social psychology's discoveries of people acting in surprising and demoralizing ways: people's understandings of the world. . . are strongly influenced by what they take to be other people's perceptions. . . "[31] Obviously wrong answers have been elicited with surprising frequency from experimental subjects asked to compare the length of lines, when they witness the wrong answer being given unanimously by six or more people ostensibly taking the test with them.[32] A "bystander" phenomenon has been observed in a variety of situations. Individuals have been found to be less likely to respond to an apparent need or emergency by giving or seeking help, the more other people are present and not responding. It is thought that the presence of others who apparently do not see any response as required in the situation undermines the subject's perception of the situation as demanding a response.[33]

Sabini and Silver suggest that this same thread runs through the experiment I discussed in section 1.1 in which seminarians who thought themselves late

[28] Ross and Nisbett, *The Person and the Situation*, pp. 50, 56, 58.
[29] Sabini and Silver, "Lack of Character?" p. 545.     [30] Ibid., p. 549.     [31] Ibid., p. 559.
[32] Ibid., p. 554.     [33] Ibid., p. 555–7.

on their way to give a talk were far less likely to pause to help someone who evinced symptoms of physical distress. I do not think, however, that this is a case of understandings being influenced by what are taken to be other people's perceptions. Sabini and Silver diagnose it more accurately when they speak of the social influence in this case as "anticipation of embarrassment."[34] I would add that the aversion to embarrassment in this case is specifically an unwillingness to disappoint the expectations of people to whom the subject has made some commitment or granted some authority. Aversion to embarrassment, reluctance to disappoint the contractually based expectations of an acknowledged authority, and influence of the authority's apparent perceptions of what is appropriate all seem to deserve a place in explanations of the shocking behavior of most of Milgram's subjects. My preferred generalization of these explanatory factors is that we are strongly motivated to be, and to seem to be, in tune with our social surroundings, as I put it before.

I agree with Sabini and Silver that "commonsense actors" are aware of this type of motive but have not been accustomed to treat it as having "great motivational significance."[35] Situationist studies show that in some circumstances it is a very powerful motivation indeed. For moral philosophy as well as common sense, the demonstration of its power may be counted as news. How disturbing is the news?

It is not news that the moral virtue of human agents typically is vulnerable to certain types of temptation. On the aversive side fear, and on the attractive side physical appetite and the lure of sensory pleasure, are probably the standing sources of temptation to which moral psychology has historically paid the most attention. Their power is not news to us, and does not seem disturbing to traditional conceptions of moral character. As Sabini and Silver point out, readers of Alfred Kinsey who accepted his (erroneous) finding "that a majority of men by age forty had been unfaithful to their wives" did not generally conclude "that character is an illusion," though they may have inferred that weakness of character was more widespread than they had thought.[36] Since we recognize that fear and sexual passion can be extremely strong motives, we do not infer that good motives overpowered or undermined by them must necessarily have been too weak to be counted as virtues. Once the situationists have helped us to see the power of motives of social conformity, I think we should likewise refuse to infer that good motives overpowered or undermined by them must necessarily have been too weak to be counted as virtues.

Perhaps we should consider adding to the traditional list of cardinal virtues. To deal with temptations of fear, the list has included courage. To deal with temptations of desire, it has included moderation. What is the virtue of dealing well with temptations of social conformity? We can hardly raise that question without realizing that we do not have a stock answer to it. Perhaps

---

[34] Sabini and Silver, "Lack of Character?" p. 558–9.          [35] Ibid., p. 561.
[36] Ibid., p. 548, n. 36.

*independent-mindedness* is the virtue we are looking for. Or perhaps it is more specifically *moral autonomy*, a deep groundedness in certain moral ways of viewing people and situations, with a developed ability to interpret situations accordingly and confidently. Contrasted with such a virtue would be a vice of excess that might be called pig-headedness or moral over confidence, and a vice of deficiency that might be called social conformism. Adopting such a framework certainly does not explain in detail why people behave as they do, or how we might acquire the virtue of independent-mindedness or moral autonomy. But I think it does offer a reasonable way of placing the phenomena discussed by situationists within the framework of a theory of character rather than a theory of no character.

## 3. CAN VIRTUES BE FRAIL AND DEPENDENT?

I have not said anything that would answer the question how robust a virtue of independent-mindedness or moral autonomy can be, nor have I seen any answer to the question compellingly justified. Experimental evidence hardly proves that none of us has or could have such a virtue in a form that cannot be overcome by situational pressures in general or by the manipulations of morally corrupt authority in particular. Such sweeping negative propositions are notoriously difficult to prove. Some critics have suggested that the rhetoric of "the power of the situation" is overblown.[37] In all versions of the Milgram experiments some subjects did resist situational pressures. More significantly, we have noted the cases of a substantial number of people who manifested the relevant quality over many months in rescuing Jews from the Nazis.

It is no part of my project, however, to defend the real possibility of invincible virtue in human life as we experience it. I don't think experience proves that any identified personal quality or trait is proof against subversion or corruption by social or situational pressures—or indeed by temptations of fear or desire. More generally, I believe that a perfect invulnerability to temptation is neither a plausible nor, on the whole, a desirable feature of moral virtue. Many of the desires we need sometimes to resist are healthy and not motives it would be better to lack. The same is true of many of the fears we need sometimes to overcome. Indeed the impulse to attune ourselves to our social surroundings is probably a necessary part of our equipment as social animals. Without it I doubt that we could learn a language, much less learn to think ethically. There are motives—malicious ones, in particular—that it is bad to have.[38] But moral temptation typically arises from conflicts among motives that are good enough in due measure.

In the Holocaust rescuers we have found actual examples of heroic altruistic virtue manifested in the face of what must surely have been extraordinarily

---

[37] Krueger and Funder, "Towards a Balanced Social Psychology," p. 26.
[38] Malicious motives are discussed in chapter 3, sections 3 and (especially) 4.

powerful temptations to conformity with an evil social project. But even of those people we have no evidence that could show that they were invincibly armed against every moral temptation they could conceivably have faced. If there are moral excellences that we have reason to admire in actual human lives, it can hardly be on the assumption that they are invincible or not situationally conditioned. In practice, especially in one's own case, it seems wise to assume that people's best moral qualities are in some ways and to some degree frail.

Some virtue theorists will be reluctant to grant this. Some forms of Aristotelian virtue theory already resist it with regard to temptations of fear and desire, holding out an ideal of courage and moderation in which fear and desire would be so tamed as never to compete with virtuous dispositions. I believe that is a mistake. A generous measure of inner harmony is certainly excellent, and a virtue. But the ideal of a character so in harmony with itself that none of its springs of action ever stand in competition with each other, is utterly unrealistic. And any attempt to impose it on oneself is likely to smother some virtues along with any vices that are smothered. In a realistic conception of virtue and the virtues we must expect them to share the inspiration of life with desires, fears, and social dispositions that do not express unambiguously virtuous concerns but are important for the richness and strength of human life and society. It is a never-ending task of virtue to build from these sources a life that is as coherent and as excellently for the good as it can be.

John Doris assumes that the concept of virtue belongs to those who are unwilling to grant this. He states that:

virtues are supposed to be *robust* traits; if a person has a robust trait, they can be confidently expected to display trait-relevant behavior across a wide variety of trait-relevant situations, even where some or all of these situations are not optimally conducive to such behavior.[39]

This is a premise of Doris's argument against the applicability of most of the vocabulary of virtue in actual life. We can certainly agree that virtues must be pretty effective in shaping the way one lives, and pretty durable, apt to last, in normal conditions, for quite a period of time. But how robust, how effective and how durable must they be? Must their strength be so great as to put them beyond the reach of luck and render them invincible in confrontation with temptation or adversity? Must their operation be uninfluenced by morally irrelevant contingencies? And how versatile, how adaptable, must they be? Must they fit a person for living admirably in every possible situation? Or can there be genuine virtues that enable people only to respond well to relatively familiar circumstances in which they have learned to live? I have granted that we have little evidence of the actuality of traits satisfying the highest standard of robustness suggested in these

---

[39]  Doris, *Lack of Character*, p. 18; cf. pp. 114–17.

questions. Must I conclude that genuine virtues are non-existent or vanishingly rare, or can the highest standard of robustness be plausibly rejected?

Doris can appeal to authority at this point, citing (as he does) Aristotelian and neo-Aristotelian affirmations of the extreme robustness of virtue.[40] But concepts of virtue and of virtues have by now a history that is too rich and complex for the views of the ancients in general, or of Aristotle and Aristotelians in particular, to be treated as definitive in this matter. It is a history in which conceptions have also been shaped in considerable measure by Christian ethical views which have ascribed virtues to people under the assumption that all of us are sinners. Such virtues as we may possess, on those views, are frail and apt to be overcome by temptation unless sustained by divine grace. Inheriting such a diversity of traditional opinions, philosophers must judge for themselves what criteria of virtue are reasonable and appropriate in the circumstances of human life. In the context of my conception of virtue and virtues, that poses the question what standard of robustness a trait of character must satisfy if it is to be *excellent*.

We do not in general think that excellence cannot be fragile or dependent on a situation. It is appropriate to admire the excellence of precision in a fine wristwatch even if the watch is not waterproof. The artistic skill of a pianist can be wonderfully excellent even though it could easily be destroyed by an accidental injury to her hands. The artistry of an orchestral conductor is not less admirable because it can be fully manifested only in a rather special (and rather expensive) social context. So why would frailty or dependence on social context be a reason for not admiring traits of character, or for not counting them as excellent?

One factor related to *frailty* is that we may well think that virtue requires *unconditional intentions* to do good and to do what is right. An intention that has as its form 'I will act humanely, provided I am in benign social circumstances' arguably is not excellent enough to constitute a virtue. But this will not yield a persuasive argument against the possibility of virtue. For intentions that prove to have been frail may not have been conditional. We cannot plausibly assume that the moral intentions that most of Milgram's subjects brought to his experiments were of such a pusillanimous form. The disturbing outcome of the experiments was that the experimenter was able to manipulate most of the subjects into doing things that were contrary to unconditional moral intentions, of a fairly general form, that they had probably had.

As for *social dependence*, human beings, like other living creatures, are adapted to live and function effectively only in a certain range of situations. Without food, for example, we cannot live at all; and with too little of it we will be enfeebled. Food is a biological necessity for all animals; but some needs are specifically human, and take, indeed, particular forms arising from contingencies of the social histories of individuals, communities, and cultures. We cannot learn to live well just by learning general ethical principles. The situations in which

---

[40] Doris, *Lack of Character*, pp. 17–18.

we must live are immensely complex, and rich in ethical considerations that may be very subtle. It would take an intelligence more prodigious than the human to recognize in detail how to apply general ethical principles on first encountering a new and very unfamiliar type of situation. For this reason we should not be surprised to find that moral learning and character formation incorporates a large measure of situation-specificity. We should (and in practice do) expect better moral performance in familiar than in unfamiliar situations.

Similarly, we should not be surprised to find that much of what we admire in human beings incorporates a lot of situation-specificity. A person who functions brilliantly in her usual life context may go to pieces in a social situation that is sufficiently diabolical, oppressive, or hostile. But that does not show that the personal qualities that enable her to live so well in the normal range of situations to which she is adapted are not truly excellent. This is true, I believe, of moral excellence as well as other sorts of excellence, and also applies where the situations in question are actual and possible temptations. The ability and willingness to resist important temptations that are part of one's actual life situation or integral to one's vocation in life is an important moral excellence, and a virtue, even if one would not manifest it in the face of other, less familiar temptations. Likewise, resistance to some types of temptation may be a virtue in individuals who succumb to temptations of other types.

## 4. MORAL LUCK

The question *how* excellent a virtue must be does not pick out the only challenge to virtue theory that arises from the apparent situational and social dependence of traits of character. There may also be issues about ownership. *Whose* must the excellence be? Ascription of a virtue is generally understood as crediting an *individual* with a moral excellence. But how much credit can you deserve for your virtues, if the existence and operation of traits of character depends on social situations? And how individual must the ownership of virtues be? In part these are questions about the place of *luck* in the moral life.

The last thirty years have seen a good deal of philosophical discussion of the idea of "moral luck," beginning in 1976 with a pair of papers by Bernard Williams and Thomas Nagel.[41] The idea applies to cases where moral significance or value is ascribed to a fact about a person that depends in some measure on factors outside that person's voluntary control. This is a controversial concept. It is widely believed that we should be praised and blamed, morally, only for what is true of us by virtue of our own free choices, and not for anything that is true of us by good or bad fortune, or luck. Some would say, therefore, that there cannot be any moral luck in the indicated sense. They hold, as Williams puts it, that

---

[41] Williams, "Moral Luck," and Nagel, "Moral Luck."

"anything which is the product of happy or unhappy contingency is no proper object of moral assessment, and no proper determinant of it either."[42]

But what are we to say about the disturbing reflection that negligence that results in a tragic accident seems to carry a heavy burden of guilt, while similar cases of negligence that turn out to have been harmless sink calmly into oblivion? What about the reflection that many a bureaucratic middle manager, whose actually useful and compulsively meticulous work life is regarded with moral complacency or even admiration by himself and his associates, would quite likely have acted as Adolf Eichmann did if his institutional setting became as vicious as Eichmann's? Must we not conclude that our bureaucrat owes his comparative innocence largely to his luck in not having found himself in such evil circumstances? Similar reflections have led Williams and Nagel and many others to conclude that there is in fact moral luck. In Nagel's vivid words, "However jewel-like the good will may be in its own right, there is a morally significant difference between rescuing someone from a burning building and dropping him from a twelfth-storey window while trying to rescue him."[43]

If an ethics of virtue is, as I propose, one that takes traits of character as proper objects of moral assessment in their own right, it can hardly avoid acknowledging the reality of moral luck. Here we may pass over issues about causal determinism and its compatibility or incompatibility with free will. We may also lay aside issues about moral responsibility for particular actions. For we are concerned with questions of character, in which we view ourselves and our lives in a more holistic and less localized way than in questions about the evaluation of actions. Our question is whether *traits of character* are influenced by factors beyond the voluntary control of the person whose traits they are, and the answer surely is that they are, and profoundly so. Whether or not individual actions can escape moral luck, and whether or not determinism is true, it is extremely implausible to suppose that any of us could have virtuous character without a great deal of (good) moral luck.

We hardly needed to wait for situationist psychology to teach us this. And if we are asking what factors beyond our voluntary control shape our characters, I think we may also bypass "nature versus nurture" debates. For those who emphasize nurture have in view aspects of the relevant individual's environment that are no less outside her voluntary control than whatever moral propensities she may have been born with. To speak of nurture in this context is to speak of moral education, broadly understood. And a major part of the study of moral education is by its very nature a study of moral luck, inasmuch as it is a study of ways in which other people can care for our virtue, and can do so effectively to some extent. Important as it is to participate actively and voluntarily in one's own moral education, that is certainly not the whole story of the process. Education in virtue is shaped by social contexts that we did not and could not have created

[42] Williams, "Moral Luck," p. 20.     [43] Nagel, "Moral Luck," p. 25.

for ourselves, and is accordingly dependent on them. Being badly brought up is surely a piece of bad moral luck. Nonetheless, saying that someone "seems badly brought up" would in most contexts imply that one does not regard that person as a paragon of virtue.

The very virtuous person may not have been brought up by particularly loving parents, but she surely encountered some virtuous people and some who genuinely cared for her. We can be even surer that she learned ethical thinking in the context of ethical practices that contained at least important seeds of enlightenment. She did not learn to be fair with no experience of fairness in other people. How much of a glimmer of virtue would any of us have if we had not begun in ethical practices that had a glimmer of it? And even when elementary ethical learning has been accomplished, how much farther off the track would we go than we in fact do if we never encountered ideas that enlarge and correct our own ethical vision? In such ways the virtuous person has been lucky. Give her credit for responding well to her good fortune—though we do not know how much her response depended on good dispositions that she was born with. It remains the case that without social settings that are morally fortunate in some degree for individuals there would be no developed moral virtue at all. At most there would be isolated prophetic words and acts pointing in the direction of virtue.

There is dependence on moral luck, not only in the *development* but also in the *persistence* of virtue. Human virtue once achieved is not intrinsically permanent. Moral firmness can be broken through "brainwashing." Personality and character can be changed by a brain tumor. The character can disappear gradually before death in Altzheimer's disease. Nor is it only our physiology on which our character is dependent in ways that may constitute moral luck. Our character is also pervasively affected by our social relationships. We learn to act, and to think and feel about our life, against a background of assumptions about our social as well as our physical environment. When those assumptions are overturned, our way of responding is apt to change too.

Our dependence on social context for the persistence of traits of character is underlined by situationist psychological research. People in general are quite responsive to social expectations and social pressures. None of us, probably, should be too sure that our behavior would not be affected for the worse if we did not know that there are certain sorts of behavior that other people will not tolerate. And do we know that we would not have gone to pieces morally if we had been imprisoned in an extermination camp like the infamous one at Auschwitz? That our social circumstances support virtue as well as they do is certainly something beyond our individual voluntary control, and thus a matter of moral luck in the relevant sense.

This is not an argument that virtue is not real. There *are* sorts of behavior that other people will not tolerate; and that being so, many people do generally act well and genuinely want to do so. Our appreciation of the excellence of certain forms of social relations, and our commitment to them, under actual conditions, may be genuine and excellent. That may be true even if the support of other people's commitment and the pressure of their demands and expectations play a major part, not only in structuring the relationships, but also in helping us to structure our lives. Our appreciation and commitment may have a significant measure of excellence even if we do not have the willpower and social creativity to sustain them in those relations without the supportive context provided by other people.

Likewise, in thinking about the moral excellences and deficiencies of people who will never experience anything like Auschwitz, there is little moral illumination to be gained by speculating about how they would have responded to an extremely malignant environment of that sort. Human beings are native to particular historical contexts. Our learning how to live is always a learning how to live in a certain range of contexts and a certain field of expectations and foreseen chances. Human moral excellence cannot be an ability and readiness to respond well to every possible circumstance. One who has learned excellent ways of being for the good is morally well prepared for certain circumstances. That such a person is not thrown into circumstances for which she is not so prepared is a piece of moral luck, reasonably expected, perhaps, but largely beyond her control. Virtue is real, and one of the most excellent things in human life. But it is a dependent and conditioned virtue. We are dependent creatures and dependent also in matters of virtue and vice.

## 5. MORAL EFFORT AND MORAL CHARACTER

The ethics of virtue and the ethics of right action differ first of all in being studies in the moral evaluation of different objects. The objects evaluated in the ethics of right action are voluntary actions. The objects evaluated in the ethics of virtue are persisting personal qualities. Virtues are qualities that engage the will, in a sense explained in section 1 of chapter 2, and they do involve voluntary action. For one does not fully have a typical virtue unless one manifests it sometimes, and not too infrequently, in voluntary action. (The rather specialized case of virtues, if any, that typically show themselves only in feeling need not detain us here.) Virtues, however, are not simply patterns of action. They are in large part dispositions, or states that give rise to dispositions, to act in certain ways or from certain motives, views, or commitments. They involve attitudes as centrally as they involve actions. Such states and dispositions are not themselves voluntary actions, and they are not directly and straightforwardly within our voluntary control. What is evaluated in the ethics of right action is straightforwardly voluntary. What is evaluated in the ethics of virtue is not. That is what makes issues of moral luck more clearly inescapable for the ethics of virtue than for the ethics of right action.

Of course it is not only actions that are within our voluntary control in ways that are relevant to ethical evaluation. So are outcomes that we are clearly able to bring about by voluntary action. If I am clearly able to affect you for good or ill, and do so, we would not normally consider it a matter of luck that I am liable to praise or blame for the outcome. This is the basis of a popular way of trying to free moral praise or censure from dependence on luck. If you are morally praising or criticizing someone for something other than a voluntary action, you can try to show that what you are morally evaluating her for is an outcome of her voluntary action and was thus at least indirectly within her voluntary control.

In this vein some who write on virtue have insisted that one's own moral effort or voluntary choice must play a part in the acquisition of any trait that is to count as a virtue. This can be seen as an effort to avoid or minimize acknowledgment of moral luck—or at any rate to assure that objects of moral evaluation are in some degree voluntary. Linda Zagzebski gives a particularly full and nuanced defense of such a view, arguing at length that "intrinsic to the nature of virtue is the way in which it is acquired." Specifically she holds that "it is part of the nature of virtue in the standard case that it is the result of moral work on the part of the human agent, and that it be acquired by a process of habituation." She does not claim that this is true of all cases of virtue "without exception," but insists that exemplary or "standard" cases of virtue must develop through a history of one's own moral choices. Her view is motivated, at least in part, by the thought that "virtues are qualities that deserve praise for their presence and blame for their absence."[44]

The relation of virtues to the ways in which they are acquired is complex. Zagzebski is surely right in saying that virtues are "states of excellence that develop over time in a person." They have histories in the individuals that have them. They develop and change (or at any rate *can* change) over time. They are not mere predispositions of a sort we might already fully possess when we are born. In that sense they are not "natural faculties, capacities, and talents."[45] Moreover, the history of a person's development of a virtue will practically always include voluntary acts of that person, some of which will be morally good acts characteristic of the virtue.

Still it seems likely that some people are innately more predisposed than others to some particular virtues, or more gifted for them. Indeed, important elements of some virtues are present in many individuals from early childhood, but not in a uniform way in all individuals. Even among persons similarly situated, it seems that some develop certain virtues (for instance, of sensitive responsiveness to the emotional needs of others) with little or no effort and others fail to develop them even with considerable effort.

More poignantly, there may even be virtues (for instance, of unselfcenteredness) which it is useless, or even counterproductive, to try hard to develop. It

[44] Zagzebski, *Virtues of the Mind*, pp. 104, 106, and 125.    [45] Ibid., pp. 104 and 106.

would not follow that *other* sorts of virtuous activity do not contribute to the development of virtues of the latter sort, but their development does not exactly lie within one's own voluntary control. More broadly, I think it is not true, as Philippa Foot has suggested, that "virtue must be within the reach of anyone who really wants it."[46] I do not believe that everyone who really wants to be patient is, or that everyone who really wants to be self-controlled with regard to food and drink, or anger, is. And surely someone who really wants to be wise can mistake excessive caution for wisdom. The truth in the neighborhood of Foot's suggestion, I think, is just that anyone who really wants a virtue already has thereby a module of virtue, though perhaps not the one he really wants. And I think we must add that the virtue must be desired from good motives, and in a way that is not too self-centered, if the desire is to be a virtue. And those motivational facts are not straightforwardly within the subject's voluntary control.

Whatever moral effort may be involved in the acquisition of virtue will not eliminate moral luck from the process. Moral improvement, becoming morally better in some respect than one had been before, is something that I suppose most morally serious people of middle age or older have had as part of their adolescent or adult lives. We may tend not to think of it as involving moral luck, because actual experience of such a change in one's own life is likely to involve quite a lot of conscious and quite voluntary choice of the better way. But considerable (good) moral luck is pretty sure to be involved.

There is first of all the luck of having "time for amendment of life"—that is, of living long enough to change in the relevant way. This is never assured by our own efforts without a lot of favorable circumstances that are not mainly our own doing. In the second place, circumstances of many different types can play a major part in the moral change seeming desirable or imperative—or in its seeming, and being, possible. Among these circumstances is very likely to have been some inspiration or experience or change of situation which one did not procure by one's own efforts, or not for relevant moral reasons. Perhaps one changed jobs, or moved to a different city, and new relationships invited one to "turn over a new leaf." Or a revelation of someone else's feelings or point of view may have led one to see things differently. If, in the third place, one was supported in sustaining the change for the better by other people who cared about it, that is obviously a sort of moral luck, and one that can be very important.

Is this good luck morally problematic? The nature of moral improvement gives particular reason to think that luck in it is undeserved, since it is a sequel to moral deficiency. At the same time, love for the good gives one obvious reason to want such changes to occur in people's lives, to do what one can to contribute to the lucky circumstances that may help them to happen, and celebrate them when they do happen. It has famously been claimed that there is actually "more joy

---

[46] Foot, "Virtues and Vices," p. 167. This is not something Foot flatly asserts, but I think it is clear in the context that she accepts it.

in heaven over one sinner who repents than over ninety-nine righteous persons who need no repentance" (Luke 15:7). Is that an exaggeration? One might have thought there would be more than enough joy in heaven for both. Indeed. But moral improvement does seem to warrant special celebration. Why?

One possible reason is that those who are repenting have special need of such support. Another reason involves some skepticism about the idea of righteous persons needing no repentance; that idea may suggest too much complacency. It is plausible to view human life as a pilgrimage in which there is always reason for moral improvement, and hence more reason to celebrate improvement than status quo. But perhaps the most fundamental reason for the famous saying is that, in comparison with the status quo, the case of moral improvement offers additional good to celebrate. The additional good is worth celebrating whether or not it was deserved. And that, I believe, is true of virtue: good character is worth celebrating even if there is much to criticize and deplore in the history that led to it.

It remains true that we should often admire a person for having overcome great difficulties in developing a good moral character. But admiring her effort is not the same as admiring the character that has come about through the effort. In evaluating virtue and evaluating the "moral work" done in acquiring it we are evaluating objects of different kinds, different in at least two respects. In the first place, the moral work consists of voluntary actions, whereas virtue centrally involves attitudes and dispositions as well as actions. And, in the second place, virtue consists in personal qualities that *persist* through some considerable period of time, whereas the moral work in question is evaluated as part of a process of *change* that may result in virtue. Despite a flurry of talk about "narrative ethics," there has still been relatively little attention in ethical theory to the evaluation of life histories or processes of change; and there deserves to be more.[47] It is not that, however, but evaluation of persisting character, that is the business of the department of ethical theory that I conceive the ethics of virtue to be.

To evaluate a person's qualities as constituting virtue or virtues is to evaluate them as excellent in themselves, as I argue in previous chapters. The voluntary actions through which one worked to become virtuous, and the process of moral improvement of which they were part, may also be excellent in themselves. We may admire someone who strives unsuccessfully for moral improvement in certain respects, inasmuch as the excellence of the efforts is independent, to some extent, of the success of the improvement project. Similarly we may insist that the excellence of the persisting qualities that constitute virtue is not a function of the value of voluntary efforts that may have contributed to their development. I think in fact our interest in moral improvement itself testifies that the qualities that we aspire to have as persisting elements of character are envisaged by us as

---

[47] Interesting explorations of evaluation of life histories, and of moral effort, in Sorensen, *The Factors of Moral Worth*, have raised my consciousness on these subjects.

admirable in their own right, and not merely as products of admirable efforts. No doubt the excellences of such different objects are different in various ways and may rightly evoke somewhat different responses. Kurt Baier, distinguishing the objects of evaluation somewhat as I have done, and refusing to classify one as having "greater moral worth or value" than the other, nonetheless seems to suggest that only moral effort rightly evokes a "moral tribute."[48] I would not differentiate the excellences in that way. I think saying that someone has a good character normally *is* a moral tribute, though not exactly the same sort of tribute as praise for voluntary efforts at character improvement.

## 6. VIRTUE AS GIFT

In view of the deep and pervasive involvement of moral luck in the acquisition and persistence of virtue, it is inappropriate and misleading to think of virtue primarily as an individual achievement. But that is no tragedy. We may well have a richer as well as less self-centered view of virtue if we regard it largely as a gift—a gift of nature or of grace, or both, and normally also of people with whom one has lived. It is not a gift received without effort, as many of the best gifts are not; but effort would not have been enough. And it is to be treasured no less for being a gift than for having involved some effort. Gifts are not in general less precious, less desirable, less beautiful or excellent, than earnings. A Mozart piano concerto can have the intrinsic value and excellence of beauty no matter how effortlessly Mozart may have composed it. Why shouldn't something similar be true of moral virtue?

Our conception of the value of virtue, however, will need to reflect its dependent and conditioned character. Virtue is fitted to be first and foremost an object of admiration, aspiration, and gratitude—not of competitiveness and personal pride. Realistically, we must recognize that virtue is a matter of gifts as well as of effort, and that the gifts are not equally distributed. But they are gifts for all of us, not just for the individuals in whom they are realized, and we can all be grateful for them. Whatever good moral luck there is, it is there for all of us to enjoy. The ownership of moral luck can be shared. For the important thing with excellence isn't soloing in it but participating in it.

The social dependence of virtue may indeed suggest that we rarely if ever do really solo in moral excellence. In many cases even outstanding individual moral excellence can be seen as a matter of playing a leading role in an ensemble of people being for the good together in an excellent way. For example, people who endure a terminal illness with admirable fortitude are often being upheld by a lot of loving and admiring attention from other people. They may be very unlucky in their health and at the same time very lucky morally. Their fortitude may be

---

[48] Baier, "Radical Virtue Ethics," p. 135.

a social as well as an individual achievement. This does not mean that the excellence is not theirs individually in a special way. It is, but it is not only theirs. It is also excellence shared with those who support them, and should be seen as more rather than less precious for that.

This suggests the following response to one who complains of unequal luck in the gifts of virtue. "You're welcome to join us in being for the good. There's plenty of good to be for, and plenty of excellence to admire, enjoy and support. No way of apportioning excellence among individuals who participate in it in those ways is as important as whether it's there for us, including you, and whether you're for it." There's something right about this response. The attitude it proposes would be virtuous. But this is not a completely satisfying response, because those whose moral luck has been worst may be unable to adopt the recommended attitude. What is most disturbing about moral luck is the downright bad luck, and not the unequal distribution of degrees of good luck.

Bad moral luck is a part of the general problem of evil, and an essay on the nature of virtue is probably not the place to attempt a solution to that large problem (or family of problems). What must be considered in a theory of virtue is whether our appraisals of virtue and vice, and our responses to virtue and vice, adequately reflect the facts about moral luck. What moral burdens is it wrong to allow bad luck to carry in its wake?

It may be illuminating to consider that question first in relation to bad moral luck in consequences of *actions*. What might it be wrong to allow bad luck to carry in its wake in the case of two drunken and reckless drivers, one of whom causes a fatal crash, while the other gets home without untoward accident? We surely should not say that the unlucky one is a *worse person* than the other; nothing in the story suggests such a judgment of character. Did one of them do something *morally wrong* that the other did not do? No, both of them did the same morally wrong thing. Did one of them *act worse* than the other? No, so far as the story I've told goes, both acted badly in the same way.

We can say that one of the two is *responsible* for a terrible catastrophe, and the other is not. The sense in which that is true is best understood, I think, in terms of our *ownership* of risks that we take, and of their outcomes. But what consequences should we draw from such responsibility? That is the most obvious place to look for something disturbing in our recognition of moral luck.

Here is one question that is at least controversial. Does the crash-causer *deserve punishment* in a way that the luckier driver does not? And, more broadly, can anyone be justly punished on grounds that involve moral luck? That's a serious question for theorists of punishment, but I think it is not of major importance for a study of the evaluation of character. It's very doubtful that bad character, as distinct from wrong actions that may arise from it, provides good grounds for infliction or aggravation of punishment in any case. If an exception to that can be justified, I think it would most likely be from considerations that would not be undercut by moral luck, such as those of reforming the offender or protecting society. And there seems to be little reason why an aversion to punishing on grounds involving moral luck should lead us to withdraw or avoid an ascription of bad character in any particular case rather than conclude that the bad character does not in this case justify punishment.

Another focus of controversy in this area is *blame*. Can one of our two reckless drivers be more appropriately *blamed* than the other? Both of them can be blamed for drunken and reckless driving; but it seems that one of them can rightly be blamed for another person's death, and the other can't (not having caused such a death). Some might reject the latter, unequal assignment of blame. Some philosophers think that 'blame' signifies a rather special act or attitude that cannot, logically, find an appropriate object in anything so affected by luck as not to be in the control of the person blamed. I'm not sure that I am really acquainted with an act or attitude of that particular sort that would fall easily under the concept of blame. In discussing what sort of consequences may rightly be allowed to follow from an unfavorable assessment of character I will therefore try to avoid resting much on a concept of blame.

I do think that some bad traits of character are also attitudes that can be appropriate objects of reactive attitudes that I personally find it natural to classify as forms of "blame," though I see no need to insist on that classification here. Suppose, for example, that I had a deeply ingrained view that persons of some racial, ethnic, religious, or sexual identity have, at best, moral rights that are much inferior to those belonging to me and "my kind." Or suppose I simply had deeply ingrained hostile desires or wishes regarding such persons. Members of the disfavored group, learning of my attitude, would be entitled, I think, to feel *wronged* by it, *resent* it, and *reproach* me for it, even if I had not acted on it except by allowing it to be perceived as my attitude. Having such an attitude is not straightforwardly something of my voluntary choosing, nor directly or completely under what we normally think of as my voluntary control. But it is still, more broadly, a matter of my *being against* some things I ought to be for—indeed, being against some *people* in ways in which I ought to be for them. I think it is reasonable for people to resent anyone's being against them in such a way, even if they assume that accidents of personal history were involved in the development of the attitude.[49]

But it is not clear that *all* bad traits of character are appropriate objects of resentment, anger, or reproach. Folly seems not to be so, apart from its manifestation in offensive attitude or action. And a deficiency in personal excellence, as such—for example, a superficial or pusillanimous conception of one's own good—is not an appropriate object of resentment or anger except on the part of a person, if there is one, to whom one owes it to be more excellent.

---

[49] The topics of this paragraph are discussed much more extensively in Adams, "Involuntary Sins."

Of course it can hardly be denied that all bad traits of character are appropriate objects of *criticism* or *dispraise*. To classify a trait as bad *is* a way of dispraising it. The business of life often calls for evaluative comment on matters involving luck, and such comment often amounts to praise or criticism of a person. The ascription of athletic or musical talent, which all regard as matters of luck, is typically taken as a sort of praise of a person; and denial of such talent will often be perceived with pain as criticism of a person. Similarly the ascription of virtue is praise of a person—though not in any sense implying that no luck was involved in the acquisition of virtue. And the ascription of bad traits of character, however acquired, will certainly be taken as criticism of a person. If my character is praised, *I* am praised; and if my character is criticized, *I* am criticized. If you say that I'm foolish, you may not exactly be blaming me; but in many contexts it's not clear that I'd rather be thought foolish than blamed. Bad moral luck is bad, but it doesn't follow that we don't have compelling reason to evaluate traits of character.

Though the most urgent worries about moral luck may be about bad luck, we have as much reason in the present context to think about good moral luck, inasmuch as the main project of this essay is a theory of virtue rather than a theory of vice. Corresponding to the question whether it is right to *punish* a person for bad character as such, is the question whether it is right to *reward* a person for virtue or good character as such. And in both cases, luck is pretty sure to have been involved in the development and persistence of character. My theory of virtue has no stake in the appropriateness of rewards for good character. Virtuous *actions* may deserve a reward, if they put others in the agent's debt, but I think not just because they are virtuous or excellent. The moral significance of virtue is not a matter of *earning* something, or of our *owing* something to the virtuous. This is not just because of moral luck; it flows from the nature of virtue as a sort of excellence. To think a person should be *paid* for being excellent is to undervalue excellence, to forget its nature as intrinsic value. Virtue needn't *deserve* a blessing; it *is* a blessing. To be sure, it is generally good for desires of the virtuous to be satisfied, but that's because what they desire is good.[50]

What responses to virtue are appropriate (and perhaps indeed virtuous)? The most obviously so are *admiration* and *praise*—not because the virtuous person has an entitlement to them but because it is good to appreciate what is excellent. And if it is right to think of virtue as a gift, then it should also be right to be *grateful* for it, or at any rate to be glad of its presence in the world as a wholly or partly unearned benefit that we enjoy. I take these to be clearly appropriate responses to another person's virtue.

One may well be hesitant to enter into such laudatory attitudes toward supposed virtues of one's own, as we rightly fear self-deception and simple excess in moral self-congratulation. The topic of morally appropriate attitudes toward

---

[50] Cf. Engstrom, "The Concept of the Highest Good in Kant's Moral Theory."

one's own character deserves attention. Here we may focus on the virtues of gratitude and humility.

To be *grateful* is in large part to be glad of what others have done for you, and in a way glad of your indebtedness to them. If we are grateful, the value and significance of such moral excellence as we may exemplify may be enhanced rather than diminished by its dependence on what others have done. That a personal quality is the more to be treasured for being a gift of God's grace and a token of contact with the divine is a familiar religious idea, and it has an obvious non-theological analogue. If our moral development owes much to the way in which our parents and other important people in our lives cared both for us and for moral goodness, does that *detract* from the value of whatever has been achieved in our moral development? Is it not much more a precious part of our moral history? Would it not be ingratitude, and a blindness to some of the greatest values in human relationships to wish not to be indebted to others for guidance, encouragement, and example that have been important to our moral growth?

*Humility* is sometimes conceived as a disposition to think ill of oneself. I have no wish to praise it under that description, under which it might easily be incompatible with clear-sighted intellectual honesty. We certainly can say, however, that humility is characterized by not *over*estimating one's own excellence. Even more crucially, humility is characterized by not overestimating one's own importance, especially one's importance in the moral scheme of things. If you are humble, you do not think that what happens to you *matters* more, objectively, than what happens to other people, even if you *care* more, in many contexts, about what happens to you. You will tend to be very conscious that other people matter to themselves in the same way you matter to yourself; and that will seem to you an important fact. You will also be suspicious of any inclination you may have to magnify the significance of good traits of your own in comparison with those of other people.

I think there is a form of humility that is also a form of love of excellence, a form of humility that focuses on the excellence there is or can be much more than on the excellence of one's own part in it.[51] If one is humble in this way, one will want to participate in excellence that transcends one's own or extends beyond one's own. In this context one will relax one's interest in the thought that one's own excellence might stand out in some way amidst the general excellence. Such humility may demand of me that I focus more on the excellence of what *we* are doing and have done than on the excellence of *my* part in it. If I think that I have participated in a particularly excellent collective performance, for example, I may spoil or cheapen my enjoyment of that excellence if I let my mind go very far in trying to distinguish my own excellence in the matter from that of others.

---

[51] The vice to which this virtue is most obviously opposed will be a form of self-centeredness, as discussed in chapter 7, section 3.

Something further can be said in a metaethical perspective that is Platonistic or theistic or (as my own is) both. In such a perspective it makes sense to say that the chief focus of our admiration ought to be on the transcendent, archetypal supreme Good, rather than on ourselves or each other. Human excellences can indeed be of great value, but are not more than ways in which we may image transcendent goodness. Their imaging is only fragmentary, in relation to the transcendent good. We need to value them as what they are, but not as more than they are. In such a view a response to the problems of the dependence, fragility, and fragmentariness of human goodness may be framed by the thought that the reality of our virtue is much less important than the reality of transcendent goodness.

# 10

# Do the Virtues All Imply Each Other?

## 1. THE IDEA OF THE UNITY OF THE VIRTUES

In chapter 8 I tried to identify qualities that are promising candidates for recognition as virtues or potential parts of virtues, despite the social psychologists' evidence of behavioral inconsistency in moral matters. However, I explicitly did not argue that any human being is consistently virtuous in *all* respects, or has all virtues. In fact I believe that human moral excellences or virtues are real but typically *fragmentary*.

I face a challenge on this point from classical conceptions of virtue. The ancient doctrine of *the unity of the virtues* enters the literature, with some fanfare, in Plato's *Protagoras* (329C–334C, 349B–360E). Socrates is presented there as arguing (1) that virtue is one, in a sense that implies that 'justice', 'temperance', 'piety', and other words commonly taken as names of particular virtues do not really name distinct properties differing in nature from one another. He holds that they are "all names of one and the same thing" (329C), which is virtue—capital *V* Virtue, as I called it in chapter 2, section 4.[1] This is the claim that best deserves to be called the thesis of the *unity* of the virtues.

It implies—and in support of it Socrates is at pains to argue—(2) that one cannot have any of the virtues except insofar as one has all of them. This claim also sometimes inherits the name 'unity of the virtues', but is probably better called the thesis of the *mutual entailment* of the virtues. I take it that John Cooper is on solid ground in stating that "all the major Greek philosophers" held the latter thesis, but that only some of them (notably Socrates and the Stoics) held the former, stronger unity thesis.[2] A third thesis that can be inferred from either or both of these is (3) that one cannot have virtue (capital *V* Virtue) without having *all* the particular virtues. Call this the thesis, of the *necessary completeness* of virtue (it will be the subject of chapter 11, section 1.

I do not accept any of these theses. My sense from oral discussion as well as reading is that Socrates' thesis (2), the mutual entailment thesis, though probably

---

[1] In this chapter I will sometimes capitalize 'Virtue' in this sense.
[2] Cooper, "The Unity of Virtue," p. 233. I have found Cooper's article extremely helpful in understanding ancient treatments of the subject.

not now a majority view,[3] retains great appeal for many philosophers. That thesis is the part of the classical conception that most obviously stands in contradiction with my view that real virtues can be *fragmentary*. It will be the main subject of this chapter. I think it will be helpful, however, to begin by attending to Cooper's plea for a sympathetic hearing for Socrates' stronger thesis (1). It holds, in Cooper's words, "that really there [is] only a single unified condition, virtue itself, of which the particular virtues that we normally distinguish from one another are (in one way or another) actually only aspects."[4]

Cooper contrasts two ways of approaching the study of ethics. One is mainly explanatory, "the study of 'the moral concepts' as they function in ordinary life." The other is "a first-order practical, moral quest." Cooper grants that the strong unity thesis may not look very plausible as an explanatory account of the ordinary working of virtue concepts. But he suggests that it may look much better if, like "all the ancient philosophers," you are pursuing a personal moral quest, "investigating how best to live yourself, with the intention of then doing your best to live that way."[5]

If one is attempting to formulate an ideal of human perfection, as a basis for doing all that one can to lead the best human life, it will certainly seem very attractive to suppose, at least as a defensible initial position, that there is some unified condition to be defined and sought.[6]

I agree that it is desirable to think of virtue as an ideal, and as the object of a practical, moral quest. I also believe that even today most philosophers who focus their attention on virtue do view it as the object of such a quest. But I doubt that the object of such a quest is best conceived in the strongly unitary way proposed by Socrates.

How is the ideal of virtue conceived, in Cooper's rationale for the extreme thesis of the unity of virtue? Most obviously, it is to be, as he says, "an ideal of human perfection." I take it to be part of the Socratic treatment of virtue as an *ideal*, in the first place, (1) that it is to be a strongly dominant ideal, providing the organizing structure for one's whole ethical life, and overriding any other considerations that might compete with the perfection of one's virtue. (2) As an ideal of *human perfection*, moreover, virtue is to constitute a "fully good life," as Cooper also says,[7] and it is assumed that humans can achieve this perfection. (3) The fully good life is supposed also to be "the best life."[8] And I take that to mean one uniquely best kind of life for human beings as such. Otherwise there

---

[3] A careful recent critic has stated that "most commentators on [the mutual entailment thesis] have tended to dismiss it" (Badhwar, "The Limited Unity of Virtue," p. 306). Cooper finds the issue of the unity of the virtues neglected in recent discussions of virtue ("The Unity of Virtue," p. 233).

[4] Ibid., p. 233.     [5] Ibid., p. 234.     [6] Ibid., p. 235.

[7] Ibid., p. 235.     [8] Ibid., p. 234.

might well be several kinds of fully good life, characterized by somewhat differ-ent virtues which would not all be necessary for each other or for virtue as such. Finally, (4) virtue, as strongly unitary, is presumably conceived as a state that has a *causally unitary* role in human psychology. Any distinguishable aspects that it has will be inseparable, each dependent, causally if not logically, on the others. Where we find one aspect of it, we should expect to find the others. It will serve as a naturally unitary factor in psychological explanation.

I disagree with this Socratic unitary conception of virtue on all four of the points just noted. My characterization of virtue as excellence in being for the good is an expression of a very different conception. (1) When being for the good is excellent, its own excellence will not be the chief good that it is for. There are a great variety of important goods, actual and possible, in the world; and a variety of them will commonly engage the virtuous agent's interest and energy at least as powerfully as the good of her own virtue. Virtue should cer-tainly be a very important and precious goal, but should not be an absolutely overriding end for the virtuous person. In pursuit (or defense) of a great good more external to oneself it can be good, or even obligatory, to do something one knows is likely to leave one less virtuous than one would otherwise have been—embittered, perhaps, or more callous. Likewise it should not be assumed that the aspiration for virtue is to provide the organizing structure for one's whole ethical life.

(2) I think there is no such thing as *complete* human virtue; no such thing as a *fully* good human life if that means a human life that could not be morally improved in any way.[9] The quest for virtue cannot yield more than an always and necessarily incomplete and fragmentary approximation to a transcendent good-ness (the goodness of God, I would say) which is its reference point. The human goodness that is actually possible, being always fragmentary, will not always con-sist of the same fragments. Moreover, if what should interest us most in the virtues of actual human beings is not something they completely embody but ways in which they challenge and inspire us with glimpses of an ideal that tran-scends them, then the greatest attention and admiration may sometimes rightly go to exemplars of virtues that are too extreme to fit in a well-rounded character that would be virtuous in every respect.[10]

(3) If a transcendent or infinite good provides the primary ideal or reference point, excellence in being for the good will nonetheless involve being for partic-ular finite goods occurring in the world. Which such goods, and which ways of being for them, are available to us, is a matter of historical contingency and vari-ability. It is thus historically contingent and variable what forms virtue can best assume—or, indeed, assume at all. For this reason there is not one uniquely best available form of virtue for all human beings as such. And even if one kind of

[9] For fuller development of this point, see Adams, *Finite and Infinite Goods*, pp. 51–8.
[10] As argued more fully in Adams, "Saints."

virtue is best in a given context, I do not think it follows that no other is excellent in that context. One of my aims in this book is to articulate a conception of virtue that will facilitate appreciation of the diversity of human excellences to be found in our situation of religious and cultural plurality. And if different forms of virtuous life are possible (and indeed actual) there may be particular virtues that are found in some but not all of those forms of life, as I will argue in chapter 11, section 1.

Finally (4), I do not believe that virtue is a single causal principle, or that there is a single psychological cause from which all the virtues flow. Indeed, the empirical evidence we have reviewed in chapters 8 and 9 suggests that rather diverse causal factors must contribute to any virtue that we are likely to be able to attain, and that virtue is one much more in aspiration than in its causes. In particular, I believe (and will argue further in section 3) that wisdom, which is favored as the unitary principle in the ancient doctrine of the unity of the virtues, is not, and does not itself have, a single causal principle. This does not mean that it is misguided to aspire to a unity of virtue. On the contrary, I believe that goals of moral integration and consistency are among the most important in the development of virtue, though not always more important than other goals that may compete with them. That theme will be developed in parts of chapters 11 and 12.

Our main concern in this chapter, as I have said, is specifically with the ancient but now controversial thesis of the mutual entailment of all the virtues. Argument for that thesis has commonly proceeded roughly as follows, along lines laid out by Socrates in Plato's *Protagoras* (329C–334C, 349B–360E). It is assumed that a trait is not a virtue except insofar as it reliably leads one to act rightly or well, so that it is not enough to *know* what is just if one is to have practical wisdom, for example, but one must also *do* what is just. And if practical wisdom is to lead you reliably to do what is just, or more broadly what is right and good, you will need to have courage and temperance to choose what is most importantly good in the face of distracting fears and desires. Likewise courage, it is claimed, is not merely ability and readiness to act in the face of danger, for that can be mere rashness if one is not acting in pursuit of what is truly good and right. True courage, it is inferred, requires practical wisdom to judge what risks are worth running for what ends, temperance so that one's risk-taking will not be squandered in the service of frivolous or unworthy desires, and justice so that it will serve the right. And similarly for the other virtues.

Is that correct? Whether each virtue entails all the others may well depend on how the notion of a virtue is defined. We have some choice about that. We could define the notion in a way that is favorable to the thesis of the mutual entailment of the virtues. One way of doing that would be to make it true by definition that a virtue must be a trait that actually, in each case in which it is a virtue, tends to issue in right action. I have given reasons, however (in chapter 1, section 2), for not accepting such a definition. One reason is that I think our interest in virtue is not just an interest in right action, but also in the moral quality of attitudes and traits of character in their own right. Another reason is precisely that thinking of virtue in terms of goodness rather than rightness helps us to recognize that a person's character can be good in some important ways and bad in others at the same time.

I prefer a definition that implies rather that particular virtues must be traits that are excellent in themselves in such a way that they *can* constitute part of the excellence of a comprehensive Virtue. Or we could say that they *will* constitute that more comprehensive excellence *if* other excellences are present in due measure. Such a definition leaves the way open to deny the mutual entailment of the virtues. I hope that the plausibility of this approach will be confirmed by the argument of this chapter. I will argue that there are indeed *some* entailment relations among virtues or types of virtue, but that it is not plausible to hold that *every* virtue implies *all* the virtues. I will employ a "bottom up" approach, considering in some detail what entailment relations there may be among certain particular virtues or modules of virtue. I will focus on courage, as typical of the structural virtues, on practical wisdom as the principal moral virtue among personal qualities that are primarily cognitive, and on benevolence as typical of motivational virtues.[11]

## 2. COURAGE

### 2.1. Courage's Relation to Other Virtues

If we are asked to suggest a virtue one might think we could have without having all the other virtues, or even without being for the good in the most important ways, courage might come first to mind. Does courage really require justice? Or can courage be a virtue in the absence of justice? For instance, what should we say of the courage of a soldier fighting for an unjust cause?

Some virtues, which I have called *motivational*, are defined by goods that one is for in having them, and in that sense by their motive. Motivational virtues are rather straightforwardly ways of being for the good, or at any rate for something importantly good. If we viewed courage as a motivational virtue, it might not be hard to argue that one cannot be courageous except in a good cause. But I believe courage is a *structural* rather than a motivational virtue. That is, it is not principally a matter of what one is for, but of how one organizes one's life around whatever ends one is for. I take courage to be a matter of one's ability and willingness to face fears and risks in governing one's response to them in accordance with what one sees as demanded by aims that are in fact among one's most important. The importance of one's aims is to be measured in this context by the value one sets on them or the commitment one has to them. As Gary Watson

---

[11] For the categories of structural and motivational virtues, see chapter 2, section 4. Regarding cognitive qualities as candidates for the role of virtues, see chapter 8, section 3.2.

remarks, "If I refuse to save you from the fire out of utter indifference to you, rather than fear, that would not bespeak a lack of courage. (Suppose I routinely face such dangers for things I care about.)"[12] We should add, however, the proviso that the courageous person's valuing of aims and judgment of what they demand is not too different from what it would have been apart from fear. For lack of courage can be manifested in distortions of one's judgments of probability and value.[13]

Courage in this sense constitutes an admirable strength of self-government, and one that is plausibly counted as a virtue. And it can be manifested in fighting for an unjust cause, if the decision to fight and face dangers takes account of the fighter's main aims, unjust as they may be. For this I think it is not necessary that the aims that ground the decision be aims that the fighter wholeheartedly embraces or approves of; it is enough that he or she be really committed to them.[14] Given the frequent messiness of human life, coherent living sometimes requires resolute pursuit of aims about which one is ambivalent. It is an important personal strength, and an excellence, to be able to live coherently in that way. Suppose the aims resolutely pursued by particular soldiers are not compatible, all things considered, with justice and comprehensive virtue. Still their courage may have an excellence which, with better motives, could be part of the excellence of comprehensive Virtue. That is a reason for counting their courage as a virtue.

My account of courage as a kind of strength of rational self-government may face the objection that one's choice, and organization, of one's main values could be cowardly by being unduly influenced by fear. The objector would hold, for example, that someone who values his own health and longevity too highly, as one of his central values, may be thereby a coward. No matter how consistently and rationally he governs his response to dangers in accordance with his main values, that will not be counted as courage, because his main values are distorted by fear.

I think the case needs a bit of filling out. Suppose the person in question has views and aspirations rather like those of the ancient Epicurean philosophers. Above all else he values a tranquil life for himself, free of illness and physical and emotional pain. In thought and will he embraces that as his central value. Like all of us, however, he is not able to avoid all dangers, all threats to what he values. Like anyone, he must sometimes accept some risks and pains if he is to have the best chance of achieving his main aims, even his aims of tranquil living. Suppose he does accept such risks resolutely and readily when it is clear that doing so is rational in view of his main aims. Then he has the kind of strength of rational self-government that I have been calling courage. Is it excellent in him? I

---

[12] Watson, "Virtues in Excess," p. 73, n.28.
[13] Cf. Wallace, *Virtues and Vices*, pp. 68–76.
[14] This qualification is inspired by the discussion of Tim O'Brien's reflections on his military service in Vietnam, in Miller, *The Mystery of Courage*, p. 40.

think so, though it may be that his main aims and values do not provide scope for
*outstanding* courage.

One might still think, however, that in making the avoidance of unpleasant-
ness such a central value, our imaginary Epicurean manifests an excessively *fearful*
attitude to life. Conversely, one might say there is a kind of *courage* that is manifested in thinking that a more ambitious and adventurous life is worth living, at
the risk, and even the cost, of more pain. I agree there is a virtue that is at stake
here. It is not strength of rational self-government; that the Epicurean can certainly have. It is more plausibly seen as a kind of moral faith—faith that a life
of higher aspiration is worth living. What is *excellent* about that? Perhaps it is an
excellence of *appreciation* of the values to which one might aspire, and of *tenacity*
in the pursuit of them. It is not clearly contrary to ordinary usage to call it a form
of *courage*.[15] But it is so different from the strength of rational self-government in
the face of danger that the Epicurean may have, that it may not be a good idea
to use the same name for both of them. In the present, virtue-theoretical context, I have chosen to keep 'courage' for the danger-related strength of rational
self-government.

While I do not accept the Socratic argument that the virtue of courage requires
practical wisdom of every sort, it is *not* my opinion that it is compatible with
every form of folly. It does require that responses to danger be governed by the
agent's judgment of what is demanded by *important* aims. To the extent that we
think this requirement is not satisfied in typical cases of playing Russian roulette,
for example, it is plausible to count the behavior as rash (or suicidal) rather than
courageous. Frivolity is not courage.

In opposing courage to at least some forms of folly, my approach to the concept
of courage, like that of Socrates, may be rationalistic in a way that is somewhat
revisionary. Ordinary talk and thinking about courage takes *physical* courage to
be the primary case of courage. Indeed, specifically *military* courage was probably the original case, and that heritage probably still influences ordinary ways
of thinking and speaking. Both historically and currently, ordinary thought and
talk about courage are doubtless influenced by urgent needs that social groups
have for many of their members to face physical dangers. Accordingly, someone's
knowingly facing grave physical danger for a cause of which we approve will commonly be praised as a manifestation of courage without much examination of the
action's place in the psychological economy of the person.

From Socrates on, however, philosophical discussions of virtue, and of courage
in particular, have not simply accepted common judgments of military courage.
I can't simply accept them either. The requirement that virtues be excellent leads
me to give courage a definition that commonly accepted examples of physical
courage may or may not satisfy. One might try to hang on to common views of
physical (and especially military) courage by saying that anyone who is *not too*

[15] Cf. Adams, *Finite and Infinite Goods*, pp. 388–9, and Tillich, *The Courage to Be*, pp. 5–6.

*unwilling* to face (physical) dangers has the virtue of (physical) courage. On this definition, one who is generally *too willing* to run physical risks is thereby courageous, though perhaps lacking in prudence. This may accord with some widely accepted judgments, but it seems wrong to me. The virtue of courage must be an excellence, not just the absence of a particular fault; and being too willing to run risks is not a form of an excellence, but just a form of the vice of imprudence.

Consider the mirror image. Could we define a form of prudence—call it "prudent caution"—as just not being too willing to run risks, and plausibly count it as a virtue? Being too unwilling to run risks is obviously one of the main possible forms of this trait. So if we count prudent caution, in this sense, as a virtue, we will have to count the vice of cowardice as a possible form of a virtue—which few will accept. Because courage is more widely admired than prudence, it is easier to evoke intuitions against the definition of "prudent caution" as a virtue than against the "not too unwilling" definition of courage. But I think reflection on such examples as that of Russian roulette will support my judgment that the one definition is no more acceptable than the other. Both fail in roughly the same way to pick out an excellence. For that reason I believe that courage's willingness to face danger must be responsive to perceptions or judgments of what is demanded by aims that are among one's most important.

Could one plausibly claim that a direct behavioral disposition to behave in accordance with a certain traditional code of honor when facing physical dangers is a form of the virtue of courage? That would be another way of trying to hang on to less rationalistic conceptions of physical (and especially military) courage. Assume for the sake of argument, though I think it would often deserve to be controversial, that the traditional code embodies an excellent conception of honor. A disposition to conform to the code will still be lacking in excellence to the extent that it does not reflect the subject's most important values and commitments.

Suppose, for instance, that the disposition is grounded in a sort of fear. According to Plutarch, those paragons of allegiance to a militaristic honor code, the ancient Spartans, "seemed to regard courage not as fearlessness, but as fear of reproach and dread of disgrace."[16] Such fear could motivate a genuine virtue if it reflects the high value an individual sets on honor as conceived in a good social code. But suppose that is not the case. Suppose the fear of social disapproval, or the intensity of the fear, is not an expression of the agent's central values. He fears the censure of his present companions, perhaps, but if given free choice of a way of life, he would choose one that has nothing to do with them, their goals, and their standards of evaluation. We may suppose that he knows that, or has beliefs and desires that should enable him to know it. Nor has he committed himself in any stable way to a course of action that demands that he face danger. Before

---

[16] Plutarch, *Lives*, vol. 10, pp. 66–7, from the life of Cleomenes, chapter 9, cited in Miller, *The Mystery of Courage*, p. 23.

every battle he considers that he may well decide that an easy escape from danger is worth the price in social disgrace, but in the end he is always overcome by fear of public shaming, and seems to fight bravely.[17] In such a case apparent physical courage may well represent a personal weakness rather than a strength or an excellence or virtue. It may indeed represent a personal weakness disturbingly similar to the weakness displayed by subjects who allowed themselves to be manipulated into morally appalling behavior in Stanley Milgram's experiments on obedience (described in chapter 9, section 1.2).

On the conception of it that I advocate, the virtue of courage requires at least a minimal motivational integration of the self. It requires a developed ability and willingness to take one's most important aims into account in dealing with fears and dangers. That is something one can hardly have unless there is enough stability in one's aims, and strong enough relations of priority among them, for some of them to *be* one's most important aims. Personal integration of this sort is itself a structural virtue. We may indeed think it the most fundamental of structural virtues, being presupposed by all the others.

## 2.2. Is Even Courage One?

Among the traditional cardinal virtues, courage stands out as one in which we routinely distinguish modules, as I noted in chapter 8, section 2.2. For instance, we distinguish between "physical courage," which deals well with physical dangers, and "moral courage," which deals well with social dangers.[18] It seems quite possible to have one of these without the other, and I think either can be a virtue without the other. We recognize that a police officer who is ready to risk his life in the line of duty may not find it in himself to act on his beliefs in the face of likely disapproval from his associates. I think most people will find it plausible to classify his physical courage as real courage, and a virtue, even in the absence of moral courage. Such separability of kinds of courage might be hard to accept if we supposed courage to be a unitary and invariant psychological cause, but there is plenty of reason not to suppose that.

In chapter 8 I called attention to the difference between physical and moral courage in the context of a discussion of direct behavioral dispositions. But in fact courage is probably always a psychological structure too complex to be simply a behavioral disposition, and the separability of the kinds of courage is rooted in the structure. It is not evident that the virtues are all members of a single natural kind. Many of them are not normally defined by their mechanism or inner workings, but rather as qualities of excellence in fulfilling certain functions. As functional states, they can be realized in quite different ways. What concretely constitutes virtues is often quite complex, and may be very different in different

---

[17] This may not be a merely fantastic example; cf. Miller, *The Mystery of Courage*, chapter 6.
[18] Cf. Badhwar, "The Limited Unity of Virtue," p. 314.

cases of "the same virtue." That seems particularly likely to be true of the structural virtues.

It may be less true of the motivational virtues. They are defined principally by desires or intentions that are central features of their inner working, as benevolence is defined by a reliable and not merely instrumental will to do good to other people. But the proportion of virtues defined in that way may be smaller than we would at first expect. Generosity, for instance, seems close kin to benevolence, but is not defined by a single motive; for the diversity of goods at which generosity may aim is very wide. Not only help to the needy, but also patriotism, patronage of the arts, and praise of another's merit can be generous. Generosity may be defined as an ability, readiness, and tendency to give or put oneself forward freely in support of ends one regards as good, without being overly constrained by any of the bad or good reasons there are for holding back. This is a broadly functional definition, which leaves unspecified the motives and other inner workings, which surely may be quite different in different cases of generosity.

In chapter 8 I distinguished a number of psychological (and socio-psychological) kinds to which virtues can belong. Here I want to ask a somewhat different question. What psychological kinds can be part of the machinery of virtues? The following is a list that is not intended to be exhaustive; some of the listed kinds may overlap each other. They include: desires, intentions, attitudes, beliefs, ways of looking at things, hopes, fears; dispositions to act, think, feel, in certain ways; and abilities to respond in certain ways. Factors of these types may be ingredients in a virtue without all of them being virtues themselves. Even if the belief that you are physically strong and healthy, for example, does not count as a virtue, it may still be part of what concretely constitutes the inner workings of your courage or your generosity in some contexts. It may be part of the machinery by which you control certain fears or maintain the inner freedom to give of yourself.

Let us take a closer look at such complexity, continuing to use *courage* as our example. We may define courage functionally, as an ability, readiness, and tend-ency to deal with fears and risks in a way that takes full account of one's most important aims and the value one sets on them, or the value one would set on them if not overpowered by fear. For further analysis I will first take up ways of dealing with fears and risks, and then ways of valuing and of organizing valu-ations.

Any form of courage will involve *ability* to deal with fears. This may or may not be *learned*; and if learned, it may or may not involve conscious *strategies* for overcoming fears. Concretely there is quite a variety of psychological states that may or may not be involved in controlling fear. Among them may indeed be *fears*; appropriate fears can help us to control fears on which it would be less appropriate to act. Fear of disgrace, as noted in section 2.1, may often be a factor in sustaining courage. It is not the noblest of motives, to be sure, but it is not altogether unvirtuous, if it is grounded in a just assessment of what is truly shameful. And which of us is able to live exclusively from the noblest motives? However, there can certainly be courage without this fear.

A seemingly opposite factor in much courage is *self-confidence*—by which here I mean confidence, not of escaping danger, but of being able to do what one has to do. More broadly, *hope* is a major factor in most courage. One runs risks because one hopes some significant good may be accomplished thereby. But even this is not absolutely essential to courage, for there seems to be despairing courage as well as hopeful courage. What should we say of someone who has both hope and hopeful courage but would not be able to stand courageously for her beliefs if she despaired of all good outcomes? No doubt she lacks a particular kind of personal strength that the person of despairing courage possesses. But it seems overly fastidious to deny therefore that her actually operative hopeful courage is a virtue.

Our more usual decomposition of courage into types appeals to the fact that the ability to deal with fear is likely to be specific to certain types of fear. Physical courage deals well with physical dangers, and moral courage deals well with social dangers. Dealing well with one but not the other could result either from individual predispositions to fear some types of danger much more intensely than others, or from differences in habituation and learned skills of self-government. One person has learned how to govern her action in accordance with her main values in the face of physical dangers, and has habituated herself to do so. Another has acquired the corresponding skills and habits in relation to social dangers. Either seems to be possible without the other.

We might discriminate more finely. We react quite differently to different types of social danger. One who deals well with fear of conflict and fear of moral censure might not be able to deal well with fear of losing friendship or popularity. Arguably physical courage too is divisible into factually separable modules based on differences in ability to deal with different types of physical danger.[19]

Situationist research suggests that such division might become very fine-grained indeed. Doris, who has no psychological objection to traits that are defined narrowly enough, seems to mock the idea of treating very fine-grained traits seriously as forms of courage. He says that a factually justifiable attribution of courage might have to be something like "sailing-in-rough-weather-with-one's-friends courageous."[20] This would be ridiculous, I agree, as an ascription of virtue if the implication were that it describes the *only* form of courage a person possesses. There is nothing in the situationist argument, however, to suggest that that is the normal case. The situationist conclusion is rather that we should expect to find people who possess some modules of physical courage and not others, in

[19] On this point testimonies of military experience cited in Miller, *The Mystery of Courage*, are quite convincing.
[20] Doris, *Lack of Character*, p. 115.

patterns that might take quite a bit of psychological research to understand. But that is quite compatible with there being plenty of people who manifest physical courage in a majority of the relevant types of situation that they encounter. Given the probable correlation between familiarity with dangers and an ability to deal with them, it seems likely that they will show physical courage in an even higher percentage of the individual occasions for it in their lives. It is surely reasonable to say that such people have a considerable measure of physical courage.

The physical and the social do not exhaust the types of danger. For example, people who deal well with fears on those two fronts may find that fear of financial risks impairs the rationality of their investment decisions. If the strength opposite to this weakness is not called "financial courage," that may be because we view it as less likely than "physical" or "moral courage" to be engaged in actions that cry out for moral assessment.

Probably few if any of us have no type of fear that we fail to manage well. Consider, for another example, parents who are "overprotective" though they know they shouldn't be. They could be paragons of physical, moral, and even financial courage, and yet lack something of what we might call the "vicarious courage" involved in dealing well with fears for persons one loves. And what about the fear of unfamiliar social contexts and of deep and pervasive social change? That very understandable type of fear is important, and causes much havoc, if not in all historic situations, at least in ours. It might therefore be reasonable for us to identify as a distinct virtue the ability and willingness to deal well with this fear. Such examples suggest ways in which even rather generally courageous people are likely still to have one or more modules of courage that they lack and could and should, perhaps, acquire. The acquisition, I think, would be likely to involve some fairly situation-specific learning.

Similar issues arise if we attend to the role of *valuation* in courage. Courage is a matter of dealing with fears and dangers, not in just any way that seems good at the time, or that impresses other people, but in a way that takes adequately into account one's valuation of one's most important aims. There are different forms of valuing that may be involved in a coherent order of values that courage takes into account. The most obvious, I suppose, is *caring* about goods for the sake of which one may face danger. How much one cares about such goods can clearly be an important part of the mechanism of courage. But so can a *commitment* to act on certain principles, or to pursue certain ends. One can certainly care about the ends one is committed to pursue, but these are distinct motives, with different structures. One can *care*, for instance, without believing anything in particular about one's own attitude; but full subjective *commitment* involves the *belief* that one is committed.

It is an important fact that one can care a lot about an end—enough to run serious risks for it—without being *committed* to pursue it. And I think the strength of one's subjective commitment to pursue an end can be out of proportion to the strength of one's caring about the end. Perhaps one cares more about the commitment itself than about the end—though commitment without any relation at all to caring for an end to be served by the commitment seems likely to be rather a monstrosity. With these differences in mind we can distinguish between a *conscientious* courage that is willing to run serious risks in order to abide by sufficiently important commitments, and a *teleological* courage that is willing to run serious risks in order to pursue goods about which one cares enough. It seems quite possible that a person who relies heavily on conscious commitments in controlling her responses to temptations might be strong in conscientious courage but quite weak in teleological courage. And it seems unduly harsh to deny that conscientious courage is a moral virtue in such a case.

Our discussion of the separability of courage from other virtues, in section 2.1, began with the question of whether one can have courage as a virtue without the virtue of justice; and I argued that one can. The implication in the other direction might have seemed stronger, and I have not questioned it thus far. We may well doubt that one could have the virtue of justice without courage, thinking perhaps especially of *moral* courage. However, if we are prepared to recognize mutually separable modules of courage as virtues, we may well think that one could have justice as a virtue while lacking one or more of those separable virtues of courage.

Separability of justice as a virtue is obviously affected by how we carve up the territory. Suppose we define the virtue of justice very inclusively, as a disposition to act justly in all circumstances, where acting justly is treating others as one owes it to them to do, respecting their rights, and upholding or promoting just causes and institutions. Then it seems likely that it would require courage, moderation, and practical wisdom, as the ancients argued. Even on that very encompassing definition of the virtue of justice, however, it hardly seems to require *all* modules of those virtues. Lack of *financial* courage, immoderation affecting mainly one's own health, and poor judgment in some areas of personal life, would not normally be counted against a person's reputation for justice, nor do I think they should be.

In the case of *physical* courage the issue of separability may be more difficult, and may push harder against an extremely inclusive definition of the virtue of justice. Imagine a person who is not able to handle certain types of physical danger at all well, having shown cowardice with respect to such dangers, which has impeded her pursuits of some purely personal projects. She has never had to face such dangers for the sake of justice, but her personal history suggests it is likely that if justice did require the corresponding sort of physical courage of her, she would fail the test. In other respects, however, her justice is exemplary. She is sensitive to the rights of others, punctilious in respecting them, willing to yield personal advantage for the sake of justice, and vigorous in discerning and supporting just causes. Would or should we say that she is not a just person, simply because her deficiency in physical courage would probably lead her to act unjustly in some circumstances (though that hasn't in fact happened)? We wouldn't, and I think we shouldn't.

Now suppose a time comes when justice does require physical courage of this person, and she fails the test. Should we say this shows her to be unjust, or only (in some respects) a coward? I think it is more illuminating to say only that she showed (physical) cowardice. Although her act was unjust, there is no reason to say she lacks a sense of justice, or zeal for justice. Nor have we been given a compelling reason to doubt that these are excellences in her character. Her problem is that she has not learned to deal with (certain) physical dangers, and thus lacks (a module of) physical courage. It would be less illuminating to classify as injustice all deficiencies of character that predictably lead, in some circumstances, by whatever mechanism, to unjust acts.

## 3. WISDOM

There is one of the traditionally recognized virtues that holds pride of place in classical arguments for the unity of the virtues, and that is practical wisdom. From Socrates' time to our own, such arguments have often been arguments for a relation of mutual entailment, or even identity, between practical wisdom, or knowledge of what is to be done, and every other virtue.[21] Practical wisdom is understood as including wise attitudes and wise actions as well as wise beliefs and good reasoning. But wise thought and attitude and action, it is argued, exhaust the territory of the other virtues, which now appear as mere aspects of practical wisdom, and thus of unitary virtue. Given the prominence of such ideas, our treatment of the supposed unity of the virtues can hardly be complete without a discussion of practical wisdom and its place among the virtues. We will examine issues, first, about the unity of practical wisdom itself, and then about its relation to other virtues.

### 3.1. Is Wisdom One?

Is practical wisdom indissolubly one? It seems not, for it seems possible to be wise about some matters and not about others. As Neera Badhwar aptly observes, "human understanding is not an all-or-nothing affair in any other sphere of skill or knowledge. We do not, for instance, believe that philosophic or scientific knowledge must be either complete or else non-existent."[22] The understanding and discernment involved in practical wisdom depends heavily on relevant experience, as Badhwar rightly insists. For this reason (and perhaps others too) one wise in statecraft, for example, may not be wise in parenting.[23] Indeed history

---

[21] Plato, *Protagoras* 349A–361C; and, for a recent example, McDowell, "Virtue and Reason."
[22] Badhwar, "The Limited Unity of Virtue," p. 313.
[23] Ibid., pp. 314–15.

affords plausible examples of that particular combination. This suggests the following line of argument. I do not believe that all the virtues are merely forms or aspects of practical wisdom. But suppose, for the sake of argument, that that is what they are. It still will not follow that the virtues all entail each other.[24]

On such a view, for example, courage might be identified with wisdom as shown in not overestimating the importance of dangers that inspire fear, and temperance with wisdom as shown in not overvaluing goods that inspire desire.[25] It certainly seems that one might have so much of one of these types of wisdom and so little of the other as to be rightly said to have the one virtue and lack the other. Similarly, justice might be identified with wisdom as shown in recognizing and respecting people's rights, and kindness with wisdom in recognizing and caring for the needs and feelings of others. Again it seems one could be deficient in one of these without being deficient in the other. It is not necessary for my argument to claim that one could have one of these virtues, defined as a form of wisdom, while having *none at all* of the cognitive competences characteristic of one or all of the other virtues. For we do not credit anyone with courage just for having *some* ability to deal with fears, or with justice for having a *non-zero* sensitivity to people's rights. Indeed, a mere non-zero sensitivity is hardly an adequate basis for attributing any form of wisdom either.

Wisdom is multiple, not only in the diverse realms of life in which it may operate, but also the diverse sources from which it may spring. This is particularly important for our present discussion because in the classical doctrine of the unity of the virtues practical wisdom appears as the unitary causal principle of all virtue. In fact there is reason to believe practical wisdom is a product of many causes and not a unitary causal principle at all. Intellectual skills and good habits of thinking can doubtless play a part in it; I believe the study of ethical theory can help. But it is a mistake to suppose that all aspects of ethical enlightenment are, or can be, acquired by practiced and disciplined rational inquiry alone.

*Experience* may be required, fresh experience of some reality, and of the possibilities and problems of good and evil in it. Love can be such an experience. I suppose also that religious and moral *conversion*, when it has any value, is commonly grounded in such experience. As that reference suggests, the experience may often be one that we could not have procured for ourselves by rational planning.

It may also be one that we did not, would not, and perhaps should not, have wanted for ourselves. This point connects with the liberation theologians' idea of a "hermeneutical privilege of the poor." If there is such a privilege, it is unlikely to be attained by voluntary poverty as long as it is welcomed as voluntary, since

---

[24] My argument for separability of virtues, on the assumption that all of them are forms of practical *wisdom* could proceed in much the same way, and as successfully, I believe, on the assumption (perhaps more fashionable today) that all of them are forms of practical *rationality*.
[25] Cf. Kamtekar, "Situationism and Virtue Ethics," pp. 480–1.

part of the revelation is likely to be in the unwelcomeness of it. It would not be surprising if those who are not taken in by false values prevalent in the society in which they live turn out in many or most cases to be outsiders, or in other ways to have unusual social positions or personal histories that give them an unusual perspective on what is going on. Those unusual characteristics may not be associated with a very general excellence of character. In any event they are not generally produced by disciplined reflection, though such reflection may make use of them. Not that poverty or social alienation is the only ground of ethically revelatory experience. A single human life is unlikely to include all the relevant experiences. The philosopher who has all her time to think about ethics may be privileged in one way in opportunities for practical wisdom, while people who lack those opportunities may have experience that grounds a sort of wisdom less accessible to the typical philosopher.

We may reasonably expect the forms of practical wisdom to vary quite widely. Diversities of temperament, experience, vocation, and moral and religious outlook are very likely to leave some people more sensitive to some goods, and others to other goods. This may not satisfy those, such as John McDowell, who define virtue not merely as a sort of *wisdom*, but more precisely as a sort of *knowledge*. " 'Knowledge' ", as McDowell points out, "implies that [its possessor] gets things right." McDowell welcomes the implication that if virtue is a kind of knowledge, virtues must be "states of character whose possessor arrives at right answers to a certain range of questions about how to behave."[26] Such a view would dispose us to think that in large and substantive differences in sensitivity to various goods, at most one party truly possesses the knowledge that constitutes virtue.

Precisely this, however, can be taken as a reason for assigning a pivotal role in virtue to wisdom rather than knowledge. As I have emphasized, it seems to me that virtue is primarily a matter of goodness rather than of rightness. Always getting it right is an *unwise* ambition for human beings. At any rate it is unwise to expect anyone always to get it right, and unwise to let assessments of rightness crowd out appreciation of goodness. Wisdom, like virtue, is a form of excellence more than of correctness. Certainly practical wisdom must generally enhance the likelihood of getting things right, and is often manifested in discerning what is the right thing to do. But it is equally manifested in recognizing what reasons are relevant and important in a given context. More wisdom may be shown in *deliberating well* but coming to a wrong conclusion than in reaching the right conclusion through a bad deliberative process. Wisdom is also in large part a matter of having a just appreciation of what matters in life. Such appreciation is not a matter of decision-making; rather it provides a context for decisions. And the wisdom of one's appreciation is not strictly or definitively measured by the rightness of one's decisions.

[26] McDowell, "Virtue and Reason," pp. 141–2.

## 3.2. Wisdom's Relation to Other Virtues

There is reason, moreover, to refrain from identifying the other virtues with forms of practical wisdom. In virtually every ethically assessable action, I grant, wisdom or the lack of it is engaged. So too is the presence or absence of one or more of the other virtues. But it commonly seems both possible and justified to distinguish failures of wisdom from failures of the other virtues.

Contrary to Socrates in Plato's *Protagoras*, I don't think a courageous person, for example, necessarily has good judgment about which risks are worth running. In particular, I think a courageous person can have *randomly mediocre* judgment on the subject, so long as the errors of judgment do not fall too heavily on the side either of caution, evincing cowardice, or of boldness, evincing rashness. Where the errors are randomly distributed, there is a failure of ethical judgment, and thus of practical wisdom, but not of courage. Here, of course, I assume that the agent is willing and able to run risks when she judges, rightly or wrongly, that they are worth running. The ability and will to run serious risks in accordance with one's judgment is an impressive strength that will and should be admired even in those whose judgment is mediocre.

Likewise, randomly mediocre judgment in weighing against each other the goods sought by different motivational virtues seems compatible with those virtues, though not with practical wisdom. Someone who regularly gives too little weight to the goods of kindness, in comparison with those of candor and fairness, is deficient in kindness, as well as in the kindness aspect of practical wisdom. But someone whose moderately frequent erroneous misvaluations in these matters do not manifest a pattern of bias against any one of the competing classes of goods is deficient only in wisdom. Of course, cognitive deficiencies of other sorts, such as insensitivity to other people's feelings, can constitute a deficiency in kindness. However, we might still ascribe a virtue of "kindheartedness" to an imperceptive person who sincerely and seriously wants to be helpful and comforting to others.

I also believe there are bad actions, and bad attitudes, that are traceable to a lack, not of practical wisdom, but of other virtues. With regard to bad actions, this belief lands me on the controversial terrain of the debate about *weakness of will*. That debate has a historic starting point in the same dialogue of Plato as the thesis of the unity of the virtues, the *Protagoras*. That is no accident, for Socrates' argument there that no one voluntarily goes against possessed wisdom—that "no one willingly goes toward things that are or that he believes to be bad" (358D)—is part of his argument that virtue is identical with practical wisdom, and therefore one.

In Plato's dialogue this is a point about the *power* of wisdom. Socrates easily gets Protagoras to agree to the suggestion that:

Knowledge [*epistēmē*] is a noble [*kalon*] thing, and able to rule the human being; and if one knows what is good and bad, one will not be conquered by anything so as to do anything other than what knowledge commands, but practical wisdom [*phronēsis*] is sufficient help for the human being. (352C)

For these two intellectuals, and perhaps especially for Protagoras, the professional teacher of wisdom, the *honor* of wisdom is at stake here. Protagoras says it would be "shameful" for him "to say that wisdom [*sophia*] and knowledge [*epistēmē*] are not the strongest[27] thing in human affairs."

But why should we believe that wisdom has such indomitable power? As a virtue, it must engage the will, in the sense explained in chapter 2. That is, it must involve dispositions to act and care in accordance with its discernment of value. Thus it implies dispositions to wise concern and wise action as well as wise reasoning. But dispositions can be real and really influential without being invincible. Few, if any, dispositions of a human mind are invincible. Why should we think that the dispositions involved in practical wisdom are invincible, and not merely influential?

It is plausible to suppose that there are two dimensions in which we can assess the excellence of dispositions formed on the basis of perception and thought regarding value. We can ask how wise the dispositions are. The virtue measured by the answer to this first question, I believe, can reasonably be identified with practical wisdom; but you may call it ethical understanding if you prefer. And we can ask how strong the dispositions are, how reliably they govern concern and action. The virtue measured by the answer to this second question is variously called resoluteness, strength of will, and strength of character.

Much experience suggests that a substantively unwise action can be due to a failure of resoluteness rather than of practical wisdom in the sense just indicated. Sometimes, for example, I continue reading a novel late at night when I judge that it would be wiser for me to go to bed. That does not happen because I don't know any better, but because of weakness of will. It happens because in that situation my self-control (not to mention temperance) is not what I should wish—or so it certainly seems to me. As I unwisely continue reading, I feel the pull of wiser dispositions that I do have, though they fail to overcome my eagerness to finish the story. Wisdom and will are not totally independent here, but they do not move in lock step.

People who are in general equally discerning may not be equally resolute. There are surely cases in which people's perception of goodness is better than their success in living it. It is one thing to depart from the path of moral wisdom through lack of understanding; another to leave it through weakness of will. Deviation from what one recognizes as the right path, particularly if motivated

---

[27] *Kratiston*, which also means "best." Both meanings are probably at work in Protagoras statement, but I translate it as "strongest" because the language of power is so prominent in the passage.

by strong temptation, such as that of fear, is reasonably seen as arising from a shortage of resoluteness or self-control rather than of moral intelligence.

Both resoluteness and ethical understanding are excellences and may plausibly be regarded as virtues separable, to some extent, from each other. It may not matter very much whether we choose to reserve the title, 'practical wisdom', for a combination of the two, or whether we choose to align the concept of practical wisdom with that of ethical understanding. If we do the latter we will say that while having practical wisdom entails *normally* acting in wise ways, even wise people *sometimes* perform substantively unwise actions. Those actions are attributable, not to lack of practical wisdom, but to weakness of will, or to deficiency in particular structural virtues closely connected with strength of will, such as courage and self-control. We can, of course, make the conceptual move of defining practical wisdom as a more inclusive property, closer to comprehensive virtue. But that will not show that practical wisdom cannot be analyzed, as regards its causal structure, into factors that vary independently of each other to some extent.

The corresponding point about bad *attitudes* does not engage the debate about weakness of will, and can be made more briefly. An example will suffice. It seems quite possible for there to be a person who is practically wise in general, and about personal relationships in particular, having loved other people enough to have a depth of sensitivity and understanding regarding such relationships—but who, for whatever reasons, finds that he does not, and cannot, love one of his own children as he ought. In action, his dealings with the child are generally as wisdom would command; but something important is missing in his attitude, which the child, sadly, does not fail to notice. His attitude is not what wisdom would recommend. The deficiency in virtue that it may manifest, however, is not a deficiency in practical wisdom, but rather in love.


## 4. BENEVOLENCE

Somewhat different issues about the mutual entailment thesis may arise with regard to *motivational* virtues (as I am calling them). Their central feature is some particular type of good motive. Unlike structural virtues, they are all quite straightforwardly ways of being for the good, or at any rate for something good. Might it be that attitudes toward different goods are necessarily so intertwined that one cannot be excellently for any good without a comprehensive excellence in one's attitudes toward all sorts of goods? An affirmative answer to this question would suggest that at least the motivational virtues do all imply each other. In fact I believe that relations among the motivational virtues are more complex than that. This section examines a prime example of a motivational virtue: benevolence.

## 4.1. When Good Motives Compete

We begin with a particular form of benevolence: *kindness*. I take it to be a matter of being effectively motivated by a concern for the well-being of other people, and *in particular* for their enjoyment and comfort in the near future. Good motives can conflict, as when it may seem unkind to tell the truth in a given situation. In that case, we may be tempted to conclude, the virtues of kindness and truthfulness not only fail to entail each other, but actually are mutually incompatible. Theorists of virtue have generally resisted this temptation—and rightly so, in my opinion. It is plausible to think that any sound development of a motivational virtue would incorporate a sensitivity to really compelling reasons to limit its demands. An otherwise virtuous concern so strong that it must override such reasons is no longer a virtue but an idolatry. The virtue of kindness will therefore rarely demand a lie. And the *virtue* of truthfulness (as distinct from a *fetish* of truthfulness) will not insist on the unvarnished truth where it must wound feelings that there is compelling reason to spare.

At this point we meet another temptation. We might conclude that a *correct* balancing of the two interests is precisely what is required by both virtues in such cases. That would suggest that true possession of any one motivational virtue implies a reliable tendency to govern and (as necessary) to limit the operation of the motives most characteristic of that virtue in accordance with the *right* reasons. From this it may seem a short step to the conclusion that all the virtues (or at any rate all the motivational virtues), are swallowed up in one single virtue, which is simply a general disposition to act rightly in every context. I will resist this temptation too, having argued that virtue is first and foremost a matter not of being right but of being good—not just of acting *rightly*, but more broadly of acting, and living, *well*.

What is essential to a motivational virtue? First, that it aims at a certain sort of *good* and motivates action and affection accordingly. And, second, that one has a pretty reliable tendency to govern and (as necessary) to limit the operation of the motives most characteristic of the virtue in accordance with reasons that one *regards as* important, good, and sufficient. The latter, in my opinion, is all the self-limitation that a trait of motivation must have if it is to be a virtue and not an idolatry. It is not essential to the particular motivational virtue that the agent be responsive to the *right* reasons. No doubt there is some sort of failure of virtue if one is commonly wrong in one's evaluation of reasons for limiting or not limiting the operation of a good motive in particular cases. As I argued in section 3.2, however, if one's judgment in weighing such reasons is randomly mediocre, and not persistently biased against one of the competing goods, it is most plausible to count that as a failure of practical wisdom, and not of kindness or any of the other motivational virtues.

A focus on the good rather than the right in judgments about the virtues is helpful here because there are typically more ways of being good than of being right. The way of virtue is less strait and narrow than the path of duty, though virtue can certainly inspire more than duty commands. An action or a character can be good in one way and bad in another; but actions, at any rate, are normally just right (in conformity with duty—with all duties) or wrong (contrary to some duty). What is right is generally in some way good, and what is wrong is certainly in some way bad. But one can be good in important ways in being wrong, and it is also all too easy to be bad in important ways (self-righteous, for example, or unfeeling) in being right. An action wholly or predominantly motivated by kindness may be imprudent, unfair, or untruthful in a way that makes it wrong, all things considered. But the motive of kindness, in itself, is still an excellence, an excellent way of being for the good.

It is relevant here to consider the psychological dynamics of learning to be virtuous. The kind person who is too unwilling to tell painful truths may need to learn to value truthfulness more highly, but does not need to unlearn or reacquire the motive of kindness. In kindness, rather, such a person already is in part what a virtuous person should be, and has something to build on in becoming more virtuous. That seems to me to be a reason for classifying the trait as already a virtue.[28] We may of course judge differently of a kindness that makes such an idol of people's feelings as to get in the way of learning to care appropriately about possibly competing goods.

## 4.2. Compromised Motives

For such reasons the extreme thesis that the virtue of kindness, or more broadly of benevolence, entails *all* the virtues seems quite implausible. Ruling out such an extreme position, however, does not answer the larger, more open-ended question, *how much* of the spectrum of forms of virtue is required for benevolence if it is to be a virtue. Going to the opposite extreme in answering that question is also implausible. Benevolence, as a virtue, cannot be coherently conceived as existing in modules that are too small or too local. The reason for this is not that more of the spectrum of forms of virtue is required for reliable generation of right action, though that may indeed be true. The reason is rather that the moral significance of one's way of being in one situation is not constituted altogether independently

---

[28] This argument can also be applied to structural virtues (and is applied to courage by MacIntyre in *After Virtue*, p. 180). The person who is brave but unjust or selfish does not need to unlearn or relearn courage. She needs to give the ends of justice, including the interests of others, a much greater place among her aims. But she has already learned to face dangers where that is important for what she values most; and that is something important to build on in learning to be virtuous. Given points made in section 2.2 about the modularity of courage, we may need to take into account a possibility that someone may have learned nothing of courage except to face dangers when impelled by certain passions that in fact are selfish or unjust. That sort of bravery would presumably not survive the eradication of the evil passions, and also should probably not count as a virtue. But I think in fact the acquisition of courage is likelier to be specific to the type of danger to be faced than to the ends to be pursued.

of actions and attitudes in at least a relevant range of other situations. I put the
point in terms of "modules" of virtue, rather than different virtues, because I do
not want to worry, in this context, about whether what is required is enough different virtues or enough modules of the same virtue. That is a question whose
answer may involve some degree of taxonomic arbitrariness.

The point will be developed here in relation to historically grounded examples:
three cases of Germans, with links to the Nazi war organization, who were helpful
in some contexts to persecuted Jews during World War II. For each case I rely
on a single source, and for one case on a source that is at least lightly fictional-
ized. The sources seem to have pretty rich documentation behind them; but my
present interest in the cases is philosophical rather than historical, and my comments about them should be understood as comments about the characters *as*
presented in the sources.

In all three cases we are dealing with characters with clear and serious moral
flaws. In one of them I believe major virtues, including a virtue, or virtues, of
benevolence, are clearly manifested despite the deficiencies. In one, ascription of
a virtue of benevolence that might be suggested by a narrow view of some of the
helpfulness seems to me deeply undercut by the character of the individual's sins.
The third case seems more ambiguous. We will begin with the one most deeply
compromised, and conclude with the one whose virtues are clear; he will also, of
course, be a further counterexample to the thesis of the mutual implication of all
virtues.

(1) The story of Eduard Wirths includes what certainly must be regarded as
crimes against humanity.[29] As the SS's chief physician at Auschwitz, in charge
of medical services in the camp, he not only participated in mass murder, but
organized the method of perpetrating it. He personally selected thousands of
prisoners for the gas chambers, insisting on doing such things himself. For his
own research he organized medical experiments on prisoners that were harmful to them and offered them no benefits. Can there be anything good to be
said about him? Yes, in fact there is. Regarded as "a dedicated physician," he
was "described by inmates who could observe him closely as 'kind,' 'conscientious,' 'decent,' 'polite,' and 'honest',"[30] though some former prisoners expressed
less favorable evaluations. He instituted and enforced measures that substantially
improved health care for prisoners. He fought, sometimes successfully, within the
SS structure to end certain types of arbitrary execution of inmates. And he used
his considerable influence to save quite a number of individual Jews and other
prisoners, especially health-care workers, from death in the gas chambers.

---

[29] My account of Wirths is entirely based on Lifton, *The Nazi Doctors*, whose eighteenth chapter
is devoted to Wirths. The book is a rich source for moral philosophers because of its fullness of detail
and Lifton's moral sensitivity and refusal to oversimplify his accounts of people whose involvement
with Nazism is deeply offensive to him.

[30] Lifton, *The Nazi Doctors*, p. 384.

Although he was devoted to the Nazi cause, and had accepted the view that "the Jews were a danger to Germany,"[31] Wirths fairly openly disapproved of the policy of mass extermination that he was helping to carry out. In an inmate survivor's words, he was "a Nazi ideologist . . . who did not like the methods of the gas chamber,. . . [who] wanted the Nazis to win but not this way." Distressed and conflicted about his situation, he talked about wanting to be transferred out of Auschwitz.[32] The political prisoner who served as his secretary pleaded with him to remain for the sake of the prisoners, arguing, "In the past year you have saved here the lives of 93,000 people" (by improving health care).[33]

There seems to be no doubt that Wirths had medical ideals that were important to him, and acted as a conscientious physician in some contexts, sometimes showing a measure of courage in doing so. There also seems to be no doubt that he had considerable sympathy and human feeling for many Jewish as well as non-Jewish prisoners, and some sort of benevolent motivation toward them. The question that concerns me here is whether we can plausibly count this as a manifestation of a *virtue* of benevolence, even a modular and situation-specific virtue.

I am inclined to think the answer is No. This is not to deny that he was morally better for having the qualities just mentioned than if he had not had them. But we have to ask what *kind* of good will he can have had toward prisoners. With regard to most, if not all of them, he stood ready in principle to order their execution if they became useless (through illness or otherwise) to the Nazi project. With regard to the Jewish prisoners, he was not only a participant but an organizer in a project aimed at exterminating them all. In this context, the modules of good will that he manifested toward prisoners do not seem to me fully humane. They amount to something less than the kind of good will one should have toward a fellow human being. This is not necessarily to say that Wirths's good will did not seem humane at all, to Wirths himself or to inmates who experienced it, in immediate, momentary situations.[34] It is rather that its humanity was compromised by what Wirths persistently willed in other areas of the larger context. Being too modular, it did not have enough of Wirths's self behind it. It was not an *excellent* benevolence, and thus was not a virtue.

[31] Ibid., p. 403.

[32] It is worth noting here that conscious distress over what they were doing, and verbal expressions of disagreement with the program they nonetheless continued to carry out, were among the phenomena Stanley Milgram observed in subjects in his experiments on obedience. (I described these experiments in chapter 9, section 1.2.) Milgram suggests that such verbal expressions of dissent served to relieve the subjects' feelings of distress without giving them more active expression (see Milgram, *Obedience to Authority*, pp. 161–2).

[33] Lifton, *The Nazi Doctors*, p. 389.

[34] In reminiscence years after the events, some of these who had been in contact with Wirths as prisoners seem to have believed that they experienced a humane good will from him. Others were more skeptical in their evaluation; one former inmate whom Wirths employed and valued as a physician, and protected, said somewhat reluctantly that "he was probably as bad as the other ones" (ibid., pp. 391–2).

It is easier to think of his better qualities as virtues in the context of his rural medical practice in his pre-Auschwitz years, when he continued to treat Jewish patients "after it became illegal for Aryan doctors to do so,"[35] although he was already a member of the Nazi Party. If they should no longer be counted as virtues at Auschwitz, is that because their intrinsic character had changed for the worse? Perhaps it had, in some ways; but I don't think that's the basis for our different assessment of his character in the two situations. It's rather that the moral meaning of the good traits that he retains is changed by a new context in Auschwitz, a new context constituted not only by other attitudes and actions of his own but also by things other people were doing, on a horrendous scale, with his cooperation. This is a case of the sort I discussed in chapter 8, section 4, involving affiliation and social role, in which the line between factors of situation and personal character is blurred. The horrifying thing about Wirths in Auschwitz, we may say, is not so much what's in him, as what he's in—what he's in voluntarily, of course.

(2) Another SS physician, the director of the Hygienic Institute at Auschwitz, called "Ernst B" by Robert Jay Lifton, on whose account of him mine is based, presents a more ambiguous case. Dr B refused to participate in selecting prisoners for the gas chambers; so far as Lifton could discover, he was the only SS doctor at Auschwitz who never selected.[36] He not only avoided all direct personal involvement in killing; former inmates, mostly doctors, with whom he had worked reported that he treated them as fellow human beings in a way that other SS personnel never did.[37] Their testimony led to his acquittal when he was charged with war crimes after the war. He also saved many individual lives, exerting himself in a variety of ways, sometimes involving duplicity toward the SS organization, to keep people from being sent to the gas chambers.

This is not to say that he was trying to reduce the total *number* of prisoners that died at Auschwitz. That was not a practicable goal for anyone in his situation. The system worked in such a way that the number who died was mostly a function of the number sent to the camp.[38] B's refusal to select, which was facilitated by his position in the Institute, therefore did not mean that fewer people were sent to the gas chambers, as he knew only too well. It was in fact to do selections in his place that Dr Hans Delmotte was brought to Auschwitz. Delmotte's initial horror at what he was asked to do, which I described in chapter 8, section 4, was mirrored in B's feeling of guilt about the substitution.[39] The situation was one in which a quantitative life-saving motivation could do little to deliver a realistic person from moral paralysis.

There seems to be little doubt that Ernst B was in many ways benevolent, compassionate, and friendly toward the prisoners with whom he had to do. Lifton also saw him as holding an "ideal of integrity of the self," which he thinks helped

[35] Lifton, *The Nazi Doctors*, p. 386.      [36] Ibid., p. 208.      [37] Ibid., p. 303.
[38] Ibid., p. 394.      [39] Ibid., pp. 310–11.

B to maintain his level of decency and humanity in Auschwitz. In this connection Lifton speaks of an "admirable, even extraordinary" achievement.[40] This appraisal seems justified on any realistic view of the malign psychological power of the Auschwitz situation.

Why then do I call Dr B's an ambiguous case? What reason would there be to deny that he had and manifested important virtues of integrity, benevolence, and conscientious regard for the rights of other people? There is, in what I have read about him, little or nothing to suggest that his claim to such virtues is undercut or compromised by any wrongful harms done to prisoners by his own personal choices, actions, and attitudes toward them. Hours of interviews with Lifton, however, reveal aspects of his political and social affiliations and loyalties that do seem to compromise, to a significant extent, his regard for the humanity of prisoners. To be sure, the evidence for this is given in attitudes expressed in interviews many years after the war; but Lifton seems reasonable in treating it, cautiously, as evidence of attitudes B had in Auschwitz.

Nothing is more disturbing about those interviews than B's praise for the infamous Dr Josef Mengele as "the most decent colleague" that he met at Auschwitz, and his insistent plea for understanding for the internal rationality of Mengele's racist views and motives.[41] That is surely defending the indefensible. B pulled back from unequivocal condemnation of the Nazis' murderous "final solution" of what he himself seems to have agreed to some extent in viewing as a Jewish "problem." Most fundamentally, he refused to dissociate himself from his former colleagues in the SS, and in the interviews played down moral differences between himself and them.[42]

B refused to repudiate the SS colleagues whose friendship he had sought and valued in their days of power, or to dissociate himself from them after they had become objects of almost universal condemnation, hatred, and contempt. It seems possible that this was motivated by the same will to integrity of selfhood that Lifton sees as sustaining his humanity in the camp. We could discuss whether its morally compromising manifestations disqualify B's *integrity* from counting as a virtue. Integrity, or willed personal consistency, is a structural virtue, as courage is. It is an excellent personal strength, which can in principle be manifested in morally wrong choices. But one might think that carrying personal consistency to the point of defending Mengele was making a fetish rather than a virtue of it.

Our present concern, in any event, is with the demands of benevolence rather than of integrity. Was the good will Dr B showed for prisoners compromised as a virtue by his solidarity with his SS colleagues? What kind of benevolence can you have for people when you are prepared to plead for understanding of the point of view of those who are murdering them in such a monstrous way? Was not moral

[40] Ibid., p. 335.     [41] Ibid., pp. 308, 321–5.     [42] Ibid., pp. 320, 329–32.

regard for Jews as human beings already compromised simply by believing that there was such a thing as a "Jewish problem" to be solved?

Lifton comments that the "draconian attitudes" that surface in B's pleas for understanding for the Nazis:

were much less operative in him than was his capacity to respond humanely to individual Jews. Whatever these conflicts and contradictions, this capacity, when expressed in an institution whose purpose was the annihilation of Jews, was exemplary and, for many, life-sustaining.[43]

Dependent as I am on Lifton's impressions of the man, I am not inclined to object to his judgment that B manifested virtues of humanity and benevolence, with a measure of excellence, in Auschwitz. But I think we cannot regard B as an unambiguous exemplar of such virtues, given his persistent affirmation of his SS affiliation and allegiance.

We stand on a slippery slope here, and cannot easily get off it. We may find no virtue, and no virtues, at all, if we insist that they must be perfectly consistent, and totally uncompromised by any association with collective policies and projects that are in some way opposed to them. Except in close relationships, the good will of human beings toward each other, and even their commitment to preserve each other's lives, are not often totally unconditional and totally unqualified. But even normally conditional and normally qualified good will can be a significant virtue. Is such a virtue very different from the disturbingly compromised good will of Ernst B, or even the radically compromised good will of Eduard Wirths?

We may be tempted to say the key difference is that one who has good will which is a virtue will not harm, or approve of harming, people who are objects of that good will except in ways that are *right* or *justified*. That seems to me too strict a view, however, and one that makes the virtue too much a matter of choosing correctly. I think we may reasonably regard harming as compatible with a virtue of benevolence where the agent's reasons for harming claim our respect even if we disagree with them. I regard the moral value of Wirths's and B's good will toward Jewish prisoners as compromised, in greater and lesser degree in the two cases. That is due in large part to my judging that the reasons for killing on which Wirths was willing to act, and which B was willing to treat as respectable, have no moral claim on our respect. In short, I believe the status of instances of good will as virtues or modules of virtue, depends in part on one's attitude to putative reasons for actions that would be adverse to the persons who are objects of the good will.

(3) My third case, the most famous of them as well as the one whose virtues are relatively uncompromised, is that of Oskar Schindler. His exploits in saving

---

[43] Lifton *The Nazi Doctors*, p. 333.

over a thousand Jews from the Nazi death machine have been celebrated in a well-known book and a famous movie.[44] A hero certainly, he was also no saint, and had a history of involvement with Nazism. He arrived in Cracow, the scene of most of his exploits, as a war profiteer, wearing an ostentatious Nazi swastika. He had affiliated with the Nazis in his native, largely German-speaking, region of Moravia while it was still part of Czechoslovakia, before Hitler annexed it. He manifested sympathy for the Nazis' military aims before the war by serving as a spy for the *Abwehr*, the German military intelligence service, in southern Poland, where he traveled as a salesman. And he came to Cracow on the heels of the German *Blitzkrieg* to get rich on the spoils of war, taking over a factory in which he would produce items to be sold on extremely profitable terms to the German military.

There are certain virtues that Oskar Schindler seems not to have had. One of them is justice. He was capable of becoming indignant at gross injustices perpetrated on Jews, and of refusing in certain contexts to enrich himself at the expense of Jews. But he seems to have had no compunctions about enriching himself unjustly in many contexts, and what is remembered about him gives little reason to think that he thought or cared much about general principles of justice—or of honesty. His story presents no evidence of the sort of dishonesty that would betray someone who trusted him in a morally legitimate enterprise,[45] but it also suggests no very general concern for honesty as such. He lied easily, and was skilled in taking advantage of the corruption that was rampant in the SS, and in maintaining insincere friendships with Nazi officials he had come (with reason) to detest.

When he did these things in order to save the lives of persecuted Jews, most or all of us will think it was morally justified. Perhaps a more scrupulous person, entering into the necessary deceptions less easily and more awkwardly, would not have brought them off so successfully, and would not have saved the lives that Schindler saved. But even a trait consequentialist should not think that a reason for holding that the unscrupulous aspect of his character was a virtue after all. For there is no reason to think it would be beneficial in better circumstances, and (as I argued in chapter 4) the most plausible forms of trait consequentialism will hold only that *generally* beneficial traits are virtues.

---

[44] The book, Keneally, *Schindler's List*, is my source. I take it to be substantially factual. Keneally calls it a novel, but says he "attempted . . . to avoid all fiction," claiming that "most exchanges and conversations, and all events, are based on the detailed recollections" of witnesses. He had interviewed "50 Schindler survivors," and done extensive archival research (pp. 9–10). The book has a bit of a hagiographical tone. It records manifestations of Schindler's vices, but plays them down more, I suspect, than is justified. Steven Spielberg's movie of the same title, which I had seen twice before I read the book, is more interesting both ethically and aesthetically, to my mind, for avoiding hagiography, and giving us vivid views of Schindler's vices before it shows his virtues emerging. In fairness to Schindler as well as Keneally, however, I should note that the book narrates a number of incidents very creditable to Schindler that did not find a place in the movie.

[45] Cf. Blum, "Moral Exemplars," p. 200.

Despite Schindler's deficiency in virtues that centrally involve caring about principles and acting on them, it is not plausible to deny the moral excellence of some of the traits he showed in rescuing Jews. I won't turn aside here to discuss issues about his courage, which I think is clearly one of his virtues; for I wish to focus on the sort of benevolence he manifested. Appalled and outraged at what he saw being done to the Jews, he developed a consuming commitment to saving the lives of a large group of them. This was a quite particularistic benevolence. It was somewhat open-ended; he was happy to add another Jew to his "list" if he thought he (and his Jews) could get away with it. But "his" Jews were definitely not interchangeable for him with others; he had a very particular commitment and loyalty to them and to saving *their* lives. There is no indication that he worried about why he was saving these people and not others, or that he was guided by such a general and impersonal goal as that of maximizing the number of lives saved.[46]

I believe the claim of this benevolence to be a virtue is not seriously compromised by Schindler's lack of some other important virtues, or even by his vices. This is not to say that he was a virtuous person, a morally good person, on the whole. I don't know whether he was. The deficiency he showed in virtues of principle or conscientiousness such as justice and honesty, in his projects as a war profiteer, is not a small moral flaw. Neither is his persistent exploitiveness and infidelity in sexual relations with women, which seems to have pained his long-suffering, supportive wife, who also threw herself into the final stages of his rescue of Jews.[47] His life before the war seems not to have shown much sign of moral fiber, and what is told us about his life after the war seems morally unremarkable. However, I don't count that as a good reason for denying that the good qualities he showed persistently (and increasingly) during six years of war and horror were genuine virtues. His wife's appraisal is apt: "He was fortunate . . . that in that short fierce era between 1939 and 1945 he had met people who summoned forth his deeper talents."[48]

Why do I think that Schindler's benevolence toward the Jews he was helping is less compromised as a virtue by his vices than Ernst B's comparable benevolence is by his Nazi affiliations and allegiance? This is not a judgment that Schindler *did more* to help those in danger of being murdered, though I suppose he did. The point is rather that Schindler's vices, serious as some of them may have been, did not involve vicious attitudes toward the people he was trying to help, and do not qualify or diminish his concern for those people and his loyalty to them, or his respect for their humanity. It is clearly relevant that his benevolence was not compromised, as that of Eduard Wirths and Ernst B was, by allegiance to

[46] Keneally, *Schindler's List*, pp. 319–20, 122–5.
[47] Cf. ibid., p. 389.
[48] Ibid., p. 397. Keneally presents the words without quotation marks, but I take it the appraisal is hers.

Nazism. Well before the end of the war, while continuing to act the part of a Nazi in public, Schindler had divorced himself, in feeling, wish, and action, from the Nazi cause. Sharing the evening of 20 July 1944 with one of his Jewish workers, he wished for news of Hitler's death, and in the last months of the war he saw to it that his munitions factory produced no usable munitions.[49] Affiliations cannot be ignored in the assessment of character in any of our three cases.

In ways such as these examples suggest, whether a relatively enduring quality of a person's effective motivation is a virtue (a motivational virtue) depends in part on its relation to other features of the person's character and life. What is thus required for its standing as a virtue is nothing so grand as complete and perfect virtue, or the sum of all the virtues. It is simply required that the particular feature's moral significance not be too deeply undercut by particular motives, beliefs, attitudes, actions, or allegiances that are closely related to it.

[49] Keneally, *Schindler's List*, pp. 267–9, 341–5.

# 11

## Plural and Integrated Virtue

Discussion in chapters 8 and 10 has not only focused our attention on particular virtues (small $v$ virtues, in the terminology of chapter 2, section 4). It has emphasized ways in which they are separable from each other, and led us in some cases to a finer-grained individuation than is suggested by a traditional vocabulary of virtues. We should not, however, lose sight of the idea of comprehensive Virtue (capital $V$ Virtue).[1] For some of our thoughts, aspirations, and evaluations regarding ethical character are holistic. We hope that our character will not be a collection of unrelated traits, but that it will be integrated in some way. We are interested in what it is, or would be, to be a morally good person; and that is a matter of holistic evaluation. We want to know what is required for comprehensive, capital $V$ Virtue.

Some may object that holistic evaluations of persons' moral character as good or bad are bound to be oversimple at best, and are likely to be offensive or harmful or both. That is a major theme of the situationist literature, and I don't wholly disagree. Little good is likely to come of any attempted division of the human race into good guys and bad guys. It is wise to assume that we are all "mixed bags," good and bad in different respects, and that differences in moral performance reflect differences of situation as well as of character. We ought to be very reluctant to classify anyone globally as morally bad, and very cautious about classifying anyone (particularly ourselves) as globally good. We should certainly cast an extremely skeptical eye on any thought that we are so good that there is no way in which our character can and should be improved.

There are, nevertheless, holistic dimensions of excellence in being for the good—having to do with one's priorities, for example, and how one's various views and motives relate to each other. And we surely have reason to ask holistic questions involving the concept of a morally good person. Among the most obviously urgent of these questions are how we might become morally better, and whether there are ways in which we might help children to become morally good or to acquire a good moral character. We do well to set before ourselves ideals or conceptions of kinds of person we might, without ridiculous unrealism, aspire to be. We have reason to ask which of these would be morally good ways

---

[1] It will be convenient once again to capitalize 'Virtue' when used in this sense in this chapter, which is largely concerned with the relation between Virtue and the virtues.

to be, in holistic evaluation—good enough to be worth trying to approximate. In such ways as these we have a use that is not obnoxiously conceited or judgmental for the concept of a morally good person, and of capital *V* Virtue. My aim in the present chapter is to do justice to holistic aspects of this concept.

## 1. IS VIRTUE NECESSARILY COMPLETE?

One of the claims mentioned in chapter 10, section 1, as involved in the ancient doctrine of the unity of the virtues, is the thesis of the necessary completeness of virtue: that one cannot have comprehensive Virtue without having *all* the particular virtues. That thesis can hardly be false if the virtues all entail each other. For then, entailment being transitive, comprehensive Virtue will entail all the virtues if it entails the possession of even one of them, as surely it does. No similarly obvious logical linkage, however, forces us to conclude that the necessary completeness thesis cannot be true if the mutual entailment thesis is false (as I argued in chapter 10 that it is). Indeed, the claim that one must have all the virtues to be comprehensively virtuous seems initially much less implausible than the claim that one must have them all if one has to have any single virtue, such as courage.

On reflection, nevertheless, the necessary completeness thesis will seem quite implausible if we take it to mean that all the virtues are strictly required for having any degree at all of comprehensive Virtue. Consider minor virtues. Punctuality is one. A lack of it bespeaks some deficiency in conscientiousness or self-control or both. Yet a person who is in many ways courageous, generous, fair and honest may surely be quite virtuous even if notably deficient in punctuality. Indeed we would find little or no Virtue in the world if it could not exist at all where it is deficient in any respect. The thesis will be a more interesting subject of discussion if we take it to mean only that every virtue is essential to Virtue in the sense that Virtue is necessarily impaired, and to some extent undermined, by the absence of any one virtue. This is roughly equivalent to saying that the absence of any one virtue is a *vice*, in the sense explained at the beginning of chapter 3.

Even in this form the thesis seems to me false, though perhaps not unqualifiedly so. The qualification I have in mind is that there is a case for regarding *some* of the virtues as essential, in this sense, to Virtue. This applies in particular, and perhaps most obviously, to the traditional "cardinal virtues."[2] It is hard to imagine a form of human life in which excellence in being for the good would not be gravely undermined by a total lack of courage, a total lack of temperance and self-control, a total lack of justice, or a total lack of practical wisdom, or even by a blatant and *comprehensive* deficiency in any one of these areas.

This argument may not be conclusive. It is not easy to determine whether there are degrees of *mediocrity* that intervene between excellence and serious deficiency

---

[2] Cf. Swanton, *Virtue Ethics*, p. 77, on "the core virtues."

in these matters. We may wonder whether mediocrity in the area of one of the cardinal virtues may be incompatible with excellence in that area, and with that particular virtue, without seriously compromising one's standing in general as a virtuous person. Provisionally, however, and for the sake of argument, let us grant that the cardinal virtues are essential to Virtue in the indicated sense.

The cardinal virtues are not the only virtues, however. I think there are many traits that can reasonably be counted as virtues, though their absence would not necessarily constitute an impairment of Virtue in the comprehensive sense. At least three broad types of traits may supply us with examples. The *first* are minor virtues that may be regarded as supererogatory, so to speak—as enhancements of Virtue but not demanded by Virtue. An outgoing *friendliness*, for example, is a praiseworthy as well as agreeable trait, if it is genuine and untainted by hypocrisy. It is a good way of responding to values of other people's lives, and of personal relationship. I think it is often part of what leads us to think of someone as a "good person," and I see no compelling reason to deny that it is a virtue.[3] If someone is introverted, however, in such a way that no one would call her outgoing, surely that is not necessarily an impairment of Virtue.

A less conventional example, perhaps, is *playfulness*. At its best, I think, it expresses a just valuation of things. Unlike frivolity, a mature playfulness does not fail to take serious things seriously. But it also recognizes the limits of their importance, thus escaping idolatry; and it does not fail to appreciate lighter goods and more tentative or exploratory valuations. A willingness, and a freedom, to be playful in such a way may be part of what we admire in a person's way of valuing things, and I see no reason not to count it a virtue, though its absence is hardly a blot on one's record of Virtue.

A *second* class of virtues not demanded by Virtue as such are those whose significance is connected with particular *vocations*. By 'vocations' here I do not mean jobs. Some jobs are not vocations, and some vocations do not earn money. Vocations are individual ways of being for the good. I think of them in terms of goods that one is given to love, and that one does love.[4] A dramatic example of what I would call a vocationally grounded difference in forms of virtue is one that many philosophers have discussed: Sartre's famous case of a young Frenchman deciding whether to join the Resistance. It can be seen as a "conflict between resistance to tyranny and loyalty to family in an extreme situation."[5] So seen, it invites the thought that "there is an irreducible plurality of admirable and choiceworthy ways of human life, each entailing the cultivation and exercise of a distinctive complex of virtues," as Gary Watson puts it.[6] It is less clear, however, whether either way of life in the example incorporates virtues that find no place at all in

[3] On friendliness as a virtue, cf. Sherman, "Common Sense and Uncommon Virtue," p. 102.
[4] One may also think of them (and I do) as given to an individual by God, by a sort of divine invitation, perhaps in some cases by divine command; but the theological aspect is not essential for the present discussion. See Adams, *Finite and Infinite Goods*, ch. 13.
[5] Hampshire, *Two Theories of Morality*, p. 47.          [6] Watson, "Virtues in Excess," p. 64.

the other.[7] In what follows I have chosen much less dramatic examples with a view to identifying virtues that have a place only in certain ways of life.

The Aristotelian virtue of magnificence (*megaloprepeia*), for example, defined as generosity on a large scale,[8] is surely not part of every human being's vocation, nor did Aristotle think it is. Another example, which may better engage our intuitions, is one that many who pursue an intellectual vocation recognize and are accustomed to admire. I refer to a caring—not to say, fanaticism—about precision in expressing oneself that is rooted in love for the goods of one's subject or one's art. It is a crucial virtue for philosophers, and also for poets.[9] Among those devoted to such vocations it is a trait of character highly admired.

The passion for precision has a value and significance in the context of an intellectual vocation that it does not have in many other patterns of life. It has, most obviously, an *instrumental* importance for intellectual work. A teacher of philosophy, or of Latin, must care very much about the precision of what she says if she is to give her students their money's worth. But an intense focus on precision would be counterproductive or at best irrelevant for many other enterprises, from snow removal to kindergarten teaching. What is more important, however, for classifying the love of precision as a virtue, by my lights, is that it also has a *non*-instrumental significance and value, an excellence, as a way of being for the good, a way of loving something of great value. It has this significance in the context of an intellectual or artistic vocation in a way that it does not in many other contexts. Helping other people is at least as excellent as artistic creation, but its excellence does not in general require great precision.

This argument may encounter the objection that an intellectual's passion for precision is just an example of the more general virtue of caring about one's work. That is a virtue that may reasonably be demanded of anyone who has work to do. But I think the passion for precision is different from that. For one thing, one who loves precision in his intellectual vocation may not have much of a general desire for excellence in whatever work he does. He may (perhaps wrongly) see nothing but a source of money in his "day job." The passion for precision is a matter of *love* for certain specific sorts of excellence, whereas the general desire to do one's work well is typically a manifestation of *conscientiousness* that often involves no particular love for the work one is doing.

This in turn suggests another way in which one might try to avoid granting that a love of precision constitutes a virtue specific to certain vocations and not generally demanded by Virtue. One might argue that it is merely a form of a less specific virtue of loving some form or forms of excellence that is a requirement of Virtue as such. That it is a form of such a broadly defined virtue I will

[7] This point is made by Hampshire and Watson.

[8] Aristotle, *Nicomachean Ethics*, II. 7 (1107b16–20). On magnificence and its relevance here, cf. Swanton, *Virtue Ethics*, p. 71.

[9] Cf. Eliot, *Complete Poems and Plays*, p. 128.

not deny, but I think we are accustomed, and with reason, to identify virtues with more specificity. The ways in which love for forms of excellence may find a home in our lives are surely diverse enough to constitute separate traits that need to be cultivated individually, with little or no automatic carry-over from one to another.

I think it is reasonable to count them as separate virtues, but there is a significant methodological issue here. On my view Virtue is a matter of being for the good, and many virtues—at least all the motivational virtues—will be forms of being for the good. Should I conclude that being for the good is the only motivational virtue? I think that would be contrary to the point of having the concept of a plurality of (small *v*) virtues, which is to help structure a fine-grained anatomy of Virtue. Still there is a certain inescapable arbitrariness to judgments on these questions, and it is clear that with a finer-grained discrimination of virtues we will more easily discover particular virtues that are not generally demanded by Virtue as such, while that will be harder the more we lump virtues together as merely forms of a small number of more comprehensive virtues.[10]

The suspicion may even arise that it is only because they are broadly rather than narrowly individuated that the "cardinal" virtues seem to be indispensable for Virtue. After all, we have seen that it is possible to have some but not all forms of courage and some but not all forms of practical wisdom. I will not pursue this suspicion very far because I think it is not very promising. We would probably find that in any ethically attractive decomposition of courage or wisdom or other cardinal virtues into more narrowly defined virtues, some of the subspecies of each would seem as indispensable as courage or wisdom more broadly defined. This seems likely to be true, for example, of some types of moral courage and of sensitivity to the rights of other people.

Assuming reasonably fine-grained distinctions among virtues, we may go on to the *third*, and perhaps the most interesting and important, class of virtues not demanded by Virtue as such. These are virtues that are specific to particular religions or moral cultures. As an example I shall discuss the Confucian virtue of *li*, or propriety, understood as expressed largely in ritual forms. I rely on the account given in Lee Yearley's interesting comparative study, *Mencius and Aquinas*. Yearley characterizes *li* as an actualization of "a yielding to others or a deference toward them."

> Propriety [he says] covers two kinds of activity that most Westerners think differ substantially. One kind is solemn religious activities, such as funerals. The other kind falls under what we call etiquette or, more accurately, reasonable and humane learned conventions; for instance, the appropriate ways to respond to people at a formal gathering. Ritual, then, covers everything from the solemn performance of an elaborate rite to the "excuse

---

[10] Cf. the misgiving suggested (as a worry, not a decisive objection) with regard to unity theses regarding the virtues in Watson, "Virtues in Excess," p. 66, that "once unity is found to be compatible with great diversity, it is bound to be merely formal, a unity in name only."

me" after a sneeze. . . .Propriety is what makes possible an actualization of the reactions of yielding or respect.[11]

Respect for other people is certainly an important part of Virtue, and it is hardly to be denied that rituals provide a way of weaving interpersonal respect into the fabric of daily life. So it is plausible to suppose that practiced, committed, sensitive adherence to a system of conventional social rituals can be part of an excellent way of being for the good. If one lived in a society in which a conventional system of respectful rituals was in place, it would very likely be reasonable to regard propriety structured by it as a virtue that it would be good for people to acquire. It is plausible to suppose that there is an excellent and virtuous Confucian way (or set of ways) of being for the good, of which *li* can be an excellent part, and in that context a virtue. I think it is much less plausible to claim that such ritualized propriety is an *indispensable* part of Virtue, or a trait whose absence, in any context, must constitute a serious deficiency in Virtue.[12] Indeed, a virtue consisting in developed sensitivity and responsiveness to the values of a particular, ritually structured system of interpersonal respect has little sense or point outside of contexts in which that system has social reality. Even in our own rather informal culture, to be sure, our ways of respecting each other have ritual aspects. But the virtue of politeness, in our cultural context, is a minor one and is not nearly as self-involving or as rich in content as the propriety structured by Confucian conceptions of *li*.

In saying this I am not interested in starting a dispute with Confucians, but rather in indicating how *li* might be seen from a *non*-Confucian point of view as being a virtue in a Confucian context. Similarly a non-theist may be able to see devotion to God as a virtue in a theistic context, as structuring a way of being for the good, even if it is not a virtue to which the non-theist would aspire. I take Iris Murdoch to have held such a view of at least some theistic devotion. A more precise theistic counterpart to *li* might be *reverence*, as typically understood in theistic traditions. It is a virtue specific to religious contexts, consisting largely (though not exclusively) in sensitivity and responsiveness to values inherent in religious rituals, inspired by respect for the greatness of God. It is narrower in scope, however, than Confucian *li*, in that it does not involve one's relation to merely social rituals.

One will not in this way classify as virtues traits characteristic of religions or moral cultures not one's own unless one takes the ethical attitudes and social practices involved in them to be sincere and reasonably enlightened. Few would maintain that *all* the forms of devotion to gods known to the history of religions have been virtuous or ethically admirable. And ritualized social patterns are always subject in principle to critical evaluation regarding their conformity

---

[11] Yearley, *Mencius and Aquinas*, pp. 36–7.
[12] Some Confucians may have claimed this. See ibid., pp. 37, 44–6.

to norms of justice.[13] I say that there can be genuine Virtue and genuine virtues characteristic of different and in some ways incompatible religions and ways of life. But I do not mean to imply that there cannot be true and false and better and worse in issues between such ways of life and between the beliefs characteristic of them.

Still it would be excessively narrow-minded to be unable ever to recognize and appreciate moral excellence in ways of life that are structured in part by religious, cultural, and social factors of which one disapproves. Here again it is important that the way of Virtue is not as strait and narrow as the path of duty. To judge that a way of life contains great excellence is not to judge that it is the best possible, nor even that nothing in it is wrong.

## 2. MORAL INTEGRATION AND VIRTUE

I have argued against the classic theses of the unity of the virtues. There are many personal qualities that can reasonably be regarded as virtues, and they are separable. It is possible to have some of them without having others. It is even possible, I have argued, to be quite virtuous on the whole without possessing every virtue. Indeed, if we distinguish virtues finely enough, it may be argued that no one could possess every virtue, because some of them are native to different ways of life that could not be lived by the same person at the same time. It would be very misleading, however, to affirm without qualification the disunity of Virtue. For there is a sort of unity that does or should belong to Virtue—a sort of unity that may be called *moral integration*.

Virtue (capital *V* Virtue, the property of being a morally good person) is a *holistic* property of persons. It is a quality of a person's *whole* way of living. In considering whether, or to what extent, one is a virtuous person, one must attend to questions such as what one really loves and what one's priorities are, which cannot be answered by looking at separate areas of life in isolation from each other.

Virtue is not a narrowly "moral" matter, not just a matter of concern about moral correctness and the good of other persons. It can be manifested in concern for any sort of good. In a virtuous outlook on life "narrowly moral" concerns will have a prominent place, but will also be related well to other excellences, and supported by wisdom and sensitivity regarding many sorts of values. Ideally, Virtue is to be shown in one's response to any situation, whether or not there is an obviously recognizable "moral issue" there. In virtually every situation one is responding to things of some value—usually to many such things. One's response to all of them, in all its dimensions, cognitive and affective as well as behavioral, is relevant to the excellence of one's being for the good, and thus to

---

[13] A point emphasized, with regard to Confucian social conventions, in ibid., pp. 44–6.

Virtue. What we do and don't find funny, what we do and don't find moving, what we do and don't find interesting, expresses something about our values. What it expresses may or may not be integrated, or even consistent, with the values with which we identify most strongly.

Unintegrated values, and an unintegrated outlook on life, may compromise the depth and consistency of one's being for the good. If I have deep resentments, for example, to which I am unable to relate my ethical beliefs, the latter may be deprived of a portion of their power. One may be tempted to *compartmentalize* one's life, confining some feelings and values to some situations, relationships, and spheres of activity, and others to others. This threatens to relegate parts of one's life to a lower level of value. It may also bring a certain hollowness into the more prized parts of one's life, as one tries to respond with only part of oneself.

This is not merely a temptation and a threat. There is a form of compartment-alization in the situation-specificity and modularity with which dispositions to types of virtuous action are commonly acquired, as was discussed in chapter 8. If people who have learned to act in accordance with a moral value or principle in some types of situation do not act in accordance with it in other types of situation, as appears to be very often the case, this is a respect in which they might well aspire to become more consistently virtuous. That would be a virtuous way of increasing the integration of their moral character. Of course there could also be a sort of integration in becoming more consistently vicious, but there is some experimental evidence that integration in the direction that is thought to be virtuous is actually more likely.[14]

Personal compartmentalization is related to social compartmentalization. Different institutions and social contexts in a diverse and economically differentiated society like ours are treated to some extent as separate moral compartments. Business corporations, schools, religious organizations, families, clubs, and informal "sets" of friends have different functions. They also have their own dominant aims, codes of conduct, and styles of personal relationship, in which they are not guaranteed to agree with each other. In that way they form autonomous spheres of life. Moving between such spheres, one is apt to face, at least implicitly, issues about how much of oneself and one's values one can carry from one to another. Should it matter to me that my parents disapprove of what my friends think is right? What do *I* think is good, and which goods do I care about most? How much do I care how much money the company makes, and why? And so forth. In a way it would be easier to keep the values of each sphere in a separate compartment in my life. But if I do that, I am an evaluative chameleon, changing my ethical colors as I move from one situation to another. If I do not have a single system of values by which I live in all the spheres in which I move, disturbing questions can be asked about me. Am I, as a person, really (fully, deeply) *for* the

---

[14] Hartshorne, May, and Shuttleworth, *Studies in the Nature of Character*, vol. 3, pp. 287–347.

goods affirmed in my stance in *any* of those spheres? Am I for any goods in the way demanded by Virtue?

We have seen quite concretely, in chapter 10, section 4, how particular virtues, especially of the sort I have called "motivational," can be compromised, in some cases fatally, by attitudes that are inconsistent with them. A readiness and willingness for sympathetic response to persons in need is a form of benevolence, and is normally a virtue. But it may not be a virtue, being deprived of much of its humane significance, if one at the same time embraces, in relevant ways, an ideology that denies the full humanity of the persons to whom one responds sympathetically.

Structural virtues such as courage and temperance demand moral integration in a different way, but no less urgently. They are forms of ability and willingness to govern one's life in accordance with one's most important aims and values. But that presupposes that one's aims and values are sufficiently coherent or integrated, with relations of centrality and priority among them that are clear and stable enough for some of them to *be* one's most important aims and values.

As I suggested at the end of section 2.1 of chapter 10, moral integration may indeed be regarded as itself a structural virtue, and a very fundamental one. It is a strength and excellence that one must have in some measure if one is to have any coherent and effective ethical selfhood at all. It does not appear on traditional lists of the virtues, and the proposal to place it there may encounter opposition, particularly from moralists who are suspicious of "the idioms of therapy,"[15] of which 'integration', arguably, is one. It should be clear, however, that in classifying integration as a virtue, and hence as an excellence, I do not intend any of the renunciation of ethical evaluation of which "therapeutic" thinking has sometimes been accused. And if 'integration' brings with it from therapeutic contexts connotations of a dynamic, of process rather than possession, that is quite salutary.

For the work of moral integration is never finished, and indeed should not be finished. Central to it is a sort of inner honesty that keeps one's thoughts and one's feelings, one's desires and one's principles, one's convictions and one's experiences in open communication with each other. Such inner openness always discloses conflicts. That is what makes it difficult. The scariness of the inner conflicts tempts us to keep thought and feeling, ethics and work, in separate pockets. Dealing with such inner conflicts is a main part of the work of integration.

But more than that. We may hope that conflict is not eternal, but there are some conflicts that are both important to us and persistent features of our lives. It is not only our convictions and commitments, but also our issues, our inner as well as our outer issues, that make us who we are. Integrity requires that our life be in keeping with our issues as well as with our beliefs and decisions. Paradoxically, indeed, a relatively integrated life is likely to be integrated partly around persistent issues and inner conflicts. This is not good if the conflict becomes important to us in such a way that we do not want it to be resolved. But if *dealing* with a certain inner issue, trying to make progress in resolving it, is one of the persistent organizing themes of one's life, that can be fruitful.

The integration of values that Virtue demands is not an uncritical syncretism, but something much harder, and at times more painful. It insists (though not impatiently) on consistency, but also seeks persistently to relate one's core values to what does not seem to make a neat package with them. There is always plenty of such recalcitrant material in our lives, and some of it may have a powerful moral claim on our attention. It is even more important, after all, that our aims be good than that they be integrated. Aspiration for Virtue is not just for conformity of the self with itself, essential as that is. It is an aspiration for excellent relationship with goods whose nature and demands are objective and not wholly or mainly determined by our preferences. This aspiration has an effect on our self-integration that is both destabilizing and creative, as it draws us, at various junctures in our lives, to refocus our lives in the light of fresh insights and fresh encounters with goods and evils.

This is particularly important in our pluralistic cultural context, which needs virtues that are in tension, in one way, with integration, and that in another way help to shape it. One such virtue that is much discussed in contemporary political philosophy is *reasonableness*, understood as an ability and willingness to take other people's viewpoints and interests fairly into account in trying to agree with them on ways of living together. A related virtue, more general and perhaps deeper in its scope, is a *sensitivity* to genuine goods that may be present in other people's views and ways of life. It seems obvious enough that *in*sensitivity in such matters is apt to close off possibilities of being *for* real goods, and thus may be contrary to Virtue. Yet sensitivity opens us to changes in our outlook—changes that may disturb the coherence of an established integration. Learning carries a threat of *dis*integration, and the more moral significance the learning has, the more disturbing the threat. For reasons of this sort moral integration must be for us ever and again a project rather than an achievement, and must be in no small part an ability and appetite for ever renewed *re*integration. I have argued for this point from the demands of a pluralistic cultural context, but a more sweeping thesis seems warranted. With or without pluralism, most human contexts present new situations that challenge existing ethical formation in one way or another, demanding sensitivity, openness, and a capacity for reintegration.

It is important here that the moral integration of a *person* is not the integration of a *theory*, though the latter may contribute to the former. Persisting tensions that would be fatal to the consistency of a theory are not necessarily fatal to the moral unity of a person. Underlying this point is the deeper one that the resources of a person for ethical discernment are not limited to the resources of a theory. Typically they include somewhat conflicting motives, feelings, perceptions, and thoughts which resist integration (especially theoretical integration) but enhance sensitivity to the wide range of values to which we are exposed. Tolerance for ambiguity and ambivalence is apt to be important for ethical perception. Such tolerance is a way in which conflicting tendencies can be held together and used together as a resource in the service of an overarching ethical aspiration. In that way tolerance can actually be a form of personal ethical integration. Non-theoretical and non-logical and perpetually uneasy as it is, it is a form of integration that is particularly suited to what I take to be our position as finite and necessarily very imperfect images of transcendent goodness.

Moral integration is commonly a project rather than an achievement, and not only for the reasons just cited. Quite apart from the problems of novelty and the demands of sensitivity, virtually all of us simply have significant emotions and desires, and in some cases beliefs, that are not in harmony with our core values. In some cases people whose Virtue is heroic or otherwise exceptional in some respects are painfully lacking in moral integration. Philippa Foot speaks of "chaotic lives" led by some people who are rightly admired.[16] Such lack of integration is doubtless a significant deficiency in Virtue, but human Virtue generally is deficient in one way or another. And it may be that inner polarization sometimes liberates, for extremes of being for certain great goods, energies that would otherwise have been absorbed in inner moderation and harmonization. Nevertheless, the advantages of integration, and perpetual reintegration, for Virtue are obvious, and we surely have good reason to pursue moral integration as a project.

The project is a personal spiritual quest. It is particularized in many ways because the holism of Virtue demands an integration that in principle includes a response to all the facts of one's life, or at least to all those that are ethically salient. Some of these will be facts of social context and common heritage that one shares with other members of one's family or national or religious community, though not with all human beings. But some will be joys and sorrows, enthusiasms and failures, adventures and epiphanies more or less unique to one's own experience. They will include particular goods that are given to one to love, in which one might perhaps discern an individual vocation in life. Thus Virtue's demand for ethical integration of the *person* is itself one of the factors that tend to assure the diversity rather than uniformity of forms of Virtue in different persons, and not just in different communities.

For many people the quest for an integrated and virtuous outlook and system of concerns will have a religious form. Indeed it is hard to escape religious forms in this matter if we understand religiousness broadly enough. If ethics has Virtue among its central concerns, it must ask quite comprehensively how it is both possible and good to be for the good. Then ethical reflection can hardly be isolated from Kant's religious question, "What may I hope?"[17] Similarly it cannot well exclude such questions as how much we have to be grateful for, and whether

---

[16] Foot, "Virtues and Vices," p. 177.
[17] Immanuel Kant, *Critique of Pure Reason*, A 805 = B 833.

desire is to be seen chiefly as a source of frustration and misery or rather of life and joy. (The latter is a question of obvious but possibly divergent resonance in Buddhist and Christian traditions.) The holistic dimension of Virtue, and its integrative aspiration, demand attention to such questions because our answers to them, explicit and implicit, condition our response to a great variety of goods and evils in all sorts of situations, and thus contribute to shaping the ways in which we can be for the good.

# 12

# Can Virtue Be Taught?

No question about virtue has a longer history in Western philosophy than the question of moral education, which opens the discussion in Plato's *Protagoras* (319A–320C). Can virtue be taught? It is no mere historical accident, I believe, that in the dialogues of Plato, questions about virtue enter the conversation so often in company with questions about education. When we are busy *being* what we have already become, it will very often seem natural and appropriate to give less attention to evaluating what we are than to questions about which actions would be right and which goals would be good ones. It is when we are thinking about how we and others (notably including any children entrusted to our care) might become morally better that it becomes most urgent to consider what is involved in being a morally good person, and thus to think about virtue.

My aims in this chapter are relatively modest. It would be absurd to pretend to offer a *theory* of moral education in anything less than a whole book. In any event I am not in a position to offer one, and am not sure whether anyone is. Ideally such a theory would rest on a rich basis of empirical psychological research, and its framing of concepts and setting of goals would be guided by philosophically informed reflection on ethical issues that are likely always to be contested. A tall order! The most impressive recent attempt at a theory of moral education that would be both empirically adequate and philosophically sophisticated may be that of the late Lawrence Kohlberg. It is valuable work, to which I have occasion to refer more than once in this book. But its empirical basis remains controversial in some respects, and it is incomplete in some important ways, as I will argue in section 3.

What I offer here is hardly more than a sketch of a map of the ground to be covered in education for virtue. Its organizing principle is a progression of three types of tasks of moral education: elementary, modular, and integrative. They are discussed in sections 1, 2, and 3, respectively. The relation of the second and third types to parts of the argument of chapters 8 to 11 will be obvious. I will not claim that the three types are mutually exclusive, much less that they jointly exhaust the territory of moral education. But they will serve to organize much of what seems to me worth saying about the subject.

I acknowledge that I have a broadly political axe to grind. Education for virtue is a subject of considerable political resonance today. There are fears in some quarters that a liberal political order and pluralistic civil society cannot provide a type of social context that is needed for the education of character and the flourishing of the life of virtue. One of my aims here is to show that such fears are misguided, and that the main tasks of moral education do not require a more extensive social agreement on ethical issues than a liberal political order can sustain.

In what follows such political issues will arise mainly in discussion of *processes* of moral education. It is well to note at the outset, however, that our views of the *aims* of moral education also have some bearing on the political issues. If we think that virtues of autonomy, of thinking and feeling for oneself in ethical matters, are important to excellence in being for the good, that may lead us to believe that exposure to a wide diversity of ethical viewpoints is salutary for education in virtue.[1] If we think that cruelty is the worst of vices,[2] we may well worry about xenophobia and persecution that may be induced by efforts to keep a society homogeneous. I believe, moreover, that one of the greatest dangers that *all* societies pose to moral education is that of themselves becoming objects of idolatry (which leads to many other ills, often including cruelty). If that is true, we have reason to think it good for education to take place in a context of diversity that encourages critical thinking about one's own society and culture.

## 1. ELEMENTARY TASKS

I take it to be obvious that all moral education takes place in a social context and is profoundly influenced by its social context. The tasks that I refer to as "elementary" in education for virtue are those that are necessary for learning to think evaluatively or normatively at all. They consist very largely in initiation into social practices and the conventions that govern them. In this regard I would emphasize the role of what we may call *ethical practices*, which are likely to present themselves to a child first of all as linguistic practices.[3] In exploring the realm of language and convention-governed social interaction, the child early encounters such words as 'good', 'bad', 'right', 'wrong', 'pretty', 'ugly', 'nice', 'naughty', and so forth. In particular encounters it is usually obvious enough to what acts or other objects these words are being applied, and in that sense what their *reference* or *extension* is taken to be. Their *sense*, however, or the way to analogize and generalize their application to other occasions and objects, is subtler and probably less obvious than that of 'red' and 'ball'. Still we all learned how to do it; it came naturally enough. What we learned, I think, was a complex of roles that these terms play in social practices, and corresponding roles that are assigned to any properties the terms may signify. In so learning we also learned to identify objects as possessing such properties—or so we and our teachers assumed.

---

[1] Cf. the argument of Mill, *On Liberty*, ch. 3.    [2] Cf. Shklar, *Ordinary Vices*.
[3] The account presented here is based on metaethical views presented more fully in Adams, *Finite and Infinite Goods*, chapters 1 and 15.

At the outset we must have assumed implicitly that the words we were learning (in this case ethical words) do in fact, or rightly, apply, most of the time, to the objects those words were applied to by the older people from whom we were learning. I take it children do this in learning the application of words more generally. Without this assumption we could hardly have learned as we did. These first steps thus involved adopting some of our elders' ethical beliefs. Here is a point at which social agreement is plausibly required as a context for moral learning. If the adults around a child do not apply the moral and evaluative terms to similar objects, the child is likely to be confused and find it difficult to develop stable ways of generalizing the application of the terms.

So does cultural pluralism pose a danger to moral learning at this fundamental level? Not to worry. The degree and kind of agreement needed at this point exists in fact in any viable society. It is an agreement, above all, on low-level generalizations. It is generally wrong to tell lies. Unprovoked physical assaults on other people are bad and wrong. It is good to be brave. It is good to be generous. Illness is generally a bad thing. These generalizations are not controversial in our society. Most of them will be generally accepted in most societies. It is hard to see how a society could do better than limp along without general acceptance of most of them.

This much needed type of ethical consensus does not amount to agreement on a comprehensive ethical theory. That agreement does not exist in our society, nor in most societies that are philosophical enough to have ethical theories. Fortunately it is not needed for moral education—certainly not at the introductory level of which I am now speaking. The consensus needed for the elementary tasks of moral education is not a matter of theory. What is required is much more an ethos of at least locally shared practices, in which people have adapted to each other's ways of thinking sufficiently to coordinate with each other in dealing with a wide range of problems of daily life. There are concepts—that of a quark, for example—that are acquired only in learning something about sophisticated theories. The concepts of the good and the bad, the generous and the cowardly, are not like that. Children acquire the conceptual foundations for ethical living long before they are acquainted with ethical theories. Many people, indeed, never become acquainted with such theories, and may still have great virtue.

Those who long for ethical homogeneity may object that differences in ethical theory entail, and articulate, subtle but deep differences of meaning in even the most fundamental ethical concepts. Agreed; but we do and therefore can live with such subtle differences of meaning—and not only in ethical concepts. As long as they do not keep us from agreeing pretty largely in our application of the concepts in low-level generalizations, they will not keep us from acquiring ethical concepts in such a way as to be able to use them, perhaps a bit idiosyncratically, in structuring our own lives and in cooperating with each other.

For the use of ethical language that we learn is not merely imitative. It is a fundamental and well-known feature of human languages that they use a finite repertoire of variations of vocabulary and atomic syntactic structures to generate an indefinite diversity of new sentences. To learn a language is in large part to learn to use its resources to say things one has not heard said before. To the extent that the language is used assertively, this is also a matter of learning to form and express opinions of one's own that are not simply taken over from other people. This applies to ethical language too. To learn to use it is in part to learn to form one's own ethical opinions, with at least some smaller or larger measure of autonomy.

How do we learn to form ethical opinions? In part by learning to *reason* about ethics, by learning to accept and give reasons, and to assess them. Children start, no doubt, by accepting reasons that adults give them, but they will not get very far in this part of ethical practice without starting to rely on their own developing sense of the roles of ethical terms. In addition to reasons, children are taught (and rightly so) to pay attention to their *feelings* in thinking about ethical matters. "How would you feel if Susie said that to *you*?" For the forming of ethical beliefs is not an entirely separate process from that of forming ethical feelings and desires, and the former will not go well if the latter goes badly. And the formation of ethical feelings and desires is doubtless much affected by social factors, including especially the attitudes of people whom we admire and who care for us. In these ways we learn to be for and against goods and evils, and to form some of the relevant beliefs and attitudes for ourselves.

A measure of autonomy is required, I think, not only by the dynamics of learning, but also by the nature of virtue. Conformism is not virtue. As argued in chapter 9, section 2, it can indeed be a vice. Excellence in being for the good demands enough autonomy to give one's ethical aspirations and commitments rich rootage in one's own perceptive and affective encounters with real goods and evils themselves, and not just with other people's opinions and attitudes regarding them. Learning an ethical practice centrally includes learning to respond (excellently, one hopes) to experienced facts that are largely unpredictable and not merely conventional. These are fundamental reasons why indoctrination in a socially fixed form of life and pattern of valuing is not an adequate form of education for virtue.

If social agreement plays a fundamental part in the learning of ethical practices, and more broadly in moral learning, so does social *dis*agreement. Learning to disagree is an essential part of learning an ethical linguistic practice, and indeed of learning linguistic practices generally. Although agreement has to come before disagreement in the learning of language, disagreeing is one of the main things we use language to do. Even in the smallest, most homogeneous groups, human beings are creatures who differ individually from each other in their experiences, perceptions, feelings, needs, and desires. As they try to live together, they have reason to communicate their disagreements as well as their agreements, commonly with the aim, though by no means always the result, of reaching agreement, and sometimes with less benign aims.

Disagreement is not necessarily a bad thing. It obviously needs to be restrained in various ways but, as philosophers of all people should recognize, some types of disagreement can be important to the meaning and value of human life. Disagreement is especially prominent as a function of ethical language—much more so than as a function of perceptual language, for example. Even if we believe (as I do) that there are real ethical facts, we must acknowledge that disagreement is particularly common about ethical matters. One who does not know how to sustain an ethical disagreement is not yet a thoroughly competent user of ethical language.

My account of the role of ethical practices in moral education has obvious implications for the *epistemology* of value. We respond in emotion and decision as well as cognition to the ethical practice of other people, and to other features of our situations. In so doing we learn to recognize and value concrete particular goods and evils, and only later, if ever, learn to theorize in a more general way about ethics.

It might be expected that a Platonic or theistic conception of value (such as I hold) would lead to a more hierarchical epistemology of value, in which ethical thinking must begin with, and be dominated by, an integrated, systematic, indeed hierarchical, ethical theory. I deny this. Conceiving of all values as grounded in a supreme Good does give reason to *seek* an integrated theory of value that reflects what one believes about the hierarchical systematicity of value. But that is not necessarily a reason to believe that ethical thinking must *start* with such a theory, or that the best hierarchical theory we can construct will be more reliable than our best sensitivity to the multiplicity of concrete particular values. In fact I believe the best theory cannot be more reliable than the best sensitivity, and that ethical theory will not be reliable unless it has much of its rootage in a good sensitivity. In the individual life, at any rate, a good ethical sensitivity must precede fruitful ethical theorizing (and in that, I think, I am in agreement with Aristotle).

## 2. MODULAR TASKS

As we saw in chapter 8, a substantial body of empirical evidence suggests that direct dispositions to ethically approved types of behavior are commonly acquired in domain-specific modules. We learn to respond bravely to certain kinds of dangers, and honestly or helpfully in certain types of social situations. If we are satisfied with the way the responses work, we are likely to continue responding in the same way to situations of the same type. Similarly we may learn to perform well in a certain social role. But such learning very often does not carry over to produce courageous or honest or helpful behavior in other types of situation or other roles or areas of life.

Situation-specific though it be, such modular moral learning is by no means worthless or unimportant. It really matters to us, for example, that even drivers who are not scrupulously law-abiding across the board can normally be counted on to stop at a red light. This sort of module of behavioral reliability is highly necessary for effective economic cooperation and an orderly society. Its situation-specificity is in some ways unproblematic. While we could hardly learn enough to know how to respond to every possible situation, it is important for us to learn to behave appropriately in those in which we actually find ourselves. Business offices, factories, schools, churches, and families have their own particular needs. That such social groups and organizations function, most of the time, as smoothly and effectively as most of them do is a tribute to their effectiveness in providing modules of behavioral education fitted to their needs. Of course this is not to say that the people involved usually conceive of what is going on in those terms.

There is indeed reason to think that considerable modularity in behavioral education is particularly suitable, and perhaps even necessary, for the development of social cooperation manageably focused on varied, and changing, tasks. Such cooperation, which is obviously of vital importance for human life, is as obviously facilitated by our tendency to adapt our behavioral dispositions to diverse contexts in response to context-specific social pressures. And we would have much less of that particular sort of adaptability if we had no tendency to learn to behave in accordance with a particular plan or pattern of cooperation in a particular domain without revising all our behavioral dispositions and evaluative attitudes at once.[4]

We cannot assume that the modular behavioral education sponsored by social groups is always morally benign. Some of the interests of any social organization may in fact be inimical to true virtue. Virtue may be severely limited if one does not question and reinterpret the values that one's social groups have been motivated to inculcate. But it would be grossly unrealistic to infer that moral education might proceed better if we simply did without such socially sponsored modules of behavioral learning.

It is in this context, I believe, that we can most plausibly find a home for something like Aristotle's conception of *ethismos* (habituation or practice). I suppose it has been historically the most influential idea about education for virtue. If one is to learn virtue, Aristotle thinks, one must when young be led by one's teachers to perform, repeatedly, noble actions. In this way one is not only to learn how to do such actions; one is also to find pleasure in doing them and shame in failing to do them, and thus come to be autonomously motivated to do them. Habits, however, tend to be quite situation-specific. If last night you did not leave your keys in the room in which you usually find them in the morning, today you may forget to put them in your pocket. Experience, I believe, gives us little reason to suppose that moral habituation will not also be situation-specific.

---

[4] The idea for this argument was suggested by an analogous argument in a biological context, in Sterelny, "Symbiosis, Evolvability, and Modularity," p. 494. I don't mean to comment here on the biological issues involved in Sterelny's argument.

There is little doubt that practice and habituation can be a valuable part of education in virtue. A major part of the structural virtues of courage and self-control is being able to control one's fears and desires, or at least being able not to be overpowered by them. And common sense is surely right in believing that these abilities can be improved by practice or by experience of exercising them—though not as right as we might wish, inasmuch as Lenten disciplines, for example, are commonly not followed by successful dieting during the rest of the year.

Not only abilities that can be improved through practice, but habits too, can be important parts of virtue. For instance, one may form a habit of thinking about certain types of considerations when trying to decide what is fair or right, or of noticing certain types of features of situations. Without these habits one might fail to recognize what would be right or good to do. Such habits participate in the sort of excellence that is necessary, by my lights, for virtue. For having, and willingly exercising, such habits may be part, not only of moral sensitivity and its excellence, but also of caring for the relevant goods and its excellence.

Virtue cannot be purely a matter of habit, however. Suppose one eats a certain high-fiber-content cereal for breakfast every day, simply out of habit, and with no thought of its hygienic benefits, because one's parents got one started doing it as a child. This is doubtless a good habit, but is not virtuous in the slightest degree, so far as I can see. Virtuous action must be done out of caring for the values at stake. In order for a habit of eating cereal to be an instance of the virtue of temperance or moderation, it would have to express a system of desires, and management of desires, organized around the realization of one's most important values. If I am right in believing that virtue is excellence in being for the good, the most crucial question about education for virtue will be how one can come to recognize and care for true goods. Mere habit formation will not be enough.

Are there effective modular strategies for the development of virtuous desires? There are tricky issues here, beginning with the possible modularity or domain-specificity of desires. It is common enough to care about some people much more than about others, to care about some common projects and not others, to care more about truthfulness in some contexts than in others, and so forth. I do believe that caring about things can be genuinely virtuous even when we care about them in these ways. Such caring is domain-specific in the sense of *relating to* some domains rather than to others. But if desires constitute the kind of deep-seated caring in which the motivational virtues largely consist, they can hardly be desires that one *has* only when one is in certain situations.

It is harder to understand the modular acquisition of desires than of abilities and behavioral tendencies or habits. Children can be trained to habitual politeness. And one learns how to face certain dangers; importantly, one learns that one can do it. For instance, one learns by experience that one can think seriously, and with some sympathy, about moral and political and religious views that are contrary to one's own without dissolving one's own structures of meaning. But how does one learn to care?

Aristotle's hope (in Myles Burnyeat's plausible reading[5]) is that through practice in acting well one comes to recognize and prize the excellence of the action,
and thus acquires not only a habit, but a love, of noble action. This may happen.
One who believes, as I do, that there are real ethical facts will be reluctant to deny
that they can be recognized and that the recognition can move us. By experien-
cing a particular type of virtuous action one may see that it is good, and thereby
come to want to perform that type of action again. No doubt there is much about
virtue that one learns only by doing, and one will probably not become wedded
to virtue without discovering that in some way it "works" in one's own life. I suspect, however, that in this discovery the *repetition* of particular types of action is
likely to matter less than the vividness with which one is able to see in a particular
case that one has accomplished something good and that it is appreciated.

We may still suspect that most exercise-based modular moral education relies
heavily on incentives less clearly virtuous. A motivationally plausible idea is suggested by Aristotle's suggestion that a youth who is learning to be noble will obey
a sense of *shame*.[6] Shame is an emotion that is commonly responsive to social
disapproval and self-disapproval. We may speculate that the pleasure that train-
ees in virtue are to take in noble actions is correspondingly responsive to social
approval, and perhaps especially to self-approval which may originally have been
inspired by social approval. Pleasure and shame of these sorts probably do play
a part in moral learning in many cases. Sometimes, perhaps, the reactions of
other people can help us to see, and care about, the intrinsic goodness or badness of actions, and thus to acquire virtuous desires. But the desire to be liked
and approved of by others, while normal and healthy in moderate degree, can
motivate bad conduct as easily as good conduct, and is not clearly virtuous. It is
a motive both powerful and dangerous. There is probably little virtuous motivation in which it does not cooperate. But if we are interested in virtue for its own
sake, or as a strength for standing against social evils, we will particularly want to
know how those components of virtuous motivation that are not dependent on
the approval of others may be acquired.

In fact I suspect it will be quite difficult, if possible at all, to "engineer" the
most virtuous of motives. But some of society's most pressing concerns in moral
education are more modest. With respect to straightforwardly behavioral aspects
of modular tasks of moral education, society is often a highly effective educator. It
operates not mainly by formal indoctrination or arranging for people to be talked
at, but much more by its social "atmospheres" and its structuring of situations.
Our economically developed, more or less liberal society is not hampered in this
by its cultural pluralism. Indeed, the modularity of these tasks is well suited to

---

[5] Burnyeat, "Aristotle on Learning to be Good."
[6] Rather than fear, which is another obvious, but not particularly virtuous, possibility (Aristotle,
*Nicomachean Ethics*, 1179b11). Burnyeat ("Aristotle on Learning to Be Good," pp. 78–9) makes
much of this.

the needs of a pluralistic society. For despite the pluralism, and its disagreements about more comprehensive ethical and religious views, there is often plenty of agreement, in the society as a whole or in the relevant units of it, regarding the behavioral modules that are most important to the smooth functioning of the group.

Partly for this reason, it is wildly unrealistic to think that the present pluralistic society of most economically developed democracies is one whose orderly functioning is especially threatened by individual indiscipline resulting from a breakdown of moral education. Many human societies have been much more fragile in that respect. Medieval European society, whose supposed moral and spiritual homogeneity has been the object of a good deal of nostalgia, was surely (and terrifyingly) much closer to anarchy than ours. This is not to say that developed Western societies have nothing to fear in the area of moral education. But a serious threat to morality's grip on us is less plausibly seen in pluralism and differences of ethical belief than in the structural complexity, mobility, and anonymity of modern urban life.

In the legendary middle American village of Lake Wobegon, where "all the children are above average," there are, as we know, at least two churches, Lutheran and Roman Catholic. Their theologies differ but their members doubtless have rather similar views about most matters of "ordinary morality." And those are the matters with which most fears of "moral decline" are concerned. Lake Wobegon is a place where everybody knows everybody else's business, and where the people who see you at work also see you at play and with your family—and conversely. You cannot divide your life into socially separate realms. Your behavior in any part of your life has social consequences in the rest of your life. That creates powerful pressures to conform to community expectations of moral behavior in all aspects of your life.

This, of course, does not necessarily imply that the community's views about business ethics are deeply consistent with its views about neighborliness. We should also remember, from chapter 9, that pressures of social conformity, while an important support of ordinary morality in most contexts, can also be very dangerous to morality, and have supported some of the most abominable behavior in human history. We have ample reason to want social pressures to produce conformity in many contexts, but conformity so produced may not be deeply internalized and may be crowned with undeserved honors if it is classified as virtue.

In a city things are different. People who see you at work very likely don't see you at home or at play. Each of these social contexts has its own norms and behavioral expectations, which it *may* be quite effective in training you to follow. But if one of them malfunctions, you may not learn its norms, and it may be easy and tempting to depart from morality in its area of life. Your associates in social contexts in which you may be more deeply rooted may neither know nor care very much about your deviance in the dysfunctional context.

This is an *anomie* or moral disorganization that can result from the compartmentalized social structures of urban life. It is a matter of breakdown both in situational factors that support moral behavior and in modular, situation-specific education of character. I don't think our pluralism of religious and moral views contributes much to it. Our economic situation may make a more or less urban life inevitable for most us, and it also has obvious attractions. But an urban context probably makes it easier for individuals to fall through holes in society's web of modules of moral education.

Most of what "society" can do to address such a problem, I believe, is at the level of modular, situation-specific learning. It involves bringing it about that families, neighborhoods, schools, and workplaces are not abusive or dysfunctional, so that modular moral learning in them will be effective, and that such opportunities are richly available to all. That's easier said than done, but I think it is the main task for those who would address typical worries about the decline of "virtue." I think we merely distract ourselves from the real, and hard, task when we worry about ethical and religious disagreements contributing to a decline of virtue.

## 3. INTEGRATIVE TASKS

Elementary and modular tasks of learning will not in any event constitute a sufficient education for virtue. For reasons discussed in chapters 8 to 11, modules of good behavioral dispositions will in some though not all cases constitute genuine virtues. But without a measure of trans-modular consistency, or integration into a more comprehensive ethical stance, they are unlikely to add up to comprehensive virtue or good moral character, and may fail to constitute some of the most important particular virtues. Education for virtue faces a task, or tasks, of moral integration. How can such integration be accomplished?

Best understood, probably, and certainly most studied in the history of moral philosophy, are *cognitive* aspects of integration. Lawrence Kohlberg's theory is a prime example. The main subject of his research was the development of ethical *reasoning.* He proceeded mainly by asking his subjects to give and explain their opinions about issues in the ethics of actions. And among his results are findings that tend to confirm the initially plausible hypothesis that people who are more principled in their ethical thinking tend to be more consistent, and in that way more integrated, in their ethical behavior.[7]

Some particular aspects of Kohlberg's theory are quite controversial, but moral experience surely does support the belief that people can have an articulate commitment to ethical principles of wide scope, and can apply them consciously, with some success, in dealing with quite diverse situations. This is probably the

[7] Kohlberg, *Essays on Moral Development,* vol. 2, pp. 548–52.

most clearly and generally available way of transcending modularity and achieving consistency in ethical performance, though it is certainly not guaranteed to be successful. Moreover, I don't doubt that there are broadly cognitive exercises that can help to improve the success of such rational efforts at moral consistency. These include the study of ethical theory, and other, less purely intellectual forms of reflection, teaching, and exhortation. They can help one to form or learn, and embrace, principles, policies, and commitments that generalize across previously separate modules. One can see relationships of similarity to be built on, and of inconsistency to be overcome. One can develop, by practice in thinking, one's sensitivity to reasons for accommodating modular virtues to each other differently in different situations. Such a sensitivity is a way of integrating the modular virtues into a more comprehensive stance.

But development of moral reasoning is not the only strategy for moral integration, and is not likely to be enough. Excellence in being for the good involves having feelings and desires that respond appropriately to the good, as well as acting well and thinking well about the good. Virtue's integration needs to involve all of these types of response. In pursuit of such holistic integration it is reasonable, I think, to seek resources in practices that are not purely intellectual; various forms of psychotherapy and of religious meditation come to mind.

It is characteristic of the arts, especially literature, and of much religious ritual and symbolism, to juxtapose themes of apparently conflicting moral significance. Such juxtaposition is prized, I think, largely because it is sometimes helpful in integrating feeling and aspiration, even though it offers no theoretical or intellectual resolution of the apparent contradictions. Why and how this helps is hard to understand, but I'm sure it sometimes does help moral integration. Perhaps that's because the integration proceeds best, in many cases, not by eliminating sources of tension but by relating them fruitfully.

Kohlberg's one-sided focus on the development of moral reasoning is the most obvious limitation of his research as a contribution to our understanding of education in virtue. His response to such criticism was essentially to appeal to his evidence that ethical behavior is quite strongly correlated with ethical judgment in individuals in the higher developmental stages of his typology of ethical reasoning.[8] That correlation probably exists in some degree, and is not surprising, but consistency of behavior with judgment is by no means all that should be involved in virtue's integration.

An important contemporary treatment of moral education that does not suffer from this limitation is John Rawls's discussion of education for justice in chapter 8 of *A Theory of Justice*. Rawls proposes a series of three "psychological laws" to account for successive stages of development of the sense of justice, from childhood to maturity. They are part of an argument intended to justify the claim that people living in a society that is just by Rawls's lights would not only

---

[8] Kohlberg, *Essays on Moral Development*, vol. 2, pp. 498–581.

understand the principles of justice but would probably become strongly motivated to uphold them and live in accordance with them. The "sense" of justice that these laws are meant to explain is a matter of feelings, and dispositions to act, that are appropriate to justice, rather than of understanding or reasoning about justice. The latter has its account elsewhere in Rawls's theory. According to Rawls's laws, under the right conditions, specified in the laws, the child will come to love its parents and be disposed to follow their precepts. The young person will develop feelings of friendliness, trust, and confidence toward his associates, and will be motivated to do his part in fair systems of cooperation. And the mature person will develop a more universal "desire to apply and to act upon the principles of justice" as such.[9] I think it is fair to classify this as an account of a piece of integrative rather than modular moral learning, inasmuch as a Rawlsian sense of justice is far from being situation-specific.

The central hypothesis of Rawls's explanatory account is that the affective and motivational dimensions of moral learning respond to moral features of the social environment. Specifically, if the parents in just family institutions "manifestly first love" the child and are "worthy objects of his admiration," if the young person's associates treat him fairly, and if the mature person lives in "an established and enduring just institution," then an appropriate sense of justice can be expected to develop through the indicated stages.[10] Although Rawls's discussion of the sense of justice makes frequent reference to work in empirical psychology as well as in philosophy, he offers no experimental evidence for his three psychological laws.

Some may think that a major conceptual difficulty stands in the way of experimental investigation at this point. Rawls is clear that the laws he proposes are stated in moral terms.[11] The effects to be explained are moral phenomena, and his proposal is to explain them in terms of moral properties of the social context. But this means that his laws are not stated in the value-neutral terms favored in many branches of empirical social science. It might take considerable conceptual and methodological innovation to subject his hypotheses to experimental testing that is both rigorous and appropriate.

Nevertheless I believe Rawls is right to state his laws in moral terms. The results that most concern us in moral education are *moral* properties of outcomes, and some of the specific features of Rawls's explanations seem to have a general value for moral education. It is plausible to suppose that the admirable character of people with whom one associates, their own behaving in accordance with the morality one is learning, and their loving or friendly attitude toward oneself will be main features of a context that is favorable to good and effective moral education. Good treatment by good and rightly respected people will be part of any plausible plan for moral education in general, and for education in virtue in

[9] Rawls, *A Theory of Justice*, pp. 463–6, 470, 474.    [10] Ibid., pp. 463–6, 470, 474, 490–1.
[11] Ibid., pp. 491–3.

particular. To be sure there are virtuous people who grew up ill-treated among people sadly lacking in virtue, and corrupt individuals who were brought up in morally favorable conditions. But I think the lesson to be learned from that is only that in this matter grace is better than the most plausible of plans, though that's no excuse for not following the best plans we can.

The most obvious limitation of Rawls's discussion of moral education, in relation to our present discussion, is that it is exclusively about the development of appropriate feelings and dispositions regarding *justice*. One of the major causal factors in his account is that the most reliable acquisition of the sense of justice takes place in "an established and enduring just institution." I take it the just institution in question is to be a just *state*. But the just and liberal state of Rawls's theory is emphatically not supposed to support any complete or comprehensive pattern of virtue in the way that it supports a sense of justice. How then are other parts of virtue, besides justice, to be learned?

Kohlberg's theory of moral education is limited in the same way. The moral reasoning he studied is about justice, or at any rate about "what we owe to each other."[12] At one time Kohlberg presumably did not see this as a limitation, for he held that "virtue is not many, but one, and its name is *justice*."[13] More recently he acknowledged that "other elements or components of moral action besides justice principles may be involved in actions deemed worthy by a theory of aretaic judgments for guiding judgments of moral worthiness," and that his theory of ethical reasoning therefore does not give him "an aretaic theory."[14] (An aretaic theory is of course a theory of *aretē* or virtue.)

In this respect both Rawls and Kohlberg are compartmentalizing rather than integrative in their accounts of moral education. In Rawls's case the compartmentalization is consciously willed, though only for a limited purpose. For purposes of political theory and political life, he wants to separate the principles of justice from "comprehensive moral views." He hopes all citizens of a liberal state can agree on the former, as a matter of "public reason," while he regards the latter as private matters about which citizens may well disagree. He does not, I take it, mean to deny that citizens will commonly seek to integrate principles of justice into their own comprehensive views. But, so far as I can see, he offers no help for such integration beyond taking care to frame the principles of justice in such a way as to take into account the interest people will have in more private values and in possibly divergent comprehensive views.

More than that, perhaps, is not his job as a political philosopher. But I think it is fair to say that Rawls and some other leading exemplars of liberal moral and political philosophy have met aspirations for comprehensive moral integration with more signs of suspicious caution than of enthusiasm. The suspicion has

---

[12] T. M. Scanlon's phrase, aptly chosen as the title of his recent book.
[13] Kohlberg, *Essays on Moral Development*, vol. 1, p. 39 (in an essay first published in 1970).
[14] Ibid., vol. 2, p. 515 (in an essay first published in 1984, with Daniel Candee as co-author).

sometimes been carried close to despair of the possibility of comprehensive integration of valuing.[15] In some cases a main worry animating the suspicion seems to be that adherence to ethical principles and concerns rooted in regard for the interests of other people will be compromised by more private valuations that are morally less urgent, or even amoral.[16] This is connected with large issues for theories of virtue. Like ancient Greek conceptions of virtue, my definition of virtue as excellence in being for the good does not limit the territory of virtue to that of regard for the interests of others. I believe the less limited conception of virtue has important advantages for the integration of ethical selfhood. I have defended it in chapters 5–7.

In the present context I want rather to address a worry more connected with Rawls's political liberalism. That is the fear that adherence to shared principles of justice that protect the equal liberties of citizens may be corrupted if it is not somewhat walled off from the influence of more controversial valuations. My view is that liberalism is ill served by such compartmentalization. The idea that it is needed seems to me to spring from an excessively theoretical conception of the kind of unity or integration that societies need or, indeed, are capable of. The thought that a well-ordered society requires agreement on an ethical *theory* of some sort is, ironically, an idea on which many arguments for a less liberal political order have been based. Liberals have already taken a false step if they accept this thought and frame the debate as one in which they argue merely for the scope of the agreed theory to be narrow rather than wide.

There is no liberty that is more important to liberalism than the freedom to form, embrace, criticize, reject, and revise theories of *every* sort, *especially* political theories. For this reason it is misguided to suppose the liberal defense of civil liberties is well served by drawing a perimeter of privacy around "comprehensive moral views," about which disagreement is expected, leaving theories of justice in the public realm, on the other side of the perimeter. It must be expected that in a liberal society political theories, like other moral, religious, and philosophical theories, not only may but will be objects of persistent disagreement. The consensus that a liberal political system certainly needs for its good order will have to be much less theoretical, and perhaps less tidy, than many have supposed. It will involve, most obviously, an agreement on sets of laws, especially constitutional laws, and a sharing of certain customs and habits of political behavior.

---

[15] For instance, in Wolf, "Moral Saints," and Nagel, "The Fragmentation of Value" (1977). Nagel is at most cautiously more optimistic about such integration in *The View from Nowhere* (1986), chapter 10.

[16] The influence of this worry is evident in Nagel, *The View from Nowhere*, chapter 10, as also in the discussion of priority issues in Scanlon, *What We Owe to Each Other*. In fairness it should be noted that both Nagel and Scanlon argue that the demands of ethical principles giving effect to respect for each other must be shaped to take account of the fact that we all have valuations that are more private. This is an integrative move, though it stops short of any strategy for fully comprehensive personal integration of valuing.

Fortunately, such agreement is possible and adequate. Those who have enjoyed the benefits of civil liberties, and the non-violent political participation made possible by democracy, generally recognize the advantages of the requisite agreed arrangements. And, in fact, it is at least as true of any society as it is of a human individual that its integration cannot be the integration of a theory. Even in a society ostensibly governed by an official ideology, most people are likely not to understand the ideology very well; and among those who understand it better, there will probably be implicit if not explicit differences in interpretation. There will also surely be interests and pressures within the society that are by no means in harmony with the ideology.

Perhaps no social condition has been the object of more nostalgia than the supposed cultural and religious homogeneity of Western Europe in the Middle Ages. It had, if not exactly an ideology, certainly a theological tradition that expressed a religious and ethical outlook that commanded almost universal allegiance in the society. Yet it was full of conflicts between families, nations, and political and religious leaders. And, even apart from various remnants of pre-Christian belief in regional folk-cultures, it had a quasi-religion of militarism. The norms of the latter were integral to much of the structure of the society and were obviously in tension with principles of the all but unanimously professed Christian religion, but endured alongside it for centuries. Regarding many points in the theological tradition, also, there were vigorous disagreements among its most knowledgeable interpreters. Yet the society certainly functioned and was in significant ways more successful than its contemporary competitors.

The generalizability of historical phenomena is obviously limited. I mention the example of medieval Europe because I think it makes vivid the difference between having agreement on a tradition of religious and ethical theory and having a functionally integrated society. With or without an overarching agreement in moral theory, functional integration of a society must deal with conflicting aims and interests within the society, and almost always with substantially divergent dispositions of ethical judgment. Much experience of modern pluralistic societies seems to show that such functional integration can be obtained without the overarching theoretical agreement as well as with it. I argued in the second section of chapter 11 that the moral integration of a person can embrace continuing inner tensions, and that tolerance of ambivalence in oneself can be part of a form of personal integration. An analogous point applies to a liberal society. Its integration will consist in large part in the mutual acceptance of citizens holding diverse political as well as moral and religious theories and points of view. An important part of such integration will be finding ways in which (in most cases) we can *respect* the convictions of other people even when we do not *agree* with them.

Such facts form a social context for individuals' integrative tasks of moral learning. It is easy to be tempted by the thought that if our society were ethically homogeneous, its culture might have an ethical integration that we could simply take over and make our own. In this way an ethically homogeneous society might seem to have a great advantage for education in virtue. But that is an unrealistic thought. There are severe limits on how integrated ethically a whole society *can* be, if it is even as complex as that of medieval France, let alone the ancient Roman Empire or the modern United States.

There are reasons to think the human needs that complex societies must satisfy, in order to survive, will inevitably give rise to inner moral tensions, and even to forces of moral formation that work at cross purposes. The institutional contexts of employment, enjoyment, and government in which adults continue their ethical formation in any modern society are functionally differentiated. To the extent that they are benign institutions, focused on real values, it will be good to learn in them to appreciate those values, but they will be diverse and to some extent competing values. We have reason to aspire to a higher degree of integration in our individual ethical selfhood than we would be likely to find in the institutions and culture of even a religiously and culturally *homogeneous* modern society.

Moreover, the relations of individuals and societies to values are too different, in principle, for it to be feasible for individuals to take over an ethical integration, ready-made, from society. Societies do not care about things in the same way that human individuals do, and do not have the same kind of emotional dynamics. Hence societies as such are not possible subjects of the very personal and individual kind of integration of caring about different things that is arguably the most central task of integration for virtue. The integration of societies and the integration of individuals are analogous but fundamentally different tasks, and solving the problems of one is not tantamount to solving the problems of the other.

Perhaps the tempting thought is rather that the integration a society can offer for appropriation by the individual is not the ethical integration of the society itself, but a standard model of individual integration. But then it is harder to see the advantage of a religiously and culturally homogeneous society. Even if a society is homogeneous in those ways, if it is complex enough to contain many social roles it will present a plurality of models of personal integration. And, anyway, why should a "one-size-fits-all" model of ethical integration be preferred to a menu of alternative models? A complex post-industrial society, with its information technology, provides a context in which a vast variety of goods can be valued. But no human individual can be seriously engaged with more than a fraction of those goods.

We each have our own vocation, which can be understood very largely in terms of goods that are given to us individually to love, as I have put it in previous chapters. Such vocation deserves a central role in moral integration of the self. The question for personal and ethical integration is not just 'What is it excellent for a person in general to be like?' but equally 'Who and what am I called to be? What people and what goods are given to me to love, protect, and serve? To what social projects and roles am I drawn or committed?' That is bound to give an individual character to our ethical integrations.

Even within a shared moral or religious tradition, one can hardly expect more than a family resemblance among individual ethical integrations. The vocations of a parent and of a celibate nun or monk, for example, are surely so different in the concrete concerns they would need to bring together that neither could simply take over an integration of them from the other. We each have our own task of ethical integration, in which it is far from evident that it is a disadvantage to have a variety of models to learn from.

I have been arguing that a liberal state in a pluralistic society can do at least as well as any alternative political system in providing an environment for education in virtue. But I should not suggest that no problems remain here for moral education, or that the liberal state can provide, by itself, a fully adequate institutional context for such education. Most if not all of us are surely likelier to become and remain virtuous, and continue to develop ethically, if we have social settings that support such development. Those will be settings in which our attention is continually directed to ethical issues and ethical ideals, and in which there is social encouragement for moral efforts. We should hope to find companionship in developing a coherent, integrated outlook on life in which virtue can find a home. As one's outlook develops in a particular direction, there may be particular practices and common projects that would help in strengthening and deepening both one's insight into the outlook and one's ability to live in accord with it.

What sort of community or institution would best fulfill these functions of moral education and support? Not the state, I think. There are many reasons for distrusting state intervention and control in these matters. It is dangerous to liberty, and not particularly likely to be sensitive to considerations of excellence of character, as distinct from considerations of behavior that is convenient or inconvenient to influential constituencies. The desired institution should probably be larger, more stable, more objective, and richer in varieties of leadership than the family. Like the family, however, and unlike most other institutions in which adults participate in a modern society, it should be concerned with the whole person and not just with her functioning in certain social roles. At the end of the *Nicomachean Ethics* (X.9), considering only the state and the family as institutional sponsors for education in virtue, Aristotle chose the state; we need more alternatives. Historically, the obvious alternative is a religious institution; we are close here to Kant's argument in *Religion within the Boundaries of Mere Reason*, that the moral development of humanity requires a church.

'Requires' should not be taken too strictly in such an argument. Even Kant, during his adult life, seems in practice to have made an exception for himself (as did Leibniz before him, despite a similar belief on the point). Moreover, as Kant emphasizes, some religious institutions are far from ideal as contexts for learning virtue. Some, for example, are authoritarian and conformist in ways that are hardly conducive to development of the integrative virtues of authentic feeling and independent thought. We can say, however, that the desired institution should resemble some religious institutions in certain ways, particularly in providing a context in which there is persistent discourse on ethical issues, and in which people care for each other as whole persons.

Moreover, if an institution is to help people to develop, sustain, and integrate *virtue*, and not just good behavior, it must provide encouragement and insight for excellence in being for the good in *all* aspects of life. In that respect such an institution should not be like a political or charitable association in being focused sharply on the active efforts of its members. Like many religious institutions it should be no less engaged in helping people come to terms with calamity, suffering, mortality, helplessness, and loss, so that they can still be excellently for the good in situations in which their power to intervene is very limited. For, in trying to live well, we surely have at least as frequent occasions to want to respond well to what we cannot control as to what we can. An institution that is to help us deal well with the helplessness in our lives must be as sensitive to what our actions can symbolize as to what they can cause.[17]

I have ventured here, very briefly, into philosophical ecclesiology, a subdiscipline of the philosophy of religion that hardly exists in English, though there have been major historic contributions to it in German, by Schleiermacher, for example, as well as Kant. I have not gone into the question of whether, in religious practice, character may be shaped by contact with a power of goodness that transcends our own, as that goes far beyond the scope of the present book. And I don't mean to imply that religious institutions are to be understood and evaluated solely in relation to education for virtue. Religious beliefs may give one reasons of other sorts to participate in a religious body and to want it to have certain features. Other functions, such as the worship of God, may rightly be central to the life of a religious institution. (Worship can indeed be integrative, but that is hardly its primary purpose.) But ethical education is a natural and historically important function of religious institutions. Many individuals in Western culture at present are morally unfortunate not to have a social context that focuses attention on ethical aspirations, and supports them, in ways that religious institutions often have.

## 4. SHOULD VIRTUE BE TAUGHT?

*Can* virtue be taught? It seems that what I have called *elementary* tasks of moral education are regularly accomplished. It would be an implausibly profound skepticism about morality to deny that older generations generally manage to initiate younger generations into a reasonably competent grasp of ethical concepts.

---

[17] The ethical significance of symbolic action and its relation to helplessness are more fully discussed in Adams, *Finite and Infinite Goods*, chapter 9, and "Anti-Consequentialism and the Transcendence of the Good," pp. 119–22.

Most public concern about the teaching of virtue, I suspect, has to do with the impartation of dispositions to socially accepted behavior in frequently recurring situations. I have argued that societies are commonly quite successful at such *modular* tasks of moral education, as even situationist skepticism about virtue does not deny. How much of what is learned in this way is really virtue may be doubted. Perhaps genuine virtue requires motivation and integration that are harder to teach and learn. I have suggested ways of working at *integrative* tasks of character education. But I grant—indeed I insist—that moral integration is an intrinsically difficult task for which we have no "sure fire" method, and that we are unlikely to find *totally* integrated people.

*Should* virtue be taught? Is the improvement of character a reasonable goal of moral endeavor? Some of the situationist philosophers discussed in chapters 8 and 9 have argued vigorously for a negative answer to this question. Indeed, they have argued that it would be better not to think in terms of virtue and vice at all. Their arguments for this conclusion are pragmatic. Whether or not ascriptions of virtue and vice are sometimes true, they are generally unhelpful or harmful, in the opinion of Harman and Doris.

While I regard the question of helpfulness as secondary in relation to that of truth, the pragmatic issues do claim our attention too, especially in consideration of moral education. There is evidence that people tend to fulfill the expectations of people influential in their lives who have labeled them, explicitly or even subconsciously, as good or bad in some respect.[18] This may suggest that it would be beneficial to avoid thinking of people as having vices, and especially to avoid thinking of them as globally "bad people." On the other hand, of course, it suggests just as strongly that it would be beneficial to think of people as characterized by virtues, or even as globally "good people." I think it is indeed morally wise both to try to discern and appreciate virtues in people and to be very cautious about attributing vices, as distinct from objecting to particular actions and attitudes. And perhaps it would be wise to abstain altogether from thinking of anyone globally as a "bad person," or even, more cautiously and more precisely, as a *morally* bad person.

It will be asked what we are going to say (seriously, really) about the likes of Adolf Hitler and Josef Stalin. Certainly we can say that they were *wicked* in terribly important ways. But probably it is not true, and therefore should not be said, that there was nothing good about them—nor even, I suspect, that there was nothing *morally* good about them. It is tempting to think that in view of the enormity of evils for which they were responsible, they do not deserve to have the villainy ascribed to them mitigated by scrupulous precision. But the question here is whether we do *ourselves* harm by allowing our judgment in such matters to be guided by vindictive impulse rather than by truthfulness.

---

[18] Cf. Ross and Nisbett, *The Person and the Situation*, pp. 227–30, and Doris, *Lack of Character*, p. 126.

It would be hard to defend talk of virtues and vices if that must mean dividing humanity into purely good guys and unmitigatedly bad guys. That aggravates conflict,[19] and also dulls moral discernment. I think it is virtually always factually unjustified. But it is surely not the only use of the language of virtues and vices. The most important application of the concept of a morally good person, I believe, is its constructive use in intrapersonal diachronic comparisons. What might I do to become morally better, or to help my child or friend become a morally better person—or to avoid influences that might corrupt us and make us worse? Such thinking should normally deal mostly in shades of gray, the more obviously so if one believes, as I do, that concepts of virtue are responsible to ideals that we are not likely ever to realize fully. The empirical findings of social psychology hardly show such thinking to be useless, though they underline the modesty with which we should think about what we may achieve in this way.

The importance of such modesty is a main lesson of one of Doris's most interesting pragmatic arguments. Rather than rely on character to arm us against temptation, he suggests, we should try "to avoid 'near occasions of sin'—morally dangerous circumstances."[20] More generally, he believes we should focus efforts on structuring social situations in such a way as to make better behavior likelier. Certainly it is sound moral advice, even for the most virtuous, to avoid unnecessary occasions of sin. It is also wise, I would not only grant but emphasize, to be very conscious of the fragility of human virtue—including one's own, if one is so graced as to have any. But that is no reason not to try to improve one's character. It is reason, rather, not to expect too much from such efforts, and particularly not to presume on such expectations in approaching temptations. Why shouldn't we try *both* to make morally propitious situational changes *and* to improve our characters?

Perhaps Doris would reply that it will be more profitable to concentrate exclusively on situational change because the improvement of character is too difficult. I have already said roughly how difficult I believe the improvement of character is and is not. Here I will add some comments on the thought that focusing exclusively on situational change is a more promising strategy for moral improvement. (1) Doris clearly believes that the decisive test of moral improvement is improvement of behavior. Important as behavior is, however, I do not see why we should not also be interested, for their own sake, in improving some aspects of character that are not directly behavioral, such as ethical beliefs and motives.

(2) I doubt that it is in general much easier to improve our situations than to improve our characters. The situations that most concern us here are social situations. Efforts to change them are likely to be frustrated in many cases by other participants whose goals or beliefs are different from ours. And even if

[19] Or causes unnecessary hostility, as Harman suggests ("Moral Philosophy Meets Social Psychology," p. 330).
[20] Doris, "Persons, Situations, and Virtue Ethics," p. 517.

we can implement successfully the steps we undertake, any changes we manage to make in complex systems, such as social systems, are apt to have unforeseen consequences that turn out to be more important than the consequences we intended.

(3) There will sometimes be ethical objections to what would otherwise be the most promising way of making a situation more supportive of moral behavior. The steps available to us might unduly limit the freedom of other people—for example, by restricting their choice of entertainment to what we think is edifying. And the avoidance of near occasions of sin may itself be a sin—for example, if it is our duty to do something that severely tests our courage or our patience.

Given such limitations of strategies of situation improvement, we can ill afford to renounce efforts at character improvement, if we have (as I believe) a significant chance of some measure of success in them. To this I might add (4) the ad hominem point that there is probably not a sharp line between strategies of situation improvement and strategies of character improvement. It is *social* situations, after all, that we are chiefly talking about improving. How does one change a social situation? In most cases mainly by changing the behavior of people in the situation. One may try to do that by manipulating them in ad hoc ways each time the occasion arises. But the most successful methods are likely to involve some open or unacknowledged training of the people—in short some modular character education.

Finally, it should be noted that improvement of our moral condition or performance is not the only important interest served by thinking in terms of virtues and vices. We are not only active creatures, seeking to control and reshape and draw sustenance from our environment. We are also reflective and contemplative creatures, seeking a just appreciation of the values in our own and each other's lives. For such an interest the assessment of moral character is important for its own sake. It would not necessarily be less valuable for being always cautious and contestable (as arguments of social psychologists may contribute to showing that it ought to be).[21] It may be likened in that respect to criticism of art and literature, in which permanent disagreements may enrich our understanding of the object more than any unanimity could. This is not to say that virtue is subjective and merely "in the eye of the beholder," but rather that it is perspectival, in the sense that it is only at certain angles that it presents an image of transcendent good.

---

[21] Ross and Nisbett, *The Person and the Situation*, pp. 125–39; but cf. critical comments on this subject in Krueger and Funder, "Towards a Balanced Social Psychology."

# Bibliography

This bibliography mentions only works cited in this book. Page references in the text and notes are to a reprint or English translation if one is listed in the bibliography. I have usually quoted from a published English translation, but I have sometimes emended the translation, and have sometimes given my own translation—normally without noting the fact, as this is not a work of historical scholarship.

Adams, Robert Merrihew. "Anti-Consequentialism and the Transcendence of the Good." *Philosophy and Phenomenological Research*, 67 (2003): 114–32.

——. "Christian Liberty." In Morris, ed., *Philosophy and the Christian Faith*, pp. 151–71.

——. "Common Projects and Moral Virtue." *Midwest Studies in Philosophy*, 13 (1988): 297–307

——. *Finite and Infinite Goods: A Framework for Ethics*. New York: Oxford University Press, 1999.

——. "Human Nature, Christian Vocation, and the Sexes." In Coulton, ed., *The Bible, the Church and Homosexuality*, pp. 100–13.

——. "Involuntary Sins." *The Philosophical Review*, 94 (1985): 3–31.

——. "Motive Utilitarianism." *The Journal of Philosophy*, 73 (1976): 467–81.

——. "Platonism and Naturalism: Options for a Theocentric Ethics." In Runzo, ed., *Ethics, Religion, and the Good Society*, pp. 22–42.

——. "Pure Love." *Journal of Religious Ethics*, 8 (1980): 83–99. Reprinted as chapter 12 of Adams, *The Virtue of Faith*.

——. "Religious Ethics in a Pluralistic Society." In Outka and Reeder, eds., *Prospects for a Common Morality*, pp. 93–113.

——. "Saints." *The Journal of Philosophy*, 81 (1984): 392–401. Reprinted as chapter 11 of Adams, *The Virtue of Faith*.

——. "Scanlon's Contractualism: Critical Notice of T. M. Scanlon, *What We Owe to Each Other*." *The Philosophical Review*, 110 (2001): 563–86.

——. "Self-Love and the Vices of Self-Preference." *Faith and Philosophy*, 15 (1998): 500–13.

——. *The Virtue of Faith and Other Essays in Philosophical Theology*. New York: Oxford University Press, 1987.

Anderson, Elizabeth, *Value in Ethics and Economics*. Cambridge, Massachusetts: Harvard University Press, 1993.

Annas, Julia. *The Morality of Happiness*. New York: Oxford University Press, 1993.

Anscombe, G. E. M. "Modern Moral Philosophy." *Philosophy*, 33 (1958): 1–19. Reprinted in Crisp and Slote, eds., *Virtue Ethics*, pp. 26–44.

Aristotle. *Nicomachean Ethics*. Trans. by Terence Irwin. Indianapolis: Hackett Publishing Co., 1985.

Auden, W. H. *The Collected Poetry of W. H. Auden*. New York: Random House, 1945.

Badhwar, Neera K. "The Limited Unity of Virtue." *Noûs*, 30 (1996): 306–29.

Baier, Kurt. "Radical Virtue Ethics." *Midwest Studies in Philosophy*, 13 (1988): 126–35.

Barth, Karl. *Church Dogmatics*. 4 vols. in many part-volumes. Trans. by G. W. Bromiley *et al*. Edinburgh: T. & T. Clark, 1936–69.

Blum, Lawrence. "Community and Virtue." In Crisp, ed., *How Should One Live?* ed., pp. 231–50.

——. *Friendship, Altruism, and Morality*. London: Routledge & Kegan Paul, 1980.

——. "Moral Exemplars: Reflections on Schindler, the Trocmés, and Others." *Midwest Studies in Philosophy*, 13 (1988): 196–221.

Brandt, Richard B. "The Structure of Virtue." *Midwest Studies in Philosophy*, 13 (1988): 64–82.

——. "Traits of Character: A Conceptual Analysis." *American Philosophical Quarterly*, 7 (1970): 23–37.

Broad, C. D. *Five Types of Ethical Theory*. London: Kegan Paul, Trench, Trubner & Co., 1930.

Buber, Martin. *I and Thou*. Trans. by Walter Kaufmann. New York: Scribner's, 1970.

——. *Werke*. Vol. 1, *Schriften zur Philosophie*. Munich and Heidelberg: Kösel-Verlag and Verlag Kambert Scneider, 1962.

Burnyeat, Myles. "Aristotle on learning to be Good." In Rorty, ed., *Essays on Aristotle's Ethics*, pp. 69–92.

Butler, Joseph. *Fifteen Sermons Preached at the Rolls Chapel*. Edited by T. A. Roberts. London: SPCK, 1970.

Campbell, John. "Can Philosophical Accounts of Altruism Accommodate Experimental Data on Helping Behaviour?" *Australasian Journal of Philosophy*, 77 (1999): 26–45.

Cooper, John. *Reason and Human Good in Aristotle*. Cambridge, Massachusetts: Harvard University Press, 1975.

——. "The Unity of Virtue." *Social Philosophy and Policy*, 15 (1998): 233–74.

Coulton, Nicholas, ed. *The Bible, the Church and Homosexuality*. London: Darton, Longman and Todd Ltd, 2005.

Crisp, Roger, ed. *How Should One Live? Essays on the Virtues*. Oxford: Clarendon Press, 1996.

——, and Slote, Michael, eds. *Virtue Ethics*. Oxford: Oxford University Press, 1997.

Darley, John M., and Batson, C. Daniel. ' "From Jerusalem to Jericho': A Study of Situational and Dispositional Variables in Helping Behavior." *Journal of Personality and Social Psychology*, 27 (1973): 100–8.

Darwall, Stephen. *The British Moralists and the Internal 'Ought': 1640–1740*. Cambridge: Cambridge University Press, 1995.

——. "Valuing Activity." *Social Philosophy and Policy*, 16 (1999): 176–96.

Dickens, Charles. *A Tale of Two Cities*. London: Penguin Books, 2003.

Doris, John M. *Lack of Character: Personality and Moral Behavior*. Cambridge: Cambridge University Press, 2002.

——. "Persons, Situations, and Virtue Ethics." *Noûs*, 32 (1998): 504–30.

Driver, Julia. *Uneasy Virtue*. Cambridge: Cambridge University Press, 2001.

——. "The Virtues and Human Nature." In Crisp, ed., *How Should One Live?*, pp. 111–29.

Eagly, Alice H., and Chaiken, Shelly. *The Psychology of Attitudes*. Fort Worth: Harcourt Brace Jovanovich, 1993.

Eliot, T. S. *The Complete Poems and Plays, 1909–1950*. New York: Harcourt, Brace and Company, 1952.

Engelhardt, H. Tristram, Jr., and Callahan, Daniel, eds. *Knowledge, Value, and Belief*. Hastings-on-Hudson, NY: Institute of Society, Ethics, and the Life Sciences, 1977.

Engstrom, Stephen. "The Concept of the Highest Good in Kant's Moral Theory." *Philosophy and Phenomenological Research*, 52 (1992): 747–80.

FitzPatrick, William J. *Teleology and the Norms of Nature*. New York: Garland Publishing, 2000.

Flanagan, Owen. *Varieties of Moral Personality*. Cambridge, Massachusetts: Harvard University Press, 1991.

Fodor Jerry A. *The Modularity of Mind: An Essay on Faculty Psychology*. Cambridge, Massachusetts: MIT Press, 1983.

Foot, Philippa. *Natural Goodness*. Oxford: Clarendon Press, 2002.

_____. "Virtues and Vices." In Foot, *Virtues and Vices and Other Essays in Moral Philosophy*. Cited from the reprint in Crisp and Slote, eds., *Virtue Ethics*, pp. 163–77.

_____. *Virtues and Vices and Other Essays in Moral Philosophy*. Oxford: Blackwell, 1978.

Hallie, Philip. *Lest Innocent Blood Be Shed: The Story of the Village of Le Chambon and How Goodness Happened There*. New York: Harper & Row, 1979.

Hampshire, Stuart. *Two Theories of Morality*. Oxford: Oxford University Press, 1977.

Harman, Gilbert. "Moral Philosophy Meets Social Psychology: Virtue Ethics and the Fundamental Attribution Error." *Proceedings of the Aristotelian Society*, 99 (1999): 315–31.

Hartshorne, Hugh, and May, Mark A. and (for vol. 3) Shuttleworth, Frank K. *Studies in the Nature of Character*. 3 vols. New York: Macmillan, 1928–30.

Hill, Thomas E., Jr. *Autonomy and Self-Respect*. Cambridge: Cambridge University Press, 1991.

_____. "Servility and Self-Respect." In *The Monist* (1973). Reprinted in Hill, *Autonomy and Self-Respect*, pp. 4–18.

Hume, David. *Enquiries Concerning the Human Understanding and Concerning the Principles of Morals*. Ed. by L. A. Selby-Bigge and P. H. Nidditch. 3rd edn. Oxford: Clarendon Press, 1975.

Hurka, Thomas. *Virtue, Vice, and Value*. New York: Oxford University Press: 2000.

Hursthouse, Rosalind. *On Virtue Ethics*. Oxford: Oxford University Press, 1999.

Hutcheson, Francis. *An Inquiry into the Original of Our Ideas of Beauty and Virtue*. Treatise II, *Concerning Moral Good and Evil*. 2nd edn. London, 1726. As excerpted in Selby-Bigge, ed., *British Moralists*, vol. 1, pp. 67–171.

Isen, A. M., and Levin, H. "Effect of Feeling Good on Helping: Cookies and Kindness." *Journal of Personality and Social Psychology*, 21 (1972): 384–8.

Kagan, Shelly. "Rethinking Intrinsic Value." *Journal of Ethics*, 2 (1998): 277–97.

Kamtekar, Rachana. "Situationism and Virtue Ethics on the Content of Our Character." *Ethics*, 114 (2004): 458–91.

Kant, Immanuel. *Anthropology from a Pragmatic Standpoint*. Cited by vol. (VII) and page of the Prussian (now German) Academy edn.

_____. *Critique of Practical Reason*. In Kant, *Practical Philosophy*, pp. 133–271. Cited by vol. (V) and page of the Prussian (now German) Academy edn.

Kant, Immanuel. *Critique of Pure Reason.* Trans. and ed. by Paul Guyer and Allen W. Wood. Cambridge: Cambridge University Press, 1998. Cited by page of the first (A) and second (B) German editions.

———. *The Metaphysics of Morals.* In Kant, *Practical Philosophy*, pp. 353–603. Cited by vol. (VI) and page of the Prussian (now German) Academy edn.

———. *Practical Philosophy.* Trans. and ed. by Mary J. Gregor. Cambridge: Cambridge University Press, 1996.

———. *Religion and Rational Theology.* Trans. and ed. by Allen W. Wood and George di Giovanni. Cambridge: Cambridge University Press, 1996.

———. *Religion within the Boundaries of Mere Reason.* In Kant, *Religion and Rational Theology*, pp. 39–215. Cited by vol. (VI) and page of the Prussian (now German) Academy edn.

Keneally, Thomas. *Schindler's List.* Scribner Paperback Fiction edn. New York: Simon & Schuster, 2000.

Kohlberg, Lawrence. *Essays on Moral Development.* 2 vols. San Francisco: Harper & Row, 1981, 1984.

Korsgaard, Christine. "Two Distinctions in Goodness." *Philosophical Review*, 92 (1983): 169–95.

Krueger, Joachim L., and Funder, David C. "Towards a Balanced Social Psychology: Causes, Consequences, and Cures for the Problem-seeking Approach to Social Behavior and Cognition." Downloaded May 1, 2003, from Funder's website, <http://www.psych.ucr.edu/faculty/funder/rap/bbs.pdf>.

Lear, Gabriel Richardson. *Happy Lives and the Highest Good: An Essay on Aristotle's Nicomachean Ethics.* Princeton: Princeton University Press, 2004.

Lifton, Robert Jay. *The Nazi Doctors: Medical Killing and the Psychology of Genocide.* New York: Basic Books, 1986.

McDowell, John. "Virtue and Reason." *The Monist*, 62 (1979): 331–50. Reprinted in Crisp and Slote, eds., *Virtue Ethics*, pp. 141–62.

MacIntyre, Alasdair. *After Virtue: A Study in Moral Theory.* 2nd edn. Notre Dame, Indiana: University of Notre Dame Press, 1984.

Mandeville, Bernard de. *The Fable of the bees: or, Private vices publick benefits.* London: printed for J. Rorerts [sic], 1714.

Merritt, Maria. "Virtue Ethics and Situationist Personality Psychology." *Ethical Theory and Moral Practice*, 3 (2000): 365–83.

Milgram, Stanley. *Obedience to Authority: An Experimental View.* New York: Harper & Row, 1974.

Mill, John Stuart. *On Liberty.* Many editions, cited by standard divisions.

Miller, William Ian, *The Mystery of Courage.* Cambridge, Massachusetts: Harvard University Press, 2000.

Milton, John. *Paradise Lost* (1667). Reprinted (according to the 1st edn. of 1667, but divided into books as in the 2nd edn. of 1674) in Milton, *Poetical Works*, pp. 174–448. Cited by book and line.

———. *The Poetical Works of John Milton.* Ed. by H. C. Beeching. London: Oxford University Press, 1938.

Mischel, Walter. *Introduction to Personality.* 2nd edn. New York: Holt, Rinehart and Winston, 1976.

Monroe, Kristen Renwick. "John Donne's People: Explaining Differences between Rational Actors and Altruists through Cognitive Frameworks." *Journal of Politics*, 53 (1991): 394–433.

――, Barton, Michael C., and Klingemann, Ute. "Altruism and the Theory of Rational Action: Rescuers of Jews in Nazi Europe." *Ethics*, 101 (1990): 103–22.

Morris, Thomas V., ed. *Philosophy and the Christian Faith*. Notre Dame, Indiana: University of Notre Dame Press, 1988.

Mossner, Ernest Campbell. *Bishop Butler and the Age of Reason: A Study in the History of Thought*. New York: Macmillan, 1936.

Murdoch, Iris. *The Sovereignty of Good*. New York: Schocken Books, 1971.

Nagel, Thomas. "The Fragmentation of Value." In Engelhardt and Callahan, eds., *Knowledge, Value, and Belief*. Reprinted in Nagel, *Mortal Questions*, pp. 128–41.

――. "Moral Luck." *Proceedings of the Aristotelian Society*, supp. vol. 50 (1976). Reprinted with revisions in Nagel, *Mortal Questions*, pp. 24–38.

――. *Mortal Questions*. Cambridge: Cambridge University Press, 1979.

――. *The View from Nowhere*. New York: Oxford University Press, 1986.

Nietzsche, Friedrich. *Die fröhliche Wissenschaft* [*The Gay Science*]. Stuttgart: Philipp Reclam jun., 2000.

――. *On the Genealogy of Morality*. Ed. by Keith Ansell-Pearson. Trans. by Carol Diethe. Cambridge: Cambridge University Press, 1994.

――. "Homer on Competition." In the supplementary material to the cited translation of *On the Genealogy of Morality*, pp. 187–94.

――. *Jenseits von Gut und Böse* [*Beyond Good and Evil*]: *Vorspiel einer Philosophie der Zukunft*. Augsburg: Goldmann, 1999.

――. *The Portable Nietzsche*. Ed. and trans. by Walter Kaufmann. New York: Viking Press, 1954.

――. *Thus Spoke Zarathustra*. In Nietzsche, *The Portable Nietzsche*.

Outka, Gene, and Reeder, John P., Jr., eds. *Prospects for a Common Morality*. Princeton, New Jersey: Princeton University Press, 1993.

Penelhum, Terence. *Butler*. London: Routledge & Kegan Paul, 1985.

Plato. *Platonis opera*. 5 vols. Ed. John Burnet. Oxford: Clarendon Press, 1900–1907. Cited by the pagination of Stephanus, which is found in the margins of most editions and translations of Plato.

――. *Protagoras*. In Plato, *Platonis opera*, vol. 3, pp. I.309–62.

――. *Republic*. In Plato, *Platonis opera*, vol. 4, pp. II.327–621.

――. *Symposium*. In Plato, *Platonis opera*, vol. 2, pp. III.172–223.

Plutarch. *Lives*, vol. 10. Loeb Classical Library, vol. 102. Trans. by Bernadotte Perrin. Cambridge, Massachusetts: Harvard University Press, 1921.

Rawls, John. *A Theory of Justice*. Cambridge, Massachusetts: Harvard University Press, 1971.

Reid, Thomas. *Essays on the Active Powers of the Human Mind* (1788). Reprinted in Reid, *Works*.

――. *The Works of Thomas Reid, D. D.* Ed. by Sir William Hamilton. Edinburgh, 1895. Reprinted Hildesheim: Georg Olms Verlag, 1983.

Risse, Mathias. "The Morally Decent Person." *Southern Journal of Philosophy*, 38 (2000): 263–79.

Roberts, Robert C. "Will Power and the Virtues." *Philosophical Review*, 93 (1984): 227–47.

Rorty, Amélie O., ed. *Essays on Aristotle's Ethics*. Berkeley: University of California Press, 1980.

———, ed. *The Identities of Persons*. Berkeley: University of California Press, 1976.

Ross, Lee, and Nisbett, Richard E. *The Person and the Situation: Perspectives of Social Psychology*. Boston, Massachusetts: McGraw-Hill, 1991.

Runzo, Joseph, ed. *Ethics, Religion, and the Good Society: New Directions in a Pluralistic World*. Westminster/John Knox Press, 1992.

Sabini, John, and Silver, Maury. "Lack of Character? Situationism Critiqued." *Ethics*, 115 (2005): 535–62.

———. *Moralities of Everyday Life*. New York: Oxford University Press, 1982.

Sachs, David. "A Fallacy in Plato's *Republic*." *Philosophical Review*, 72 (1963): 141–58.

Scanlon, T. M. *What We Owe to Each Other*. Cambridge, Massachusetts: Harvard University Press, 1998.

Scheffler, Samuel. *The Rejection of Consequentialism*. Revised edn. Oxford: Clarendon Press, 1994.

Schlosser, Gerhard, and Wagner, Günther P., eds. *Modularity in Development and Evolution*. Chicago: University of Chicago Press, 2004.

Selby-Bigge, L. A. *British Moralists, Being Selections from Writers Principally of the Eighteenth Century*. 2 vols. Oxford: Clarendon Press, 1897. Reprinted, 2 vols. in one, Indianapolis: Bobbs-Merrill, 1964.

Shaftesbury, Anthony Ashley Cooper, Third Earl of. *Characteristics of Men, Manners, Opinions, Times, etc.* 3 vols. London, 1711.

———. *An Inquiry Concerning Virtue, or Merit*. In Shaftesbury, *Characteristics*.

Sherman, Nancy. "Common Sense and Uncommon Virtue." *Midwest Studies in Philosophy*, 13 (1988): 97–114.

Shklar, Judith N. *Ordinary Vices*. Cambridge, Massachusetts: Harvard University Press, 1984.

*Shorter Oxford English Dictionary on Historical Principles*. 5th edn. 2 vols. Oxford: Oxford University Press, 2002.

Sidgwick, Henry. *Outlines of the History of Ethics*. Boston: Beacon Press, 1960.

Slote, Michael. *From Morality to Virtue*. Oxford: Oxford University Press, 1992.

———. *Morals from Motives*. New York: Oxford University Press, 2001.

Sorensen, Kelly. *The Factors of Moral Worth*. Ph.D. dissertation, Yale University, 2003. Available from UMI.

Sterelny, Kim. "Symbiosis, Evolvability, and Modularity." In Schlosser and Wagner, eds., *Modularity in Development and Evolution*, pp. 490–516.

Stocker, Michael. "Desiring the Bad—An Essay in Moral Psychology." *Journal of Philosophy*, 76 (1979): 738–53.

———. "The Schizophrenia of Modern Ethical Theories." *Journal of Philosophy*, 73 (1976): 453–66.

———. "Values and Purposes: The Limits of Teleology and the Ends of Friendship." *The Journal of Philosophy*, 78 (1981): 747–65.

Swanton, Christine. "A Virtue Ethical Account of Right Action." *Ethics*, 112 (2001): 32–52.

——. *Virtue Ethics: A Pluralistic View*. Oxford: Oxford University Press, 2003.

Tillich, Paul. *The Courage to Be*. New Haven: Yale University Press, 1960.

Wallace, James. *Virtues and Vices*. Ithaca, New York: Cornell University Press, 1978.

Watson, Gary. "Virtues in Excess." *Philosophical Studies*, 46 (1984): 57–74.

Williams, Bernard. "Moral Luck." *Proceedings of the Aristotelian Society*, suppl. vol. 50 (1976): 115–35. Reprinted with revisions in Williams, *Moral Luck*, pp. 20–39.

——. *Moral Luck*. Cambridge: Cambridge University Press, 1981.

Wolf, Susan. "Moral Saints." *The Journal of Philosophy*, 79 (1982): 419–39.

Yearley, Lee H. *Mencius and Aquinas: Theories of Virtue and Conceptions of Courage*. Albany: State University of New York Press, 1990.

Zagzebski, Linda Trinkaus. *Divine Motivation Theory*. Cambridge: Cambridge University Press, 2004.

——. *Virtues of the Mind: An Inquiry into the Nature of Virtue and the Ethical Foundations of Knowledge*. Cambridge: Cambridge University Press, 1996.

# Index of Virtues and Vices

# General Index